Amaranthea

Yiorgos A. Potamianos

Amaranthea

Translated by:
Philip Ramp
Edited by:
A.J. Bewsher

All rights reserved. No part of this work covered by the copyright hereon may be reproduced or used in any form by any means – graphic, electronic, or mechanical, including copying, recording, taping, or information storage and retrieval systems – without written permission of the publisher.

Typeset and printed by Q3 Print Project Management Ltd,
Loughborough, Leicestershire.
(01509 213456)

Published by Shoestring Press
19 Devonshire Avenue, Beeston, Nottingham, NG9 1BS
(0115) 925 1827
www.shoestringpress.co.uk

First published 2002
© Copyright: Yiorgos A. Potamianos and John Lucas
ISBN-13: 978 1 904886 47 1
ISBN-10: 1 904886 47 7

Shoestring Press gratefully acknowledges financial assistance from
East Midlands Arts

PART ONE

THE SCENT OF THE DESERT

In the wake of the destroyer Navarchos Koundouriotis, pulling away from the harbour of Piraeus, all of his childhood and adolescent years were being left behind.

The large flag hanging at the low stern of the warship caressed the sea as Alexis, standing by the flagpole, watched the land fade and merge into the setting sun.

The war and the German occupation of Greece had forced him to grow up too quickly, but now as he set off for foreign lands, alone, he felt truly a man for the first time. Alone. How strange! His father, his mother, his brother, his friends in the Resistance, the warmth of his home and familiar territory – these were the chocks that propped up the boat in the boatyard. As the distance grew, it was as if one by one the stout beams of support were being removed from his soul, letting him slide into the boundless sea. There was no sensation of pain. Only that curious yet sweet melancholy one feels during the most important moments of one's life.

Now the road of adventure, inquiry and independence was opening up before him. To be accountable to no-one! All the choices one's own! He hadn't forgotten that he'd wanted to leave. No matter how much he loved his native land, he was deeply embittered, for he believed he was an idealist, a true patriot, and had done his duty through and through. Hadn't he been imprisoned by the Italians? Hadn't he hidden from the Germans who had convicted him 'in absentia'?

He closed his eyes for a moment and saw again the nightmare, the waves of leftist guerrillas in Kaisariani, cursing him, punching and kicking him as they dragged him to the People's Court. Two or three young boys, not even ten years old had walked in front of him, clutching

3

toy guns shouting: "Traitor! Traitor!" Traitor? How dare they! They left him with no hope at all. He was to be the sixth one executed that day. But he had been oddly composed, even though he expected no help from anyone. It was the injustice of it all which incensed him.

Ever since he was small he had believed in fighting for his homeland. What did he know about politics? All he knew was that the Germans and the Italians had violated his country. He fought them. And then suddenly his compatriots were fighting him.

It simply isn't possible, he'd said to himself, these are Greeks, they must share the same feelings, they'd come to their senses and even shake his hand. But how can you explain anything to a mob? He'd been arrested by a fellow student – Spyros – on the day they were celebrating the Liberation and the anniversary of the war. He'd met him during the period when the national organisations had been trying to re-enter the University, after the assassination of his friend Maltezos by ideologically antagonistic groups. He simply couldn't understand. Why? Why? Why would they kill a patriot, an innocent person. And yet, when the Cadets from the Polytechnic School had come to assist the nationalist students, had arrested Spyros and were beating him to make him confess – who knows to what – Alexis had tried to restrain them, though he was seething with indignation over the murder of a young man who had been widely admired.

Many years later, he would run into Spyros at a gathering of friends and say to his wife; "You see that man? He wanted to put me in front of a firing squad. But looking at him now you'd think he was the nicest person around". A while later they spoke to each other as if the past did not exist. They never became friends, but it wasn't past history that prevented it. He always had a tendency to forgive and forget.

Alexis had been saved by Evert, the Chief of Police; he had been notified by friends who had seen Alexis arrested. With an armoured car and a show of force he had come and taken him away from the Civil Guard of ELAS, the leftist guerrillas.

October 28, 1944. It was the first time he had worn a uniform. He had assembled it himself: an Italian helmet – booty from the Italian surrender – shorts from an old Boy Scout uniform and his grandfather's military gear. Like a masquerader during Carnival.

He was celebrating the Liberation by marching with other people from his own resistance organisation through the streets of Athens when they came face to face with Spyros and a battalion of ELAS. Before he knew what had happened, he was a prisoner being marched off to Kaisariani.

Now disillusion was driving him from Greece. In his mind he could not separate the land from the people. He had loved Greece, he had fought for her and she had betrayed him, He was fleeing with a mixture of sorrow and relief.

He opened his eyes again. The destroyer was steadily increasing its speed and the wake it left behind seemed oddly mysterious. It was as if he had flung his confused sensations into the churning foam so that in the vortex created by the propeller they might give birth to hope. He was leaving and he had no real idea where he would end up or what he would do. The war in Greece had ended but fierce battles were still being waged on all the fronts of Europe.

The Navarchos Koundouriotis had been dispatched from Piraeus with the mission of picking up captive Italians and Germans from the islands of Mytilene and Chios and taking them to Egypt. Alexis had embarked with the idea of attending the Naval Academy in Alexandria – but perhaps he would try for Captain in the Merchant Marine.

That first evening the First Mate had invited him into the Officer's Mess for coffee. He was young in years but he had been to war. He was undaunted by the stripes the ship's officers wore. But when he saw that travelling with them to Mytilene was the heroic commander of the submarine Papanikolis, who had sunk three Italian ships in one day, he was as proud as could be.

Iatridis, one of those people who are always fun to be around, had become Governor of Mytilene after the Liberation. He made them laugh with his stories about the ladies of the island who had lined up to receive the ... blessings of the hero! What a shame that he should later die so young and needlessly on his motorcycle on a street in Perama.

The second evening – they had already called at Mytilene and Chios and had taken on approximately two-hundred captive Italians and

Germans – three ship's officers gathered in the mess again, the Captain, the First Mate and the doctor, and once more Alexis was invited to join their little party.

The sea had begun to get rough. A strong north-westerly was blowing and the Koundouriotis was beginning to roll. Commander Boudouris, a member of a great naval family of Hydra and captain of the Koundouriotis, had come down from the bridge with the intention of questioning a German prisoner to pass the time. He sent his orderly forward to have the highest ranking German sent down. This proved to be a mere Sergeant who after a while made his appearance; frightened, he sat down at one end of the table. Since Alexis knew German he was to act as interpreter.

"How do you feel now that the war is over for you?"

"The war is over for all of Germany so it doesn't matter to me that I'm a prisoner of war."

"But Hitler is still waging war and saying he'll win."

"Hitler's crazy, he's been the ruin of us all."

"Don't you believe in the magical power of the Fuhrer anymore?"

"I was never a Nazi.

The Commander interjected:

"The little innocents, now it seems none of them was ever a Nazi!"

"Why doesn't Germany surrender?"

"We'll hold back the Russians, till the English and Americans have occupied all of Germany."

"What if you can't hold the Russians back?"

"Then the Americans will stop the Russians from entering Germany." Wishful thinking!

The weather was growing steadily worse. They had to hold onto the table to keep from falling over. During one roll the radio slid from its place and landed against the bulkhead. They laid the two empty chairs down on their sides so they wouldn't topple over.

The German was beginning to turn green with seasickness. At a certain point the commander started to hand him an orange but the ship made such a mighty roll that as the German stood up to take it he did a flip right over the table and ended up on the other side in the Captain's arms, which brought the questioning to an inglorious end.

The sea didn't calm down for two days and nights. The ship bucked madly along. Even the sailors were nauseous. The cook was out of commission right from the start and in any case not one pot or pan was left in its proper place. A chunk of "halva" in the officers' refrigerator got cut into four, into eight, into sixteen, into thirty-two, and lasted for three whole days – not that anyone had much of an appetite.

On the third day – the sea still just as heavy – they began a zig-zag course that took them through the mine-fields. And then the coast of Egypt finally appeared in the distance.

Alexis braced himself by holding onto the small gun mounted in the stem, as excited as any traveller entering a harbour for the first time. He was one of the few who wasn't seasick. "I'll make a good sailor," he thought to himself. He sighted the buoys in the channel outside Alexandria; he had been told that a rough sea demanded caution because it was shallow here and many boats had run aground in their pitching and tossing. The north-westerly howled against the starboard side of the vessel, forcing it off course until it was past the channel that led to the harbour.

Under full reverse engine the ship began to keel over farther than it had during the whole trip. When the sea on the port side stern of the destroyer reached the gunnel, Alexis was sure they were going to capsize. He was ready to jump into the sea but was waiting for someone else to make the first move. He kept an eye on the First Mate holding on for dear life to the door of the poop deck; he had turned deathly green. Then, miracle of miracles, the Koundouriotis righted itself like one of those Russian dolls that always manage to spring back to an upright position, and slowly made its way back on course. In proud and stately manner, it sailed into the harbour of Alexandria.

Alexis felt as if his heart would burst. He shouted "Alexandria!" into the wind, delighting in the magic of the word. As they moved slowly along, he saw British warships that had fought battles in every ocean of the world. He spotted the flagship of the British fleet, the legendary battleship George V which had hunted the Bismarck in the Atlantic; he saw Egyptian 'feluccas' with their large lateen sails and men in jelabas' at the rudder, while opposite, rising up on the horizon, were the first minarets he had ever seen.

A dream composed of the heroism of war, the mystery of the East and the magic of discovery.

During docking manoevres they bumped into King Farouk's yacht, thus putting the finishing touch on his introduction to Alexandria.

By the time the boat had docked the crew was beginning to recover after three days of storm and little food and set about securing the boat, and an hour later headed for town.

A platoon of English soldiers came to pick up the prisoners to take them to one of the army camps in the desert. Alexis waited for the Mate, before going ashore. He didn't have a passport and would have to sneak off the boat.

They waited till night fell before getting into a small truck belonging to the Naval Command that would take them out of the harbour. They stopped at the checkpoint at the gates. Alexis had burrowed into the rear of the truck, hidden by five sailors. Fortunately, the Egyptian police simply signalled to the driver to pass through.

It was the third time in his life that he had felt such an intense sensation of freedom. It was not just a figure of speech when they said: "I breathe the sea-breeze of freedom." It was as if the air around him had become lighter, as if each breath was filtering all anguish and fear from his mind. It was like awakening in relief after a long night fraught with nightmares.

The first time he had felt this way was when he'd come out of the Italian prison and was on his way home. The second time, was when he'd caught sight of the first English paratroopers, while he and his mates were surrounded by the resistance fighters of ELAS, in the hotels of Omonia.

And now? The most beautiful moment of all. Streets opened before him that he would be able to walk along, looking, seeking, learning, no longer needing to glance behind him to see if anyone was following him. If someone called out his name on the street he would know it was a friend. For the moment he wasn't seeing all that much anyway, wedged into the truck like that. He and the mate were dropped off in front of the house where the latter's in-laws lived; they would be putting him up.

Agamemnon had married a charming, dark-skinned Alexandrian Greek girl, Kiki. He had met her during the war – he had been wounded and she, a volunteer nurse. She lived with her father, her mother and her little sister in her family home, a two-storey detached house to the rear of a well-tended garden in Camp de Cesar which along with the Ibrahimia were the classiest districts of the Greek colony.

She had not known her husband would be arriving that evening and, when she opened the door, burst into joyous tears in his embrace. Alexis, embarrassed, waited outside with his ditty bag containing the few clothes he had brought with him on his shoulder.

"I've brought a guest, my cousin's son, who'll be staying with us for a while if you don't mind. He's crazy enough to want to join the Navy. But we'll talk about all that later."

The unfeigned joy with which they received Alexis and welcomed him into their home, moved him deeply and made him feel at ease. From that moment on he would feel that the Greeks of Alexandria were embracing him with love, and even admiration! He had come from Greece, had gone through the occupation and now would be able to supply first-hand information about the years during which the homeland had been cut off. It was like the return of a hero, except that he didn't feel like one with his homeland well behind him.

He'd unexpectedly found himself in a friendly environment, and when that same evening he went out into the town and heard more Greek spoken than any other language, he really felt at home. They had told him to take the tram-line at Camp de Cesar station and go to the terminus at Ramleh. He had quickly changed into some worn trousers and a shirt from his bag and some time later was out amid the lights of the Alexandria of 1944.

"My God, all these lights!" It had been years since he'd seen such lights. Store windows, sweet shops, cinemas with brightly-lit marquees, soldiers, sailors, airmen, English, Australians, Indians, Africans and Greeks in clean, freshly-ironed shirts and, amid this pandemonium of the "good life", the elegant silhouettes of the

Egyptians in their white, grey, red and green jelabas glided through the crowd, giving motion and colour to the strangeness of the Middle East. Everyone was speaking freely and casually and the voices around him echoed in his ears like an enchanting song in Arabic, English and Greek. He stood for a long time before a kiosk in Ramleh Square, mesmerised by the brightly coloured chocolate bars and packs of cigarettes. He scrutinised them one by one. "Craven A" with black letters on a white label against a red or green background. "Player's" with the world-famous old captain and his red beard and pipe, "Camel" with the yellow camel on both sides of the pack!

He remembered the boxes he had sold – one cigarette at a time – with his friend Aris in Syntagma Square during the occupation. They'd called them "Stukas". It had been a way of making a little pocket money and of beating inflation at the same time!

He couldn't resist any longer. He took an English pound note out of his pocket and asked for candy bars and cigarettes. What was a pound note compared to the millions of inflationary drachmas of the occupation? But then when they loaded him down with candy bars and cigarettes for his one pound, he realised how extravagant he'd been.

Since his pockets couldn't hold all these provisions, he clutched the candy bars in his hand; he couldn't bear to open them. He stroked the wrappings and when his fingers discovered the grooves which marked out the sections of the bars, he felt the same thrill he remembered from his childhood when Uncle Aristeidis had brought candy bars back to the house.

He'd got used to going without food during the occupation, so the three days on the destroyer when he'd eaten practically nothing, hadn't affected him. He had become so thin he had had to tighten his belt so the old pair of pants his father gave him before he left wouldn't fall down. But now his stomach began to rumble. He still had a pound note in his pocket; he would have to eat a proper meal somewhere before attacking the candy bars. Opposite the kiosk was a shop with little tables set out on the sidewalk and more inside a glassed-in area. Most of the clientele were military. A sign on top of the shop said "Alakefak". He crossed the street and went in. In an enormous case covering nearly the entire width of the place, was everything one's heart desired: platters of cold pork, beef, chicken, fish salad, shrimp salad, tuna fish, ham, cheese, vegetable salad, and behind the counter waiters were taking customer's orders and making sandwiches of soft buns.

He put his bars of chocolate on a table to claim it while he stood studying the case, deciding on his first meal in freedom, this first postwar meal, with pre-war food! He looked at the prices. One and a half shillings for a sandwich with those soft buns which bore no relation to the coarse corn bread of the occupation. He would be able to eat eight of these sandwiches, have a beer and still have enough change left for the tram fare back. He had no difficulty in ordering since all the waiters were Greek! "A little of this ... a little of that!"

After a while he settled down before a mountain of sandwiches – and immediately faced his first dilemma: should he start with the shrimp or the tuna? "That's one problem I never had during the occupation", he thought. He chose the shrimp and began to eat voraciously, gleefully wolfing down one sandwich after another, with sips of beer in between.

What seemed strange to him was that he hadn't forgotten flavours and tastes. It was as if he'd eaten pork with mustard and butter just the day before even though it had been four years since he'd eaten real food. His gaze wandered over the new faces around him and he was in the mood to speak to them, to communicate his joy to them, to get them to share in his celebration – to call out: "I'm free, I'm eating, I'm walking around, playing, looking at things and I'm not afraid! I am not afraid! You are all my friends, you English sailors and you Americans and you picturesque Arabs with your red fezzes."

He had to force down the eighth sandwich and there were still the chocolates to go. His eyes were bigger than his stomach which had shrunk during the war and he felt ready to burst. It was his first spree as a "consumer".

He went out to walk it off. But the candy bars itched in his hands. He unwrapped one of them and began to lick it the way he'd done with cheese during the occupation, to make it last.

He lit a cigarette and stopped to gaze at the Strand cinema. In the display photographs a tall, gorgeous girl in a swimming suit was diving, swimming and rising up through water lilies like the Aphrodite of Botticelli, with a carefree smile. "Carefree!" Here was another new sensation. He read her name again so he wouldn't forget it: Esther Williams.

Women. Up till then he had not noticed that in Ramleh Square, on the tram, or at Alakefak's, there hadn't been any women around. Not even on the carts that passed through the square piled high with drunken soldiers like bunches of grapes! There was a pastry shop opposite the cinema. He crossed the street to see if he might at least find something female, in there. Now that his belly was full, other instincts were awakening ...

He read the name "ATHENAIOS" on the sign over the entrance. Another Greek place! He didn't have any more money to spend, but he couldn't have made any more room anyway, for his sponge-cake with cherries, but he paused for a while caught up in yet another pre-war recollection. He walked inside and pretended to be looking for someone among the tables. Most of the English there, as in Alakefak, were soldiers, airmen and sailors.

A small orchestra was playing and on the dance floor were five or six couples. He noticed how well-groomed and well-dressed the two or three girls were who were dancing with their partners. But he was flabbergasted when he saw male couples dancing; a soldier with an airman, a sailor with another sailor, or an airman with a sailor! As he stood there gaping he noticed another airman getting up to ask him to dance and he turned and fled. All right, so the ladies were few and far between – but for Christ's sake what fun was it to dance a tango with a man?

As he walked out he nearly bumped into two dark and elegant European women and this calmed his fears about the lack of females and completed the image of his first evening in Ramleh Square, in the pulsing heart of Alexandria.

A scene full of lights, food, music, dancing, sweets, movies and cheerful people. Now the anticipation of a woman, that dream. What a beautiful start, what an introduction to a new life.

The following days he lived for life alone, without worrying about anything – his only aim was to enjoy those things he had missed for so many years. Almost every day he would meet his friend Andonis, who had also arrived in Egypt from Greece, at the Naval Canteen every evening just before six and go to three cinemas in a row, from 3 to 6, 6 to 9 and 9 to midnight, to fulfil yet another lust: movie shows.

During the occupation he had seen German and Italian films. He had seen Alida Valli, Christina Soederbaum, Marika Rock, Ilse Werner, and Theo Linden, but Alexis' favourite was the blonde charmer of the Italian screen, Assia Noris. He remembered how he had laughed at "Baron Munchausen" with Franz Albers or at "Seven Years of Bad Luck" with Hans Mozer – despite feeling guilty about going to see the enemy's productions. He remembered the Hungarian film "Night Vision", the first film in which he had seen the naked silhouette of a woman on a screen; that had fed his fantasy for ages, along with the film reminiscences of the older Athenians who had told him that movies meant Hollywood; Bing Crosby, Hedy Lamarr and Errol Flynn were just names to him. Laurel and Hardy and Charlie Chaplin were the only pre-war actors permitted for his tender pre-war age. No, wait! He had also seen the "Life of Schubert" at an evening performance, with his parents. As they were walking out of the cinema, in front of the pretty daughter of friends, his father had said, "Tonight is a premiere for Alexis." Alexis had flushed at being thus embarrassed in front of the blonde girl, who was older than he. Now, in Alexandria, all these famous Hollywood stars were appearing on the screens of the 'Rialto', the 'Rio' and the 'Mohammed Ali'!

Three to six, six to nine, nine to twelve! During intermission, the organists played where the contrasts co-existed peacefully in a unique cosmopolitan atmosphere which countless melodies on the theatre organ. The melodies of Alexandria of 1944, of this city which perhaps had never existed before and would never exist again. It was difficult to say just what it was that gave rise to the buoyant and idyllic atmosphere and the untrammelled joie de vivre' in a place with so many contradictions. He paused to reflect. Was it the abundance of impressions? The silent acceptance that there are always masters and servants? What did the silver service and the white gloves of the boys with their shiny red tarbushes have to do with the braziers and 'falafel' and 'foulia' which Arabs in grubby jelabas cooked on street corners? How was the "Oh, ma cherie" of the ladies with their lorgnettes connected to the "Ebn el KaIb" and "Kussomak" of the barefoot multitude? How did the languor of the feudal lords with their ten servants fit in with the squat brick houses of the 'fellaheen'?

How, without complaint, without offence, without hearts in revolt – at least on the surface – could the lace covers over the cradles of rosy pink babies co-exist with the swarms of flies that nestled in the eye sockets of the swarthy children whose mothers didn't even brush them away?

Was it the attitude of fatalism, the acceptance that nothing could be changed, nothing questioned? Why did Alexis with his open mind, accept all these comforts without a second thought? There had to be some common factor to account for all these people living in and moving about this town.

Was it the 'proper upbringing' of the Europeans, the discipline of the Army, or the good hearts and the traditional courtesy of the Egyptians which prevented conflict and misunderstanding?

Whatever it was, Alexis enjoyed the 'apres-midi dansants', to which he escorted the young daughters of his hosts, the foursomes when he accompanied their mother, the trips along the Corniche with their friends, the evenings at the "Gloria" theatre where Vembo sang wartime songs, with Mimis Traiphoros as M.C. and Menios on the accordion. On such evenings, the neighbourhood of Ibrahimia became just another corner of Greece.

He enjoyed the sandy beaches at Sidi Bishr, and Stanley Bay, and the unbelievable fun on the trams which he often rode with no real purpose, going from Ramleh to Glymenopoulo, then walking all the way up to the door of Farouk's summer palace, at Montaza.

The only time that he objected to the Egyptian establishment was when they played Farouk's anthem at the end of a movie. He would leave the auditorium conspicuously while the rest of the audience remained motionless. He wasn't sure if it was to show that as a European he was above all that, or if it was that he didn't like the round face of the Farouk with its black moustache.

One afternoon, he went to Naafi with Andonis again. "I think we should forget about the movies today and start looking for girls." Andonis suggested.

"So where have you got them hidden?"

"Someone showed me where the whorehouses are."

"So let's go. Lead the way!"

They crossed Mohammed Ali Square and entered the narrow alleyways that contained the brothels of Alexandria. At the entrance to each alley a black circle was painted on the wall with a line through the middle like the loadline on a sign of a ship.

"What do those signs mean?" Alexis asked. "I don't want to appear totally ignorant." "This whole district is nothing but brothels and that sign means it's off-limits to military personnel."

"You're well-informed, aren't you? Why won't they let the military in?"

"So they won't catch any disease probably."

"So why did you bring me here, just for show?"

"Shut up, you numskull! All the girls here have health cards but they don't allow soldiers in here because they come from all over the world and if one of them was carrying some disease, say from Burma, and he gave it to one of the girls, the entire Allied Forces in the Middle East would get the clap!"

Alexis wasn't entirely convinced but moved on, appalled by the spectacle he saw in front of the doors and windows of the red light district.

Lolling around on the stairways of houses in the alleys, were enormously fat women with breasts like udders sticking out of gaudy satin blouses, skinny old women sitting with crossed legs, their skirts hiked up, dishevelled shrews leaning from windows, and an occasional female who was just passable though you couldn't tell if her colour was a matter of race or of not washing. Most of the women were Middle Eastern, but there were darker ones from central Africa.

The alleys were unpaved and the low two-storey houses with the dilapidated white or pink plaster were not an ideal setting for making love. However, hundreds of customers, from all the corners of the world, strolled through the shadows from door to door in the hospitable alleyways.

"I can't believe you would want to screw in this place!" Alexis said.

"Just close your eyes – besides, it's really cheap, you'll see."

"If I have to close my eyes, I might as well jack off and that's even cheaper!"

Just then as they were having this nonsensical discussion, they saw a tall mulatto with black frizzy hair pulled back over large, equally black eyes and unpainted lips, who stood out from all the others, at the window of the upper floor of a house somewhat better cared for than the rest.

Without hesitation, Andonis went up the stairs. Alexis followed him and when they got close to Farida, they saw she had a gorgeous well-built body and lovely shapely legs. Andonis was really excited.

"You look just like Anne Sheridan" he told her before they started bargaining.

It didn't take long to make a deal – seven piasters, which was pretty cheap for Anne Sheridan! After excusing themselves, the couple went into the room next door while Alexis sat on a chair to wait. No more than fifteen minutes went by before the door opened and Andonis emerged with a grin stretching from ear to ear. Farida came out to get Alexis without bothering to get dressed, but he made up some excuse and turned her down.

Every time he had gone to a brothel in Athens with friends he had had to be the first one to go with the woman, otherwise it turned his stomach. Even though he knew that the same woman had been with ten other men earlier.

He wanted to hold on to the illusion that he was her only lover. He told Farida that he would be back the following day. He was always polite to prostitutes – he didn't want to offend them.

As they went down the stairs Andonis said:

"Your loss! What a dame! And if you subtract the time it took to undress her it only cost me one piaster a minute!"

"Dirt cheap, you might say – you make love sound mercenary!"

"What a dame! I tell you!"

There could be no agreeing …

Often during the evenings at home, visiting friends of his hosts (on leave from the Army or the Navy) they spoke of their own war, which they brought to life through tales of the fight in the desert or, at sea, using Alexandria as a base to ply the Mediterranean. Agamemnon, Kiki's husband, had been one of them, trying to live up to his glorious name. Only this time it wasn't the eyes of the Belle Helene of Troy that were at stake. Alexis was told about the agonising days they had gone through, when they could hear the sound of the cannon only a few miles to the west of Alexandria, being almost certain that Rommel couldn't be stopped. It seemed that the members of the Italian colony in Alexandria were already sewing Italian flags to welcome the liberators! But then had come El Alamein.

El Alamein! The magic name that changed the course of the war. The name he had heard on the clandestine radio hidden in his father's cupboard in Athens during the Occupation. The first hope in the long night of the German advance. Montgomery, Rommel! Names which had fuelled his imagination, as one by one he re-lived the scenes of those far-off battles, as if he were taking part in desert war himself he was proud that on land, on the sea or in the air, the Greeks in the Army, Navy or Airforce were always fighting in the front lines with the British allies.

Now he was learning the inside story; of the Greek destroyer Hydra that had spotted the Italian fleet in the open sea off Crete which had led to the important naval battle of Matapa in which three Italian warships were sunk. It had been the last time the Italian fleet dared venture out of Taranta and it had been bombed there by allied aircraft. And of the legendary Adrias under Captain Toumbas, entering the Port of Alexandria with its bow blown away by a mine, while all the crews on board the English fleet were saluting the gallant effort to save the ship. He had the story first-hand from Lieutenant Themelis who had been blown up high against the mast and left hanging upside down from the rigging for hours before they got him down. He would have a limp for the rest of his life.

He heard the story of the submarine Katsonis which, after criss-crossing the Aegean with its Captain, Vasilios Laskos, was sunk in the open sea off Leros on its last time out. He also heard about the

Mountain Brigade, the "Sacred Battalion", named after the first unit of heroic Greeks who started the War of Independence against the Turks in 1821. Seen at a distance, his own war seemed insignificant. When you got right down to it, he hadn't even worn a uniform! What is a war without a uniform, stripes and decorations? But then ... he fought ... underground! In Alexandria, uniforms were the dominant feature, giving the town the flavour of the war which, even though now far away, had not yet ended. He felt bad going around in civilian clothes in spite of the fact that at last he had suits that fitted him perfectly.

Time was passing and he had to make up his mind what he was going to do. Naturally, he couldn't imagine doing anything without a uniform. There was no problem in deciding what kind of military clothes he wanted to wear. He and the sea had shared a long love affair. The dark blue uniforms with the gold braid and the pure white caps would suit him very well.

His decisions were instinctual and based on pure emotion – his was a soul which accepted without question the advice of parents, priests, teachers and books. He was a born soldier! He was obedient to the precepts that had been instilled in him and his moral code was based on the same patterns. He didn't have many choices. Moreover, it was time to put his life in order. He couldn't go on accepting hospitality indefinitely; he had to start earning his own living.

And so it was that he turned up one morning at the Greek Cadet School, which had not yet transferred back to liberated Greece and was still in Alexandria, fired with great enthusiasm. Making a decision always filled him with optimism as well as pride. Pride, not so much for the actual decision he had made, but for the fact that he had made a decision at all!

But the moment he passed the guard at the gates, he had a sinking feeling: the same sensation he'd had passing through the gates of the Italian prison during the occupation.

He was sent straight to the office of the Deputy Commander who had three-and-a-half stripes on his sleeve. They improvised a test for him in Mathematics and Greek. They asked for his High School diploma and they put a sailor's uniform on him, the blue collar with white piping, the black scarf the white cord with the whistle. They put a cap on him too which had a band with NAVTIKOS DOKIMOS, "Naval Cadet", on it and told him to come back in fifteen days when the courses at the School would begin. It wasn't exactly the uniform he'd had in mind. He remembered the Cadets before the war, wearing the beautiful uniform that cadets on leave wore, with an officer's hat and a small gold sword at the side and his optimism started to wane somewhat. He took the tram to Ramleh with the idea of mixing in with the other uniforms in the square to see how he would react. Suddenly he felt very unimportant. Nothing but a simple sailor!

Not even one stripe, among all those people who had gone to war; if they didn't have stripes or stars, they at least had medals. In his own war in the resistance he had been "section chief' in his neighbourhood, and now he was at the bottom of the hierarchy. Even during the parade marking the liberation of Athens, he had felt more important in his Boy Scout shorts and his grandfather's kit. He examined himself in the window of a sweet shop and didn't care all that much for his image. The sailor's hat was too small for the proportions of his face which had grown from the chocolate and sandwiches he'd been putting away every day at Alakefak. Not to mention the beer. He began to have his first doubts. By the time he returned home that day his original enthusiasm had died down.

It was nearly Christmas. A Greek freighter had docked in the harbour and although the Captain and Mate were older, they were both friends of Alexis. The freighter would stay in harbour for a month for repairs and Alexis went to visit his friends and listen to their stories about how they had crossed the Atlantic, the Pacific or the Mediterranean in convoys. On Christmas Eve, the three decided to go out together and paint the town red. They first tried to get into the "Monseigneur", the best night-club in Alexandria, but nobody was allowed in without a tuxedo.

They ended up at the Laluna Cabaret, three cuckoos revelling in nostalgia on this Christmas far from their country and families. During the intermission between Samia Gamal's belly dance and Mohammed Fakri's singing "Tahalili Yabata", the two officers tried to convince Alexis to forget about the Royal Navy; if he really liked the sea and wanted adventure they would take him along with them on the freighter as a cadet officer. It didn't take much to convince him. Instead of four years in a school which at any moment could be shifted back to Greece, why not take the chance they were offering him to see the world? The trip to Egypt had given him a taste of it. Now he thirsted for more, to fly off to new horizons, to feel the ecstasy of seeing places for the very first time.

While his eyes followed the gyrations of Samia Gamal that evening, he was seeing in his imagination exotic girls dancing on the steps of a Siamese temple with supple movements of their wrists and hands, slender South American women bronzed by the sun whirling in the long strides of a tango, colourful Spanish women in ruffles spinning to the rhythms of flamenco, and sweetly smiling barefoot Tahitian girls wearing leis and strolling on the limitless sand beaches of Polynesia. He had been offered all of them on a single plate. He made his decision. A small change really – both careers were at sea. And his desire to wear braid and a sailor's cap would become a reality. He wouldn't be wearing the crown emblem of the Royal Navy, but what did that matter.

The next day he handed in his uniform at the Cadet School and declared his intention to leave; to his surprise the Deputy Commander of the School shook his hand and congratulated him on his decision. He found this strange but encouraging. The same afternoon he bought his new uniform with the white Merchant Marine officer's cap and when he saw his reflection in the store windows he felt proud. At last, he was somebody! People would notice him and when he went into the "Athenaios" he would feel an equal to his other colleagues in uniform. "They say the robe doesn't make the man. Well, they don't know what they're talking about!" he said to himself.

The Captain gave him his papers, which showed he was a registered seaman, and now he had a month before the boat left, to get to know Alexandria better, part of the allied effort himself now, the winners of the war, able at last to sample the dreams he had had during the Resistance. He wouldn't be going to Germany as part of the Occupation forces but at least he was in a uniform now, even though it was only in Alexandria; when you got right down to it the place felt like a colony, with the local people bowing their heads when you gave them an order.

A month. He'd have to set up a programme: to see Cairo, the Pyramids, the Nile and make a pilgrimage to El Alamein.

He would begin there since it wasn't far. A friend told him that they rented cars to soldiers without asking for a driver's license. After he had ordered a car, early in the afternoon on the Saturday after Christmas, he realised that his knowledge about driving was purely theoretical. He knew how to go forward and turn off the engine – a taxi driver in his neighbourhood had shown him how, years before – but this would be his first time on the road.

Fortunately, the car was parked on a downhill slope and he let it coast away from the rental office so they wouldn't find out he had not the slightest idea what he was doing!

At the bottom of the street he stopped and began to examine the dashboard and the other equipment. He more or less remembered what was what and began to move forward very cautiously. He turned a corner at a crawl, and without too many problems set off on the road to El Alamein. At least he knew how to steer, because from the time he was little, he had sat next to a taxi driver and been allowed to hold onto the wheel.

He didn't believe it himself when he reached the desert of El Alamein. He got out of the car and felt as proud of his feat as if he had conquered Rommel himself!

He stood in awe, staring at the endless desert and the remains of the tanks and artillery strewn like skeletons of dinosaurs on the yellow sand which was turning orange in the light of the setting sun, and forming with the reflection a diaphanous layer of mist like a luminous aura from the thousands of souls of those killed there.

It was as if the desert were beckoning to him to go on alone, on foot, aimless, toward some infinity. He grew afraid, got into the car and turned back.

It began to get dark. He returned along the same road and in one and a half or two hours at most, he would be back in Alexandria. He had passed Mareotis and was nearing Agami, Alexandria's two summer resorts with their beautiful beaches and lovely summer homes, when the engine began to miss and shortly thereafter it stopped. He knew nothing about engines and after trying to start it again and again he gave up in despair.

It was completely dark now. About one hundred metres further on he saw a house with lights on. He locked the car, walked down the road and opened the iron gate to the garden. It was another thirty feet or so to the three or four steps up to the bell. He heard music inside and was practically speechless with surprise when the door was opened by a statuesque British WAC with braided black hair, large blue eyes and the most beautiful smile in the world.

"I'd ... I'd like to use the telephone, to ring someone to come and get me because my car has broken down and at this time of night no-one will be able to fix it."

As he was talking he saw through the half-open door opposite, three or four WACS sitting on the knees or in the arms of American officers and another one dancing cheek to cheek with her escort whose nationality he couldn't guess because he had taken off his uniform jacket. Inside could be heard a loud male voice with a strong American accent.

"Who is it?"

"A young naval officer with a sweet smile whose car has broken down", replied the girl who had opened the door.

"Tell him to come in, we're a man short!"

"And I'm the woman without a man," the WAC added promptly. "My name is Ellen." She gave him her hand. "Oh, I forgot, you wanted to use the telephone. But it's too late – who would come all this way to fetch you?"

"I'm a guest at a house in Alexandria. I came from Greece a month ago – they'll think of something."

"From Greece? You must tell me more! Would you like to be our guest tonight? You could ring them so they won't worry. Besides... as you heard, we're a man short."

Alexis felt like he was in a dream; he couldn't say yes and he couldn't say no. With an instinct that so often guides her sex when necessary, the woman took charge of the situation.

"Come with me. Telephone them and say that one of us will take you home tomorrow morning."

"Where am I?"

"At a WAC's house near Agami."

"There don't seem to be many 'agami'* here!" Of course, Ellen didn't get the joke.

"There are six of us WACs living in this house and as you can see, tonight we're having a party. Our five friends are Americans. Another one was supposed to be here but he had guard duty and couldn't make it."

"So I'll take on his duty at the party?"

"Don't you like the idea?"

"I've always liked the unexpected."

He didn't have any choice, she made the decisions and he went along since it seemed to be to his advantage anyway. Ellen led him to the phone and then to the living-room he'd seen through the half-open door. The Americans had made considerable progress in their endeavours with the girls. As time passed, skirts went higher and more and more leg was showing.

"Our new friend is from Greece!" Ellen called out to introduce him.

For a moment the couples slackened their pace, turning their heads and looking at him curiously, but then they immediately went back to the job at hand. Only two or three of the girls said, almost in unison, "Hello George!" They all looked pretty sloshed to him.

"Why do they think my name is George?"

"Don't you know that in the Army we call the Greeks George, like the English Tommies and the Americans Johnnies?"

"My name is Alexis."

One of the Americans raised his head. "Take good care of Ellen. We let her down tonight!" Then he added with a grin; "Did you bring your cannon with you?"

It took Alexis a moment to get the meaning. Ellen quickly intervened. "Do shut up, John, Alexis isn't used to our Army jargon.

---

*in Greek: unmated/unmarried

"I wouldn't think of going out without it." Alexis quickly replied, trying to win back lost ground.

Soon he felt at ease in the group, despite the fact that they were all older than him and from what he could see they each had at least one or two more stripes than he did. Ellen wore the star of a second lieutenant but nobody was standing on rank that evening. In his crisp naval uniform, his new sparkling white cap in his hand, and the bar on his shoulder, he didn't have to envy the others, especially in their condition – half drunk, in stocking feet – and he grew more confident.

The music stopped but the couples who had been dancing didn't let go of each other. Ellen took Alexis' cap and went to put on a new record, while he looked around the room. Heavy velvet curtains on French doors to the balcony, comfortable sofas, handsome English furniture and an old crystal chandelier above the round table in the corner. He had been impressed by the old French and English furniture, the Persian and Turkish carpets, the expensive silver and Bohemian crystal in the Alexandrian mansions, but he never would have imagined that he'd find them in army quarters.

"Will you have something to drink, Alexis?" asked Ellen, who had returned. "Or something to eat? You must be hungry."

"I've eaten so much since I arrived in Alexandria but ... well, I'd be happy to have a little something, if it isn't too much trouble."

"The easiest thing in the world. Come with me to the kitchen."

As he followed her to the kitchen, he examined Ellen for the first time with desire, aroused by the sensual atmosphere.

In his mind, English girls had pale, soft skin, fine blond hair and blue eyes. Ellen's hair was dark, but her skin was as he'd imagined it and her curves, despite her delicate build, had a power verging on the magnetic, as did her long legs, and while he had often found WACs sexy, he now felt slightly hesitant.

"It seems strange to me to be pairing off with a Second Lieutenant", he told her as they entered the kitchen. "In Greece, during the occupation, I saw female German soldiers in the street – 'the grey girls' as we called them – and I asked myself whether it would be a conquest of the enemy or an act of treason if you went with one. Not that I ever chased after them, because if you got caught you were sentenced to death."

"Would you think of it as a 'conquest' to ... go with an ally?"

"To go with an ally like yourself would be a celebration of victory! Only ... I feel strongly about the chain of command and you outrank me!"

"If that's all it is ..."

Without hesitation, she took off the jacket of her uniform, leaving her wearing a skirt and a white brassiere with lace around the border which made her shapely bosom even more alluring.

He had not expected this impulsive action but Ellen quickly made him feel at ease. "I'm not ashamed of my body. And if it makes you feel better not to see me in uniform, then isn't it better all round if we simplify things this way?"

It all seemed very simple indeed! What kind of woman was this who helped you forget about taboos and prejudices? Was she just being maternal toward him? He thought she must be two or three years older than him. Now, without her uniform, even her eyes had taken on a motherly tenderness. She approached and caressed his cheek and head.

"All my friends say that I make the best apple pie in the whole British Army! Would you like a slice?"

"Did you get the medal you're wearing for your pie?"

"No, I got that for screwing a general."

Another cold shower! This lady blew hot and cold. What a woman – one minute she was mothering you and caressing you tenderly, and the next she was talking like that! But then her mood switched once more;

"Another old army joke. Don't get upset! My, aren't you the sensitive one! But I do like you. Don't take it seriously if every so often I tell an uncouth joke. Two years in the army makes a person cynical. I think we're going to get on just fine. Just a sec and I'll bring you some apple pie. Or would you like me to make you a sandwich?"

"Apple pie is just the thing. I'm stuffed to the gills with sandwiches. I've been eating ten a day at Alakefak since I arrived. I've put on fifteen kilos."

"You must have been skin and bones!" she cried, her expression softening again. "I've heard that in Greece you were starving during the occupation."

She took the apple pie out of the refrigerator, set it on the kitchen table and sat down across from him.

"If you think it's easy for me to eat apple pie when there are a couple of ... cream puffs ... on the opposite side of the table ..."

"Do you want me to put my uniform on again?" she asked slyly.

"No, no, but ... I just want you to know that to eat apple pie under these conditions is nothing less than heroic."

Ellen smiled. "Tell me about the occupation in Greece."

Romantic music and the easy laughter of the group could be heard through the closed living-room door.

"It's hard for me to tell you in a few words and I don't want to spoil your mood ... but if you insist."

He would play her game. She wanted to appear protective, to console, to lend him the warmth of her presence. He would let her have the role that she had chosen and he would become the tormented young man whose eyes had seen too much, the child fallen victim to the madness of adults, who had had to live heroically, to fight and suffer, who was only now at last able to lose himself in the caresses of her womanly embrace. All he had to do was tell his story in an offhand manner, as if he had never taken it seriously. On the other hand, how could he not be serious?

"Ellen, I would like to tell you about the people who died in the streets, and the ones on the verge of death licking the garbage cans and the young men mowed down by German firing squads, and the villages that were burned to the ground, but these are heartbreaking stories. It's better if I talk about the things that made us survive: the coarse yellow corn bread, the four-decker sesame sweets, the cabbage we used for soup one day, salad the next, pseudo-meatballs the day after that and sometimes ... even for dessert. Then there's the water – it came on for two hours every Wednesday and we would fill the bathtub to use all week for drinking and washing. I can tell you about the black market, about the hidden radio we all gathered around, even friends from the neighbourhood who wanted to hear Big Ben. That's how I improved the English I'd learned from my teacher, who was, believe it or not, a friend of Al Capone! And about how our hearts lurched when we heard German boots under our windows or our delight when we heard about Allied victories, our optimism, our conviction that the Allies would win the war, no doubt about it; and then there was that special kind of euphoria that surfaces when you are fighting for something you know is just and right, without hesitation, without question, and which does not allow fear to turn into anxiety."

He lowered his head for a moment and then went on:

"Being here, in Alexandria, surrounded by 'largesse' from Heaven, I don't know anymore what I want. Up until now I have been walking down a road with no question marks. It's questions that cause you grief."

He paused on that word, waiting for sympathy as a prelude to love, the love that he realised he was in search of.

Ellen had reached across the table and taken hold of his hand. Now she squeezed it harder and as she did her breasts seemed to swell provocatively. The music continued to play next door but the laughter had stopped. The stairs that led to the next floor would creak every so often. Ellen got up and came round the table to him. She took his head and hugged it to her breasts. His reward!

And he hadn't even told her about his own personal adventures yet! Even though Mama was asking the questions and the boy was doing the answering, he thought it would be impolite to talk only about himself.

"So where were you in the war, Ellen?"

"In London, in the Blitz. But let's leave that for later. Let's go up to my room."

It was clear that she didn't want to talk, or at least to remember.

The bedrooms were on the upper floor. Ellen's room was all blues and whites, the upholstery and curtains, bedspread and tablecloth, in matching colours, blue lacquered furniture and a wide brass bed with enormous square pillows the like of which he had never seen before.

"You know, Ellen, I have always slept with my arms around a pillow. When I was a child I pretended to embrace movie stars every night before I fell asleep."

"I hope it's not the pillow you plan on embracing tonight!"

She slipped out of her skirt and shut off the ceiling light, leaving only the blue bathroom light on. She came to him, turned her back, and stood there, as if she was waiting for him to protect her now, as if asking him to embrace her. She was wearing lace underpants that matched her brassiere and in an instant she had become a woman, not a mother any longer.

Instinctually, she wanted the man to take the initiative. Alexis understood that. He embraced her from behind, cupping her breasts with his hands and kissing her hair.

Ellen accepted his caresses and his kisses, moving her head and murmuring like a cat purring in its master's hands, Then suddenly she wheeled round and began to kiss him passionately.

Before they stretched out under the sheets, Alexis whispered:

"... – *Tonight, the room*
should not have too much light. In deep reverie
all receptiveness, and with the gentle light –
in this deep reverie I'll form visions
to call up the Shades, the Shades! of Love."

"That's lovely," she said, "who wrote it?"

"Cavafy. Our great poet from Alexandria."

That night he came to know what a real woman's love was, perhaps for the first time, and made love without inhibition and felt at ease and sure of himself.

They awoke at first light and looked into each other's eyes. They smiled and got up to open the window, facing the sea beyond the wide sand beach.

"Somewhere over there is the mouth of the Nile and then the Pharos, one of the seven wonders of the world, rising six hundred feet above the earth, beacon of the city of Alexandria for sailors," Alexis whispered dreamily, "and somewhere here, between Pharos and Mareotis, Man suspected for the first time that the Earth revolved around the Sun! When I was in Greece I was seeing the Mediterranean from the other side ... now it's Greece on the other side, way to the North.' He stared nostalgically at the sea for some time. Greece, his family, his friends, the war, seemed like a far-off dream to him, after a night of love-making in a strange land.

Thus they stood, naked before the sea. Ellen had the relaxed and satisfied expression of a woman after making love and the woman turned into a child just given a marvellous gift – it was Alexis who was now the protector, the master. The circle had closed. A mother before they went to bed, a woman in bed and a child the next morning. She put on a white robe and sat on the bed cross-legged. She had let her hair down and it half covered her face; Alexis took it that this too, was a symbol of submission, like the veil worn by Middle Eastern women. Alexis slid back into bed, holding his head above the pillow as he listened to Ellen speak.

"Now is the time for you to hear my story. What you told me about the time Greece was occupied got me all excited. I wanted to take you in my arms, make love to you, make you want me all for yourself. Now I can talk about myself and get your affection, I have stories to tell too. They seem so far away this morning. Those terrible nights during the Blitz... losing my fiancé, ... I was twenty-one ... he was a pilot ... shot down over the Channel. All the injured and dead we dragged out of the rubble, the air raid sirens that wrenched at your nerves. I waited endless hours for news of him. Not to mention my anguish over my own family on the west coast of Scotland – and the only thing that saves you is the strength you seem to draw from the common danger, from shared experiences – that, and the lack of choice. Others decide your fate, and you accept the blows more readily, since there's no feeling of guilt, no feeling that you could have changed things through your own actions. Just like Biblical catastrophes. Those who survive, start over, re-build, learn to live again without being driven mad by the ruins around them."

Alexis parted her two curtains of hair to get a better look at her face and to repay her understanding, her tenderness and love. In her sadness, Ellen was even more like a child.

"Now the war is further away, people have withdrawn. One's bound by one's own egotism, one's own interests, the framework within which one moves, and there's no longer any trust. It's women versus men, children versus their parents, customers versus merchants and the sick versus doctors. If you are wounded in the war and they take you to an inexperienced military doctor in a tent on the front, he seems like a god to you and you trust him totally – you have no choice. But now, if you go to the most famous doctor in Alexandria, there is always someone better! And so the agony of choice is born: what if I didn't do it right? What if I made the wrong choice? Isn't that a tragic question?"

Alexis interrupted her, to lighten things and cheer Ellen up a little. "Well, I made the right choice last night anyway! But now it's time to think about getting that car fixed. Just imagine how worried the rental agency will be! You know what I was thinking? That I have become a colonial too. I haven't thought about that poor Arab once. Give me a slap and bring me to my senses."

"Would you mind if I gave you a kiss for that confession?"

"You are an Englishwoman from an Empire that rules half the world, don't you feel different from the locals?"

"I'd be a liar if I said I didn't feel superior, or that this dependent relationship didn't suit me. It gives you security and comfort and keeps you from thinking. You'll see, you'll begin to feel that way yourself, and Egypt isn't a real colony, when you come down to it,"

"I'm afraid that I'm feeling just like that already."

"Wait till you go to Kenya!"

"Have you been there?"

"For a few months. I felt like a Queen. I had two servants, one male and one female, just for myself, and I can assure you that I did not for one moment think that each of us wasn't in his proper place. I hear steps on the stairs. The Americans will be leaving, they have to be back at their base this morning."

"Do … you often have these parties?"

"Don't go all jealous on me. The answer is: No, and you can believe it or not."

"I believe you because I want to believe you."

"Meaning?"

"That I don't believe you."

"We've had a splendid time together – don't go and spoil it. What jealous creatures men are!"

"Aren't you on duty today? Aren't you going to put on your stripes?" Alexis said to her, nettled.

"My girl friends and I have a week's leave starting today – hence the party. If you must know, I've been thinking of going to Cairo for a few days. Have you been?"

"No, have you?"

"Never, and I do want to see it before I go – we may be sent to Europe in a few weeks. Why not come with me?"

The sudden invitation to Cairo mollified him. "To Cairo? When are you going?"

"Perhaps tomorrow, on a military flight. You could go by train or fly Misr-Air. I'll reserve rooms at the Mena House, near the Pyramids. You'll find me there."

"Rooms?"

"Have you forgotten that I'm a WAC? I have to watch my reputation."

"I hope I didn't ruin it for you last night."

"You're dead set on a quarrel, aren't you?"

"I thought you English had a sense of humour!"

"Well, do you want to come or not?"

"I'll come, but I'll have to inform the Captain of my ship and then telephone you. What about the car?"

"Let's have breakfast first, then we'll think about repair shops."

That morning he sat in the kitchen and drank coffee with the five other WACS and Ellen. The Americans had left.

"Let me introduce my friends to you again. Last night they weren't in any condition for introductions. Mary, Fay, Diana, Margaret, Jenny."

They were still wearing their colourful bathrobes, but were already made-up and well-groomed, as if they'd been to the beauty parlour. "It must be a part of military training," Alexis thought. They were like a delightful spring bouquet picked from a greenhouse kept with love.

They greeted him politely, no smirking, no suggestive remarks and in fact went to great lengths to coddle him, frying eggs and bacon and making toast. First one and then another would fill his cup with coffee.

They were chattering and laughing among themselves, discussing what they were going to do with their leave, six charming women who had all spent a night of love-making and were starting off the day renewed in body and spirit. Now and then they turned toward Alexis and asked him the sort of questions you ask someone you have just met.

"This is how it must feel to have a harem," Alexis said at some point.

"Except that the only one of us you have a right to is Ellen," Jenny piped up.

Ellen gave her a severe look. "I'm beginning to think this breakfast wasn't such a good idea. These friends of mine are too pretty to trust!"

"You act as if you didn't trust me either. At least that's what I see in your eyes," said Alexis.

Taking a last sip of coffee he rose and so did Ellen. The girls gathered around him to say good-bye and it was a long time before he forgot their fragrance, as one by one they kissed him on both cheeks.

"You're right not to trust us, Ellen," said Margaret, "he's such a sweetie!"

After Ellen had called a garage about the car, she said to him as he went out the door: "Try to be at Mena House tomorrow afternoon. I'll be expecting you."

And he headed toward his car with the light step of one who has had a beautiful experience, full of optimism, of expectations. He said to himself that now life was beginning – this was how he had imagined a man's life should be. He was wearing a uniform (an indispensable feature), he had spent a night with a woman who was straight out of a dream, and had discovered new places and people.

He thought about his Captain who wanted him to put in at least two hours a day on board ship – not to actually do anything but to learn the ropes.

He had no appetite for that today. He wanted to be by himself, to re-live the past night, moment by moment, For the first time, it occurred to him that there were only men on the freighter and that all the time he would be travelling there would be not one female form to look at. He couldn't imagine another morning without a bouquet of fresh young girls around him! He remembered that he had seen pin-ups of naked girls on tropical islands in the men's cabins on the boat – he didn't at all care for that kind of substitute.

Would this be a new prison? He'd left the Cadet School to be free: could he have fallen into another trap? Was he going to pay a heavy price for his travels? An opening to the wide world, they'd told him, and all that just to wear a uniform? Wasn't there any other way of travelling? And why was a uniform so important when you got right down to it? It might have helped a little in the conquest of Ellen but during the night he had been loved with his uniform off and now he was in the mood to go to Cairo in civilian clothes. He didn't need a uniform anymore. As for work ... the Lord provideth! For the moment he still had some family money and his regret at not having worked yet, lessened with the thought that after going through a whole war he had the right to enjoy a few more carefree days. The warrior's respite!

He lied to the Captain that day, saying that he had to go to Cairo on family business, and the next day, dressed in civvies and carrying a small suitcase, he arrived at Alexandria airport.

It would be his first time in a plane. All in all there were eight passengers who went out on the air-field but Alexis didn't see any plane. After they'd walked for some time, a tiny aeroplane appeared, practically a toy, with only one propeller. He had to stoop to enter it, and sat in one of the eight seats, four on each side. He hadn't expected to make his first flight in a miniature, but despite that he was excited about his aerial baptism.

The pilot's cabin wasn't separate, and you could watch everything that went on. Moreover, the pilot and co-pilot sitting next to one another were the entire crew. There was no stewardess, no steward. The aeroplane taxied down the runway and in a few minutes, having used the whole length, it lifted off and flew so low that they could see the desert, the Nile, palm trees and even camel caravans.

As Alexis looked down, all the images that he had ever connected with the desert passed through his mind: the Three Wise Men and their gifts, the Mufti's troops on their camels fighting General Gordon, the Bedouins in their black capes, Lawrence of Arabia, and all the fairy tales of his childhood ... the One Thousand and One Nights.

The navigation instruments must have been very primitive. Every so often the pilot stuck his head out of the window to see how hard the wind was blowing! The wings weren't of metal ... their frame was covered with canvas painted the colour of aluminium which had come unglued here and there and the bits, flapping in the wind, didn't give one the greatest feeling of security.

It was nearly time to reach Cairo. He looked out of the small window again and his heart leapt. He could see the Pyramids!

The aeroplane descended slowly and did a turn around the Pyramids before landing at Cairo airport. He tried to make out Mena House from the air but he couldn't see anything that looked like a hotel. It was around four in the afternoon when he got into the bus for the city and nearly five when he took the tram from the centre to Giza.

He passed the large square of Kasr el Nil, the two bridges over the Nile and a large boulevard with mansions and gardens. From the window of the tram, though it had the same cosmopolitan atmosphere as Alexandria, Cairo seemed more Middle Eastern, more Arab, more mysterious to him. Perhaps because more men and women were wearing 'jelabas', perhaps because there were more minarets jutting grandly up above the roofs of the city and the Citadelle.

He got off at the end of the line as he'd been told. He had no trouble finding Mena House with its lush gardens, exactly as he had imagined the gardens of the Orient in the technicolour dreams he'd often had as a child. He was startled. In a recurring childhood dream, he had walked in the fairy-tale garden of Yul Baba amid broad-leaved trees and dark red rose bushes, to reach the majestic stairs of the palace; he climbed it and stopped in front of the imposing gate. Somewhere in Arabia ... the tall black servant with the enormous tarbush on his head bowed, and asked him what he wanted: "I seek Aisa," and the answer was always the same: "She has taken to the desert". He would wake up disappointed that the dream never went any further. And that he had never met Aisa. But he was left with that pleasant sensation of the magic of the gardens and the palace – and now here was the palace, the gardens, and Aisa waiting for him.

He hurried toward the entrance to the hotel – and there before him was the tall servant with the dark red cape over the jelaba and the gold tarbush who bowed. Alexis stared in confusion at this unexpected ritual, but recovered quickly, went up to the reception desk and asked for Ellen, not without some trepidation. When they told him she was expecting him in the bar, not that she had gone to the desert, he relaxed. He sent his suitcase to the room that Ellen had reserved for him and the tall Arab with the red cape led him to the bar.

He gazed around at the hotel's decor, with its Islamic arched and carved wood, the 'mushrabiya', multi-coloured mosaics and old Arabic wooden furniture in Rosetta and Damietta style with inlaid ivory and pearls. It was as if for the first time his dream had crossed the threshold and gone through the gate of the palace, into the interior of the mystery itself.

Ellen was sitting on a stool at the bar with her back to the door and didn't see him come in. She was dressed in a green silk jelaba with gold piping around the throat and the edge of the cuffs, and was talking to the bartender. Her loose hair covered her bare shoulders. Her legs were crossed and under the jelaba he saw she was wearing a nearly transparent pink dress of pleated cretonne, cinched at the waist with a belt of the same material, which showed off her supple body. He approached quietly and whispered to her:

"*Hair as though stolen from Greek statues,*
always lovely, even uncombed,
and falling slightly over pale foreheads ..."

The impression he had expected to make on her with his recitation went awry because Ellen wheeled around abruptly, almost angrily: "My hair's uncombed?"

"Oh Aisa. Cavafy says it, not me. And by the way, I've never asked you how an Englishwoman like you can have such black hair and such white skin?"

"What did you call me? Aisa? Have you forgotten my name?" She really seemed quite irritated.

"But you are the woman of my dreams, or should I say dream?" He was forced to explain the whole story before she finally laughed and they ordered two Scotches from Ahmet.

"Don't forget, I'm Scottish, and you have to pay homage to my national drink. Besides, it will put us in just the right mood to see the pyramids by moonlight. As for my black hair – you should know that we Scots are Celts."

"Can you believe this is the first time I ever sat in a bar? In Greece we have coffee-houses instead, where we drink Turkish coffee between the throws of dice, or rounds of backgammon."

"In England and Scotland the pubs are an institution. During the war, the old men and the women who had been left behind would gather there and talk about the front until the air-raid sirens broke the meetings up. Why are you staring at me like that?"

"Your blue eyes, your black hair and your pink dress against the background of the mosaic is one of the most beautiful images I have ever seen."

"You Greeks must have a special criterion for beauty. None of the men I've ever known have treated me like this. You not only make me feel like a woman but like a woman in an enchanted place full of colour and fragrance. But let's not get too romantic, let's leave something for our ramble. Have you been up to your room?"

"Not yet, I came straight here to you."

"Then let's go – we have adjoining rooms – so I can get a wrap. The evenings can get quite chilly here."

"Do you mind if I call you Aisa tonight? I want my dream to become a reality."

"Call me Aisa, if you like, and I shall grant you the most beautiful oriental night that you can ever have imagined in your wildest dreams I've been here since noon. I've checked things out and have decided on our programme – do you mind?"

"Why should I mind? All those years on my own, I never even managed to get through the Palace gate!"

They went to their rooms, and without prior appointment, found themselves on their adjoining balconies looking out at the gardens of his dreams. Without a word, they turned toward each other, they looked at each other and then leaned over the iron railings and kissed. As Ellen's hair floated in the empty space between the two balconies, Alexis parted it with his hands. "Look, it's as if you had two black wings and were ready to fly away!"

"You're the one who might have to fly, the way you're leaning over the balcony."

"I'll hold on to your hair. I can't help it, your hair mesmerises me."

"Did you see the lovely gardens and the fountain on the terrace with the little tables and lamps? We'll come back and eat on the terrace later. I'll be waiting for you at the front door."

With a pale blue shawl around her shoulders and clasping her shock of dark hair, Ellen had become even more like something out of a fairly tale.

He wanted to take her hand as they walked up the dirt road to the pyramids but he was afraid of suddenly waking from his dream. Dignified and aloof in the light of the moon that was beginning to rise, Ellen was well aware of the image she was projecting; all her senses were open to everything around her and she was ready to face the first pyramid, that of Cheops, which loomed up larger and larger as they approached it along the uphill road.

At that moment Alexis felt that he was nothing more than a small part of Ellen's world and, next to the great pyramid which was already framed by the other two, he was a mere pebble in the moon-bathed desert. He immediately disliked the pyramids.

When Ellen said in admiration: "Don't you find them incredible?"

Alexis only muttered: "I find them overbearing. Three lines which start out from the earth and meet at a point without leading anywhere! They look like your sharp little nose pointing at the sky."

Ellen looked at him unable to tell if he was serious or joking. "How can you change mood like that? What does my nose have to do with anything?"

"I don't like the pyramids – I don't even care for geometry"

"Is my nose overbearing? Don't you like it?"

"You were putting on such airs as we walked up the hill – as if you were Nefertiti at the very least."

"Is that so! Come let me kiss you. And tell me right now that I have the most beautiful nose in the world."

"You have the most beautiful ... sharp little nose in the world, but I still don't like the pyramids or the obelisks."

"Phallic symbols bother you, do they?"

"I don't know, it may be that. The obelisks especially – they look castrated."

"I suppose you Greeks only approve of your own temples and columns?"

"A column has a base and a pediment chiselled by an artist's hand and it connects the soul of a person with heaven; it's not just one block of stone on top of another which meet somewhere up there leading nowhere. Leaving aside the fact that hundreds of thousands of slaves worked to build these tombs for the Pharaohs – it upsets me."

"I've never heard such strange talk in my life. Stop it now, don't ruin my evening. Just look at the desert, that scattering of palm trees to the rear, the sleeping camels and the moon casting its wings on the sand."

"Ellen ... Aisa ... don't you think I feel the magic of it all? It's just that on the way up here you seemed so distant that I was afraid the night might take you from me, that I'd lose you in the desert. The night I met you I had just been at El Alamein where I thought the desert was going to swallow me up. The desert frightens me. Perhaps it was a dread of the desert that created the feeling of death in the Egyptians and made them build these enormous monuments with their vast chambers for the dead, larger than their palaces in life."

"I forget you're a seaman; so you're out of your depth here."

"It's wonderful to see something important for the first time with a woman like you!"

"It's wonderful to experience ecstasy with someone you love. Don't let my words frighten you: right now I do love you."

Why right now? Why make him worry about tomorrow? He hadn't asked her to love him. Better if she hadn't said anything. So, "right now" he had to make sure. He used her shawl to pull her gently to him and tested the heat of her kiss. She held him so tight that he groaned: "Aisa!"

And she: "This is a dream – our dream!"

His dream had become hers.

There was no-one else there that evening. They walked around Cheop's pyramid and far off, where the ground fell away to the rear, they suddenly saw the rough shape of the Sphinx. As they approached, its mass was outlined against a backdrop of white houses of an unlit

Arab village, and, bathed in moonlight, it caused Alexis' feelings of awe to grow. They stood in front of the "beast" with bated breath.

"You will call me incorrigibly classical again. But isn't it beyond any analogy of nature and man? Isn't it inaccessible?"

"Isn't God inaccessible?"

"Not the Greek gods! When there were fewer of us, we had a lot of gods and they were close to us. We even knew where they lived! Now that there are so many of us, we've combined them all into One, far away, somewhere in infinity, and there are some that would like to abolish this One as well."

"I didn't realise I'd made love to a polytheist!"

"We had sphinxes in Greece too but they were at least female and humbler. Art should never be inaccessible and overbearing."

"And a voice was heard from the Golden Age, Divine!", Ellen declaimed ironically.

To get his own back Alexis said: "I'm not saying that. You people in the west have your noteworthy achievements as well ... it's just that you were so far behind us!"

Then, once again, silence and reconciliation. They walked further into the desert and stopped.

"In the desert, where there are no roads, you don't know where you are going. And I have to find my own way. During the war, each day took you by the hand in the morning and left you in the evening and you didn't ask about tomorrow because the next day would take you by the hand once more. But now I have to make my own decisions. I came from Greece with memories but also with indignation about everything I had left behind."

He told her the story then about how he'd escaped from the jaws of death. "Now here on this peaceful night I am faced with the agony of choice, as you put it last night in Alexandria. Then, I was fighting with comrades and we shared our feelings. But now the future seems like this desert, without pattern, without end, and if you weren't next to me at this moment, I would be feeling the weight of a vast loneliness."

"But I am next to you. Perhaps this will sound strange to you, but being with you I've found a new meaning in life. Though you're younger than I am, you've revived me and opened a world of poetry to me that I will keep for the rest of my life. I would like to see you again, say ... at thirty-five, before you lose your present romantic freshness, but with the taste and experience you will have acquired by then. If I like you the way you are now, I can imagine what you will look like with the polish of the years to come."

"There you go bringing me face to face with the future again. But you're right. I don't have the experience to face the uncertainty of the temporary. Today, the idea of a tomorrow without you clouds my soul. I have to learn to enjoy the moment without anguish and to keep the curiosity of discovery stronger than any anguish about the future; the curiosity of quest has to be more powerful than the sensation of the moment. To learn, learn, always to learn."

– And may you visit many Egyptian cities
to learn and go on learning from their scholars.

"Cavafy again, of course! Deep down you're a poet. Why do you keep on trying to find out what you are?"

"Poet? That's all very fine, a poet, but I don't want to deal with life only as a poet, on the sidelines. I don't want to be a spectator, to hear music and not be able to play, to read a book and not be able to write, to watch a runner and not be able to run. I want to participate, to work both with my hands and my mind. Rimbaud said: 'Today, the hand of the worker and hand of the writer are of equal worth.' That's the way it is for me: they're both of equal worth. But I want what I do with my hands to be poetry."

"That's to my benefit, too!" Ellen said coyly. "Last night your caresses put me in seventh heaven. Go on the way you're going, don't change, you're on the right track. And speaking of tracks, how about going back by way of the village?"

They slipped into the labyrinth of dirt lanes that formed the village, trying to find the way to the large avenue that would lead back to Mena House.

Ellen had him tell her in detail his experiences at Kaisariani, and she squeezed his hand tightly at the critical points in the story. She had become the mother again. The framework was set by now. In a while, in his room or hers, Ellen would once more be transformed into a woman who would bestow on him another night of love before turning into a child once more – closing the circle one more time. He almost smiled to himself when he realised that he could predict her reaction.

The only sign of life in the village, which had settled down for the night, were a few Arabs in long jelabas' and with canes in their hands, sitting in front of the doors of their houses; they stared at them curiously as they passed by. Ellen was nervous and held on tightly to Alexis.

"We should have gone back by the Pyramids. I'm a little afraid of these people in the dark."

Suddenly, an Arab got up and started shouting and shaking his cane.

"What's he saying?" Alexis asked. Ellen, who had spent more time in Egypt, translated: "I think he's shouting, 'Esma, come my child, come!'. He seems to have taken a fancy to you.'

"At least you've nothing to fear. Act as if you don't understand and walk on as if nothing were happening. Hold my hand."

The Arab followed them keeping his distance.

"Do you know how to get out of here?" Alexis asked.

"You seem to think I come here every day. There are no lights to be seen around here anywhere."

"If we keep going straight, we'll emerge at some point, since the desert is behind us – I'm sure of that."

"What will you do if he attacks us? Remember, others usually join in as soon as a quarrel starts."

"You can be sure I'm not going to try and be Lawrence of Arabia!"

"Shall we stop and talk to him?"

"In what language?"

"I don't know, but surprise is always the best tactic."

"You're right. I don't think we can be so far from the road. The village didn't look all that big from up there. Any time now we should run into the paved road to Mena House. Listen: I'll shout out loudly the only Arab words I know, he'll be startled, and the moment he pauses, run ahead as fast as you can. I'll stay behind for a while as a diversion and then I'll run away myself. In any case, he won't be able to run fast enough in a jelaba to catch us."

"All right, but if I don't see you in a couple of minutes, I'll run to the hotel and call the police. What are you going to shout?"

Alexis shouted as loud as he could. "Allaaaaah Akbaaaaaar! Allah is great!"

Then to Ellen: "Run! Now!"

Ellen began to run. Alexis wheeled around suddenly and as he'd expected the Arab had frozen at hearing this mere strip of a lad calling out the name of "Allah" in the middle of the night; what surprised him was that the Arab then started running off in the opposite direction. Two minutes later Ellen and Alexis were hugging each other on the public road, overcome with laughter at the turn their romantic walk had taken.

"I promised you one of the most beautiful nights ever. I didn't think we'd have an adventure too", Ellen told him.

Mena House wasn't far away and the night was still young. On the terrace in front of the hotel, at the bottom of the steps that led to the park, an orchestra with violins was playing the same music he'd heard at Ellen's place on that first evening. The tables were all frill except for the one Ellen had reserved earlier.

The elegant waiters in their crisp white robes and red fezzes did a kind of ballet between the tables as they balanced silver trays on high and leaned forward to serve with silent movements. The only light came from the table-lamps' tiny lampshades.

They were both hungry after their night walk. Alexis picked up the menu and thought that it was the first time he'd seen such an elaborate card with the name of the hotel in gilt letters. He ran his fingers over the raised letters with the same sensual pleasure as when he'd caressed the chocolate bar in Alexandria. He read it carefully:

– *Soupe veloutee Richelieu*
Tranche de dorade 'A la grecque!'

(He felt very proud of the 'A la grecque!')

Canard sauvage du desert au vin blanc

(He didn't know they had duck in the desert!)

Bombe a la vanille
Fruits de l'Orient
Café

As he was reading, he remembered another menu written on the wax paper of the table at Barba Thanassis' taverna in Erythraia,

outside Athens, by the joker of the party, during a night of high spirits only a few months ago:
   – *Canadian soup with insects in season*
   Croquettes a la grasse
   Cornbread a la mode
   Triple decker sesame cake
   He began to laugh. Ellen watched curiously as he wrote in French, on the back of the Mena House menu, the menu from Barba Thanassis' taverna, and then they both laughed together.
   "You didn't tell me you knew French, Ellen."
   "My mother is half French, from Normandy. But then what do you know about me – very little when you get down to it. It's only the second time we've seen each other. Don't forget we didn't do ... much talking that first night."
   "Yes, but two people say a lot to each other when they make love. At least that's how I felt with you. The way you embraced me, the movements of your head, the shuddering of your body, the sweet nothings you whispered, and above all, the way your expression became spontaneous – a change from the cynical woman you were trying to be when I first entered your house, with your little jokes like 'I got a medal because I screwed a general!'"
   Ellen watched him and listened to him, deeply moved, not only because of the way he was talking about her, but also because she was getting to know herself better, as if looking into a mirror! As a woman she was most interested in plumbing the depths of the soul and she didn't try to hide her interest.
   "I'm finding out who I am by listening to you. It may seem like I have my feet on the ground but I'm quite confused really."
   "But you do have your feet on the ground. I saw you earlier when you were standing in the light of the moon and you seemed to be talking to the pyramids – as if you ruled the endless desert – as if you stood alone between earth and God!"
   "I didn't mean to interrupt you. Go on ... go on."
   "You are 100% female. In your soul, your body, in your sweet glance, in the grace of your hands, in the way you toss your hair back. You cover the whole gamut of love – of mother, woman and child."

"The moon, the palm trees and banana plants, the violins, the pink table-cloths and the red wine, your words ... it's like a fairy tale. Get up – let's dance – I want to hold you tightly and I can't do it across the table."

There were only two or three couples on the dance floor.

"We have a Greek saying that goes: 'A hungry bear won't dance!' We haven't had a bit yet but ... I suppose we'll survive!"

"Honestly, you're the limit! You spoil the atmosphere even with your jokes."

"We have another saying: 'One on the nail and one on the horseshoe.' It keeps you off your high horse!"

"You ...!"

They got up and danced. The orchestra was playing the 'Comparsita' tango.

Ellen leaned on him and began to softly hum: "Da, da, da, da, dada, dada – da, da, da, da, – da."

"I'm jealous," she said.

"Who are you jealous of?"

"Of all the women you'll know after me."

"See, you're just like me – you can't enjoy the moment without going off into something else."

"It would be nice if we could flip a switch and turn off thought whenever we liked."

"Would it make you feel better if I said that no matter how many women I might get to know, you will always be part of me, as my first dream that came true?"

"No, it would not!"

Then, she added maliciously: "I'll forget you the day after we say good-bye and I'll sleep with the first man I meet no matter how ugly, short or old he might be."

"Did you say 'old' to chide me for the fact that I'm younger than you?"

"Perhaps. It seems strange to me that you have got such a hold on me in such a short time and that I should be hearing from an adolescent who has just reached manhood the most beautiful words I have ever heard. And where did you learn to tango so well? During the occupation?"

"That's another story. Even when we didn't have enough food to eat, my mother and father raised me with 'French, piano and dance', as they said then. My mother played piano, my father the violin. My father would cuff me if I didn't answer him in French, to make me practise it. As for the dancing, a group of young people gathered once a week at a neighbour's house and Madame Newland, a very unattractive dance teacher, of uncertain age and nationality, taught us to tango, waltz, fox-trot and rumba. I was a good student in everything but the tango, because in the other dances I could keep her at a distance. But with the tango she held me so close I got the steps wrong. That Balalaika record, the only tango they had at that house, became a nightmare for me, But at least I didn't forget the basics and with you the nightmare has turned into a beautiful dream."

"There we go again! You use the word 'dream' again and again. I've never met anyone so dream conscious."

"Do you know how often a dream has saved me?"

"Tell me."

"In prison, for example. When the Italians locked me up, it was my dreams that kept me on the outside."

"You were in prison?"

"During the occupation, anybody with dignity spent some time in jail!"

"Will you tell me why they jailed you?"

"Yes, but not now. Anyway, in the larger 'prison' which was Greece during the occupation, I dreamed of liberty day after day. You see, sometimes we must extend ourselves into the future Then there were the evenings before my school examinations when, lying on my bed, I'd be looking out at the stars through the open window and I'd dream up a story giving each of the stars a human form; they loved each other and made war just like people. The next day when the teacher wrote on the blackboard, 'The star-strewn heaven', I'm sure you can imagine how I felt!"

"You must be a medium; I'm beginning to be afraid of you."

"Maybe ... but right now, I am truly holding Aisa in my arms! ... I think they've brought the food to the table."

"A dream's a dream, but you never forget about your stomach!"

She gave him a peck on the cheek, they went and sat down. Everyone around them was talking in whispers: even the waiters seemed to be walking around on a layer of air, like well-synchronised puppets, so as not to disturb the magical calm of the oriental night. With a glance or a squeeze of the hand, Alexis and Ellen signalled to each other when to dance, when to eat, to clink glasses or to steal a kiss.

At about midnight, Ellen took him by the hand and they walked down the terrace steps toward the gardens.

"I promised you one of the thousand and one nights – what does it matter if we are in the gardens of the Pharaohs or of the Yul Baba of your dreams? In the Arabian nights, the tales are about a place that is a mixture of Persia, Arabia, China and Egypt. They mention Kings who are not known to history. Sultans and caliphs, fishermen and viziers who are lost in the geography of the Orient. Each one of us has lived through different nights, different dreams. Maybe now is the time for you to talk about your own fairytales, the ones you lived or dreamed about. Start by telling me what Sultan put you in prison during the occupation?"

"I'll tell you. Only you must swear to me that every night for a thousand and one nights, you will listen to one of my stories, like the Sultan listened to Scheherezade. The one night you promised me, is not enough for all of my fairy tales."

"If it depended on me, if it was my decision alone, I would gladly give you all one thousand and one nights, and then again as much. But others give the orders, and don't forget, there is still a war on, and when peace comes the fairy tales may be no more."

"At least let's count the nights, starting today, and counting from one thousand and one ... let's see how far we get."

"Starting from one, we can reach the infinite! Starting from the end, we know there will be an end."

"What if we start at one and don't ever reach a thousand and one? We'll never be able to say that we lived through the fairy tale of the thousand and one nights? Listen to me, my system is better, and let's hope we reach zero!"

"Then let's have it your way."

"Sometimes I wonder if it's your English common sense or your Cartesian French logic that is prevailing!"

"At this moment, it is Aisa the Eastern lady speaking – she is dying to hear the first tale before making love to you till dawn."

Ellen sat down on a small bench under a palm tree and called Alexis to her. The moon spilled through the foliage of the trees making abstract shapes on the ground. Ellen wrapped herself in her long shawl and snuggled up next to him as he spoke.

"A few years ago, which seem like centuries, the Sultan of Rome, Mussolini Pasha, came out on his balcony and shouted 'Cockadoodledoo! Cockadoodledoo!' and rushed to seize Greece. He sent soldiers with plumes in their hats to show the other madman, Sultan Adolf, that he knew how to wage war too.

"But suddenly there rose up before him an enormous genie wearing a white pleated skirt and clogs with pompoms. 'Ochi! No! No matter who you are, you will not pass!' and the Italians were so afraid they ran away. But the enormous genie chased them and would have driven them into the sea if Sultan Adolf had not awoken in a foul humour one morning and immediately called for his barber, his orderly, his astrologer and his general.

"To the orderly he said: 'Bring my best boots and my grand uniform!'

"To his barber he said: 'Make my moustache symmetrical with my nostrils and make sure my hank of hair sweeps diagonally across my forehead in line with my left ear!'

"To his astrologer he said: 'Fix the stars so they have a good influence on my soldiers in the Balkans and listen carefully, I'll cut off your head if you make a mistake." "The planet Mars is not lined up with Saturn the way it should be, mein Fuhrer", the astrologer told him but the Fuhrer didn't listen to him.

"To his general Jodl the Dervish he said: 'Take 100,000 soldiers and goose-step into Greece.'

"The genie reared up again and for three weeks the soldiers of Sultan Adolf goose-stepped but didn't move an inch forward! The sultan called for his astrologer again and told him he would send him to the guillotine. The astrologer kneeled: 'Your highness, do not advance, the stars are not right, I told you that your greed would lead you to the abyss of destruction.' 'You silly man, you don't know what you're talking about.' And he cut off his head.

"So the Sultan goose-stepped into Athens and brought along with him the Italians and they found the windows and the eyes closed, the streets empty, and the souls frozen. Slowly, we Greeks opened our eyes ever so fearfully and our souls filled with courage and we started another war, secretly, in whispers, in the dead of night, which revived hope in the vanquished and destroyed the morale of the conquerors.

"Then everything became very simple. Kostas whispered to Theodoros, Theodoros whispered to Pavlos, Pavlos to Yiorgos and so forth and so on. We organised ourselves like the caterpillars who at one moment are rolled up in a ball on the branches of a tree and the next slither out like a huge, silent snake. Like the Dragon of the East, ready to shake off the yoke of the Sultan."

For a few moments, Alexis and Ellen listened only to the silence of the night.

"It must have been June of '43. I'd just finished high school – so I could devote all my time to the Resistance. Distributing newspapers in neighbourhoods, sticking proclamations on doors, painting slogans on walls, learning to use rifles, machine-guns and pistols, to transport them to hiding places, to be prepared for the great battle for freedom. It became routine. The Germans of Sultan Adolf had already caught quite a few of us but as time went on we got braver and more reckless.

"One evening, Linos, Petros, Stelios, Nikos and I gathered at our hangout. We were going to paint slogans on the Carabinieri Headquarters on Adrianou Street. We took a bucket of blue paint and the brushes and slipped into the night during the blackout. We scampered from wall to wall till we reached the rear of the Carabinieri, making sure the sentry couldn't see us; we set Stelios and Nikos as look-outs on two corners and the other three began to paint the walls with slogans that had been given to us from the 'higher echelons': "The Allies are coming", "We shall triumph", "Enemies Out!", and others I can't remember.

"We had become professional painters by that time. The improvised paint was well-made and we put just enough on the brush to make the letters clear. We were concentrating so intensely on our … calligraphy, that no-one thought of looking overhead at the balcony where a Senior Carabiniere, sprawled in a chair was watching the whole scene. Before the look-outs got wind of him, he was standing in front of us with his gun in his hand and introduced himself: Mareshal Vardanega – the Italian police. One of our more composed members replied, 'Pleased to meet you', before he froze too. The look-outs faded away like smoke!

"Later, as we stood in front of the desk of the Chief of the Carabinieri, the interrogation started. A couple of feet further on was a tall and cold-looking 'torturer' with a whip in his hand – leather, with knots in it.

"Do you see that?" Petros said.

"Just as long as we only see it everything is all right," Linos replied.

"I got so many beatings in school that a few more won't make any difference!" I said, more to give myself courage than anything else.

"Shut up!" the head carabinieri shouted but he didn't seem to be all that angry.

"First question: 'What organisation do you belong to?' A short Greek was doing the interpreting. We passed the first test, the first lesson, by staying mute. We had committed ourselves to secrecy two years before, not even letting our own families know what organisation we belonged to, what our aims were, where we disappeared at night. A great force is generated through the secrecy that knits a group of people, like the unknown hierarchy that governs the Mafia. The godfathers never appear and only their confidants know them – however, they are the ones holding reins. The questions continued to rain down.

'What are the names of your friends who ran away? What do those slogans you are writing mean? Enemies out! Who are the enemies?'

'The Bulgarians up north!' Petros shot back.

'Who are the Allies who are coming?'

"Uh ... the Germans, the English, the Italians and the Americans!' I quipped.

'Are you trying to mock us?'

"For the first time I heard the whip whistling over my head. But apparently we looked so harmless and innocent that the head carabinieri asked:

49

'Now you tell me, how did the English and the Germans become allies?'

'Look,' said Petros, who had a nimble mind, 'it depends on how you look at it. The Bulgarians are our enemies. Whoever helps drive them out is an ally!'

"The other two were stunned by Petros' cheekiness and even more stunned that the Mareshal didn't automatically respond with the whip. Instead of that, the head carabinieri yawned – it was late of course – and motioned for them to take us out of there. The interpreter explained that the interrogation would be resumed the following day. They took us through a small yard, down to a cellar laid with wet sand. They handcuffed Petros and me together by our ankles. Linos got special treatment. They handcuffed his feet. He was self-sufficient. As the door of the dark basement closed, I was the first to speak.

'So, Petros, what do we do if we have to take a leak? Go together?'

'I was just thinking that tomorrow I have a date with an elegant doll and that I'll be standing her up.'

'Don't let it bother you,' Linos said, 'she'll wait for you and when ... and if ... you get out of prison, you'll be a hero to her!'

'Forget it. We'll have to think and make plans.'

'This is one situation where we can't do anything but lie down and sleep like Siamese twins' I said.

'I hope you sleep well on your back,' Petros said with a grin on his face.

'Do I have any choice?' I replied.

"Creeping about we found two rocks for pillows and with co-ordinated movements lay down on the sand.

'What the hell do they water this down for? The sand is wet,' Linos complained.

'It's just piss from the other men who've been locked up here,' Petros shot back.

'Excuse me,' I told him, 'for making you move but I have to take a leak. It's your fault – you brought it up!'

"We stood up again and by hopping we went to the other side of the cellar which was about four metres by four.

'Why don't you have a piss too so we don't have to keep getting up?' I told him.

'I'll do my best!' he said and doubled up with laughter.

'What's so funny?'

'Nothing, I just thought of a joke. In Paris – you know, I'm half French – in a public 'pissoir', one of those cylindrical ones they have on all the large boulevards, someone went in and asked the fellow next to him to unbutton his fly for him. The other fellow was astonished but he went ahead and did it. "Will you pull it out for me now?" he says. The other guy looked at him oddly but carried out the request. "Please, hold it for me while I pee, would you?" Convinced that the guy was mad, he didn't want to rile him. "Now, would you put it back and button me up again, please?" "Excuse me, sir," he says to the madman, "but why can't you do all that by yourself?" "Ah, it revolts me, you see!" and Petros burst out laughing again.

'I hope it doesn't disgust you too, because I certainly won't be doing you the honours!' I told him.

"And we all started laughing then. And so the first hours of the night were spent telling jokes, since, even if we felt like sleep, what with the over-excitement on the one side and the conditions of the cell we found ourselves in on the other, the situation did not exactly lend itself to sleeping. Now and then one of us would say: 'I wonder how we're going to get out of here?' but no-one had an answer.

'I hope the interpreter notifies our homes, as we asked him to, so at least they won't be worried.'

'Maybe they'll take us out into the yard tomorrow morning ... I noticed, as we were going by, that the wall is low and the service stairs are flat against the apartment building next door,' I whispered, so we wouldn't be overheard.

'You'll get a long way with those cuffs on,' Linos said, 'I guess you read a lot of detective stories. Get it through your head, you don't get out of here so easily. You should be happy they haven't put us up against a wall yet.'

'Execute us for a handful of slogans? It's a good thing the look-outs held onto the posters and got out of there, those rascals,' I said.

'Do you think they'll give us a beating tomorrow, to make us talk?' Petros asked.

'How should I know, they don't look all that tough. It's like we were little kids and they felt sorry for us,' Linos said.

"In the end we all dozed off and were awoken by footsteps in the morning. We opened our eyes and for the first time realised that in the corner of the cellar there was a small grating of thick iron bars in the ceiling that looked out on the sidewalk outside. We got up and hopped over to stand under it; a few early morning people passed by overhead going to their jobs. It was a strange feeling knowing that just a few centimetres separated the free people from us prisoners.

"Aren't you tired of listening to me yet?" Alexis said to Ellen. "Shouldn't we take a break? Anyway, it's beginning to get chilly – aren't you cold?"

Ellen, who had been curled up against him, straightened up and kissed him, wrapping her arms around him to offer the warmth of her body. The mother again.

"Just a little more. Tell me what happened next; I'm on tenterhooks."

"The next morning they unshackled us and took us to be interrogated again. To make a long story short it was the same questions all over again: 'What organisation do you belong to?', 'Who are your leaders?' We played dumb. 'We don't know. It's the first time we've done this, you can tell by the fact that we didn't know we were painting slogans on the Carabinieri Headquarters.' And miracle of miracles, there was no beating. That is, not the beating we expected. A few slaps, which seemed like caresses compared to the whip that the carabinieri had there to scare us. After the interrogation they separated us. Petros and Linos went back in resignation to the cellar. They chained me to a chair in the dining-room.

At first I thought they had put me in there for my own good, as I was the youngest, but when I saw the policemen wolfing down huge forkfuls of spaghetti dripping with sauce right in front of me and not offering me even a bite, letting me have no contact with my friends, I came to realise that this was a form of torture, to break me. Despite the fact however that I craved a plate of spaghetti, it seemed so funny that for the first time I was seeing with my very own eyes the famed spaghetti-twirlers, that I began to laugh to myself! The large photograph of Mussolini-Pasha hanging on the wall with his thick lips and pompous bearing made me feel giddy rather than despairing.

"As soon as the Italians finished off their meal and cleared the table, the Greek interpreter, a young fellow of around twenty-five, came and sat down next to me, secretly passing me a note. I recognised my father's handwriting. I opened it and read it under the table, 'I hope you act like a true Greek! Your father.' I hadn't taken the whole thing seriously but my father's note really shook me. While I had expected him to be furious with me, despite his anguish, he had written me a few stalwart words like the stalwart man he was, and given me strength – but I also suddenly realised that this was no game! This was prison and I was in it! I asked the interpreter if he'd seen my family.

'I saw them and admired them,' he told me. 'Don't worry, I'll keep them and your friends' parents informed.'

"Then he tried to justify his collaboration with the Italians.

'I know, you're suspicious of me but I was a poor kid and when you get down to it all I do is interpret and try to help fellows like you as much as I can.'

"Since he was our only contact with the outside world we had to put our trust in him, whether we wanted to or not; it was true he had notified our parents without delay.

"My stay in the dining-room lasted for three days, and for three days the platters of spaghetti passed under my nose. So I wouldn't starve they gave me a little watery broth and some bread. Every so often they'd call me into the office for interrogation and tell me the classic lie: 'Your friends have told us everything, so you may as well tell us what you know.' Even though we were inexperienced in interrogation, we knew that trick at least and were sure that none of us had talked.

"Moreover, the beating we kept expecting, didn't happen!

"I only saw Petros and Linos very briefly when they were being taken to and from interrogation and we would exchange encouraging glances. The third day, in the afternoon, all of us were collected in the Mareshal's office, and after they'd taken off the handcuffs, they told us they were sending us to the prison in Kallithea. Vardanega, the one who had arrested us, put us in the "kluva", the police wagon, and off to Kallithea! In the wagon, Vardanega started to talk to us, speaking Italian syllable by syllable, so we could understand. He told us about his village in northern Italy, about his family and the evil of war and did everything but ask forgiveness for arresting us!

'Why don't you stop the car and say we escaped?' I ventured at some point in broken Italian, using gestures.

'I can't, my boy, it's war!'

The atmosphere got friendlier.

'Why did you start the war?' I asked him.

He paused a moment and then shook his head.

'I wish I knew,' he said. 'The Greeks didn't do anything to us. It's Mussolini's fault' and he made a face.

'Don't you feel any remorse about arresting us?'

'I'm a carabiniere and I have my duty to do.'

"For the first time it went through my mind just how subjective duty is. A duty, determined by geography and hierarchy.

'You see how strange it is?' I said to him. 'Your duty is for you to fight me. Mine, to fight you. But duty should be one and the same for everyone: to fight for love and humanity.' I am not sure he fully understood my poor Italian.

"And I realised what a monster hierarchy is. A Mussolini, a Hitler, at the top of the pyramid and millions of puppets underneath who cannot or do not want to escape."

"Now I understand why you dislike the pyramids," Ellen whispered, almost speaking to herself.

"When the wagon stopped in front of the large gate that was framed by the high walls of the Kallithea prison, Vardanega looked more dejected than we were. He said good-bye, and as he handed us over to the Italian officer who was waiting for us at the gate, shook hands with us.

'From here on things get serious,' Petros said, and nobody answered.

"The first large iron gate opened and a second high wall stood before us, forming a corridor around the prison, like the moat around a medieval tower.

"They put us in an office, took away our shoelaces and whatever else we might use to try and commit suicide in a moment of despair! It seemed like a joke to us because we were anything but despairing.

"Despite the seriousness of the situation that Petros had noted, from the moment the three of us were together again, we were happy. After they had emptied our pockets, they took us through the second gate into the large prison yard, with a blanket on one arm and a thin army mattress covered with stains (which we considered the height of luxury after the wet sand in the cellar), a tin plate and a tin spoon. Slaves of Sultan Benito. There it was! We were in jail. For how long? Would there be a trial? Would they sentence us? To one year? Two years? Or would the Allies liberate us sooner than that? Would they torture us? How serious was our crime? Questions which no-one could answer but which from then on we would discuss every day with the other prisoners who had longer experience than we did.

"We stood for a while looking around. All the prisoners were in the yard at that time and we were relieved to see that they weren't wearing striped pyjamas as we'd imagined. In front of us was the main prison building but no-one took us inside. They left us by ourselves in the yard.

"We hesitantly began to make our way toward the other prisoners, who welcomed us warmly. Each new arrival was a big event in the monotony on life. It was like islanders who scatter at the pier whenever a boat arrives, wanting to see who disembarks. There were a lot of prisoners – around eight hundred we learned later – and now and then an Italian non-commissioned officer patrolling the yard.

"As we wandered around feeling like idiots with the blankets under our arms and the mattresses on our shoulders, I saw in the distance somebody I knew sitting on the ground cross-legged and leaning against the prison wall – Achilleas Kyrou, Editor-in-Chief of the Estia newspaper and a good friend of my parents!

"Suddenly, the whole scene changed. A familiar face inside the prison walls – Hope. I went and stood in front of him and he said in utter surprise, 'Child, your mother was right when she said you'd end up in jail!'

"He got up and kissed me on both cheeks. I introduced him to my friends and he introduced us to his. I remember Admiral Chrysanthis, who also happened to be a good friend of my father's, and a Police Chief, the clown of the group, whose name I don't remember.

'We'll take the boys into our cell, Kyrou said to the others and turning to us – we'll be a little crowded in there but it will be better. There are only seventeen in our block, while the other cells, although they are larger, have forty or more.'

'Don't they lock you in?' we asked.

'They lock the building, but not the cells. They let us out of the building into the yard for four hours in the morning and the same again in the afternoon.'

"In a few minutes we had learned the schedule for the day, and from then on it was like a social gathering with all these friends and the feeling of protection we got from the adults, so our worries disappeared, at least temporarily. They asked us why we'd been arrested and everyone said how small the world was; the only one who stayed silent was Linos, who looked all around him with great concentration.

'What are you looking at so intently?' Petros asked him.

'At the walls of course. Don't you know that the first commandment a prisoner must obey is that of escape; to examine his surroundings to find the weakest point so he can break out?'

'How come you know so much about being a prisoner?'

'From thrillers.'

'What have you found out so far?'

'It's too early to tell yet, but it looks difficult.'

"I had also had a look around the prison, and saw that the height of the walls and the soldiers with their machine guns manning the eight towers, didn't leave much room for dreaming! But I did notice the kitchen near the entrance. Smoke was coming out of its chimney and at the moment that was of more interest to me than any idea of escaping. I couldn't get out of my mind the memory of the spaghetti the Italian soldiers had eaten right under my nose for three days.

'The first aim of every prisoner is to try and find a way to escape, if only to keep his morale up!' Linos repeated.

'The first aim of a prisoner is to make friends with the cook,' I said off the top of my head and my joke, more than half serious, warmed the atmosphere and created a cordial bond with our protectors.

"When the bell rang for us to go inside it was like the end of a school recess.

"Can I take a recess now too and kiss you?" Alexis asked Ellen.

Ellen unbuttoned his shirt and rested her hand on his bare chest. As he looked into her eyes he kissed her with longing and held his breath till their lips grew numb and then they both breathed deeply in the crystal clear, almost tropical, night.

He started to kiss her again but Ellen put both her hands on his mouth to stop him.

"First the prison – you haven't finished the story yet. Then the kisses. Like a child needs a fairy tale before going to sleep, I need one before I make love."

"But I am the child!"

"But I am not going to bed if I don't hear the end of the story!"

"Where were we? There's not much more to tell. There were now twenty people in our room. Ten mattresses on the right, ten on the left, with a narrow aisle in between. My first contact with the morning ritual was perhaps my most unpleasant experience. The line-up for the few toilets (there must have been about one for every fifty prisoners), the tidying up of the room and the waiting to go out into the courtyard. Some watery broth from a cauldron for breakfast and then free time to get to know the other prisoners or play some improvised sports. I then became the star athlete in the prison at … hop-scotch! During the middle of the day it was back in the room for a siesta and then, in the afternoon, back into the yard for another recess. Toward sunset, the bell. The same routine day after day. Every time we entered the prison building a barred door was opened for us and as we passed through we were counted one by one. One evening Petros and I stopped in front of the door, each of us inviting the other to pass through first, while the other prisoners waited in line behind us. I don't remember who had the idea but I was usually the joker.

'You first, please!'
'No, after you.'
'No, I insist, after you!'
"By the time the Italians had taken us by the ear and pushed us inside, all hell had broken loose. It seems they'd made a mistake in the count while watching our performance of good manners, and found us one too few. The Italians were in an uproar, shouting that someone must have escaped! Only we knew the truth. So we had to go out again to be recounted.

"When the count came out right the second time, they looked for the two trouble-makers who had confused them, and went through all the rooms trying to find us by staring each man in the face one by one. It was our good fortune that the prisoners were just numbers to the guards; they didn't pay any attention to faces, even though they seemed to stand before us forever. Our innocent expressions had worked their magic again.

"In the evening, before we went to sleep, we'd sit around cross-legged and try to analyse the fragmentary and often erroneous news about the Allied campaign in Italy, and the war in Russia, to get some idea of how long the war would last, and consequently our captivity. We learned the news from the few visits of relatives, or from the Italians themselves, though that was from another viewpoint. Once in a while, at night, we were woken by the screams of prisoners being tortured; these were the only really terrible moments in the otherwise rather peaceful life. Our prison was a small society. People of every age, from admirals and generals to street kids fifteen years old. Some had been arrested for resistance work, others because they'd stolen Italian army bread, others by mistake.

"Even in prison there were social distinctions. The intellectuals and officers were on one level and the common people on another. There was admiration, friendship, sacrifice, envy, all the human reactions and weaknesses, reduced to four walls, and as a result, so much more obvious, more explosive.

"All the best people were in our room and Achilleas Kyrou was the undisputed leader. So our evenings passed rather pleasantly with stories and jokes. To my right slept an administrative employee of some Ministry; he was of enormous dimensions, and getting him to bed each night was a small ritual. One had to hold him on each side to place him on the mattress, so he was able to lie down. Since he often talked to us about his wife, we couldn't help wondering how he made love with such a belly! To my left was Socrates. We quickly became friends, because he too, was good at hop-scotch. The Italians had caught him as he was trying to escape from Euboea to the Middle East, like so many others.

"The days went all the same but our imaginations travelled beyond the confines of the prison, to the fields of battle and even further, to the day when we and all of Greece would be free again. Dreaming of this celebration – for we never had any doubt about victory – we felt strong, and, to a certain degree, free. It's strange, but now I feel that you are freer when you are fighting for your freedom than when you have it and become a slave to your own self."

He expected Ellen to contradict him but she only listened, enchanted, as if his words were a melody, influenced by the magic of the night and the glimmering of the moon.

Alexis continued: "The smoke I had noticed from the kitchen chimney on the first day was driving me crazy. A month had gone by and I hadn't been able to strike up a conversation with the Italian cook. Every day I passed by the window which looked out on the yard, but he was always involved with his pots and pans and never even cast a glance in my direction. It was mainly out of stubbornness and a need to impress my friends at I wanted to become a member of the "spaghetti club". Besides the prison food, our families had the right to bring us food from home, whatever kind of food you could prepare during the occupation; once a month the Red Cross parcelled out to us a cardboard box which seemed like Solomon's treasure: powdered milk, powdered soup, powdered eggs and hazelnut butter. What a feast! I thought it would be better if I sent them to my home rather than them sending me food. But the spaghetti had become an obsession with me and when one day I saw the cook at the window getting a breath of fresh air, I asked him, using gestures, and making sure none of the guards saw me, if I could put my head through the window and smell the spaghetti sauce. Just like the 'Karaghiozi'!* He laughed, took me into the kitchen and served me an enormous platter of spaghetti covered in sauce, and that will always remain my most beautiful memory of my life in prison. When I had thanked him and started to leave he told me to come whenever I wanted to – 'But make sure that no-one sees you!' And from that day on, at every opportunity, I would sneak into the kitchen, wolf down a plate of spaghetti voraciously but also guiltily, because in spite of my efforts, the Italian cook would not let me bring my friends. 'I'll get into trouble,' he said. He spoke to me openly and like Vardanega he also tried to justify himself for fighting in Greece. He told me the war was lost for the Italians and perhaps he was trying to pave the way for himself in case his homeland capitulated. There were already such rumours about, and the news I got from the cook I took back to the room. That way I kept my conscience clear. My justification for eating spaghetti!

"The great day arrived. 'Open sesame!' And suddenly, one morning, as if someone had rubbed Aladdin's lamp, the doors opened. The Italians urged us to leave quickly. The news passed from mouth to mouth: Italy had surrendered! But what about the Germans? Those of us that managed to get out were lucky. I stopped to say good-bye to the cook but he wasn't there, I looked back at the walls of the prison. We had spent three months behind them. So long, Sultan! Your slaves have escaped!

"Ellen, I would like to be able to describe to you the emotion you feel when you are able to determine where you are going, and what I just said to you about being a slave to your own self is nonsense! It's like being suspended in the infinite and each one of your cells is rejoicing in its own way. The smile on your lips reflects the feeling of joy for the freedom which is before you as well as pride in the experience you left behind.

"Soon the Germans took over the prisons. Those that hadn't hustled right out of there were caught in the trap. My friend Socrates

---

*the dirt-poor, comic character in Greek Shadow Theatre, who was always trying to outwit the Turks.

didn't make it. I learned later that in despair he tried to escape over the high wall and was killed.

"I met the Italian cook, who was also trying to hide from the Germans, by chance one day on the street. I hid him at a friend's house. Later he left for his homeland and I lost track of him.

"As you know, the Germans shot the Italians by the thousands because they had surrendered and so they wouldn't have to take them prisoner. They killed six thousand on the island of Cephalonia alone.

"During the first few days after the surrender, we went to the Italian army camps and collected rifles, machine guns, pistols, red or dark red hand grenades, our children's toys in the occupation, to carry on the resistance. Petros found the girl, who had waited for him, and imbued with the glory of the hero spent several beautiful months with her.

"Linos went back to his books and his music.

"What I remember, more than my reunion with my family, was the big hug Lillian gave me as she embraced me when I went on my bicycle with its tires patched a thousand times, to visit her in Kifissia, the very first day out of prison."

"And where is Lillian now?" Ellen asked jealously.

"In Greece. A beautiful childhood dream. The carefree girl with the golden hair."

"Let's go," Ellen said simply.

She was ready to console him one more time, to make him forget about the war. When they reached the corridor outside their adjoining rooms, she asked: "Yours or mine?"

"Tonight it's your turn to be my guest," Alexis said.

After they had taken a bath together to get rid of the desert dust, they stood for some time on the balcony, bathing their bare bodies in the night, one of the thousand and one nights. If while making love their souls could have shouted they would have been heard throughout the depths of the Orient. They had surrendered themselves to the fairy tale.

As soon as Ellen opened her eyes the next morning she said: "Thank you."

"What are you thanking me for?"

"For the way you made love to me."

"You know, I always thought it was the woman who made love to the man; and perhaps it's because in Greece men talk lewdly to each other: 'Does she go all the way?', 'Does she put out?', or even worse to me, 'Is she a good hump?' Maybe because most of the time when women agree to sleep with you, they act as if they were doing you a great favour, the supreme concession! I want to thank you too, Ellen. Outside the fact that I have never felt such intense pleasure, I understand now that you cannot make someone love you. Besides, I feel twice the man having a woman beside me who isn't afraid to say she wants a man."

They had breakfast in the fabulous Mena House dining-room, which resembled the interior of a Mosque, with its old, bronze, Islamic lamps that hung from the cupola and its walls decorated, like the rest of the hotel, with 'mushrabiya' grillwork. After they had savoured the atmosphere that Churchill, Roosevelt, Chaing Kai Shek, Field Marshall Montgomery, Charlie Chaplin, Kings and Maharajahs had experienced before them, they took the tram to the city.

They got off before the bridge and went on foot to the point where the Nile broadens and forms a big lake near the island of Zamalek. The water slipped by slowly and picturesque 'feluccas' with lateen sails, similar to those Alexis had seen in the harbour of Alexandria, sailed past under the bridge. River boats were anchored on one bank. As a passerby explained to them, before the war these river boats went up the Nile as far as Upper Egypt, to Luxor and Aswan.

"Wouldn't a trip like that be wonderful for a honeymoon?" Ellen said.

When she saw that Alexis was looking at her in surprise, she added:

"I mean, for any couple who had just got married – what were you thinking?"

Alexis didn't say anything, but it was the first time in his life he'd realised that a relationship with a woman might lead to marriage! It was something so far in the future for him, something that only much older people would consider. He was still a child, even though he was trying to play the part of a man. But it made him uneasy again that soon the day would come when the fairy tale he was living in at that moment would end.

Beyond the river boats were four wooden houseboats. The first had a Greek flag, the second English, the third French and the fourth Egyptian.

"Shall we see what they are?" Alexis suggested.

Turning back, they crossed over the bridge to the bank and to the gangway that connected the land to the houseboat with the Greek flag. They realised it was a rowing club. The boat-house was in the lower part and the clubhouse in the upper. They found a party of Greeks who welcomed them and told them everything about the Greek Club in Cairo.

Alexis told them that he had rowed in Greece and thought about how lovely it would be to pull on the oars in the calm waters of the Nile, to pass under the bridge, to gaze at the river baths and to pass the slow 'feluccas'.

As if reading his mind, they asked him: "How long are you staying? Would you like to join?"

Alexis' eyes lit up and he turned to Ellen. "How long are we staying? When is your leave up?"

"I have to be back in Alexandria on Sunday evening. We still have," she counted on her fingers, "five days."

"Sign me on,' Alexis said, "and I'll come every morning to row."

"Not too early in the morning," Ellen observed.

"Sunday afternoon we're having a race with the other clubs in Cairo," one of the group who had been introduced as the Rowing Supervisor said. "We could still make up a two-oared boat but I haven't found a second oarsman. Do you want me to enter you?"

Alexis turned to Ellen. "I thought of going back to Alexandria by train, to see a little of the desert. Do we have time, if we leave Sunday evening? Unless you have to go back by military plane?"

"It isn't necessary," Ellen replied.

"There's a train at six in the evening that gets to Alexandria at nine," the Supervisor interrupted. "The races will be finished by then and you'll make it."

"Perfect – put me down!"

They thanked them and left He was excited primarily because he had begun to do something, even though it was only rowing. So much time had gone by since he'd arrived in Egypt and in essence he'd done nothing. Deep down this pervasive atmosphere of luxury and extravagance reminded him of the period of landaus and crinoline. However much he enjoyed it, the contrast with the occupation was too great and he felt remorse. Especially when he realised that in Greece, in his home, the picture even now was completely different. He'd talked to Ellen about that during the morning, as they roamed the well-known streets of Cairo, passing through Opera Square, strolling through Shepherd's Hotel, ending up at the Museum, looking at all the treasures of Tutankhamun and other kings that were being exhibited, though the most important finds were still hidden for fear of bombing raids during the battle of North Africa.

"Don't feel guilty," Ellen told him. "Accept what God gives you, even this holiday. You won it in the Resistance, in the war. What you went through in Greece and I in England, no matter how tormented we were, is wealth that no-one can take away from us; at the same time we don't owe anyone anything. Life owes us now. We win each moment by enjoying it. We have the right to be happy. Not only the right but the obligation. In the army they taught us that to serve is a right, not an obligation, though I had always had my doubts about that theory. Life, however, is an obligation and happiness even more so. It's a crime against God not to enjoy the beautiful moments He grants you."

"If we were having a Platonic dialogue, I would answer that under your long, black hair and behind your English face is hidden a lot of wisdom," he said laughing.

"When you talk to a Greek, you have to do it on his level! I'm not to blame. You're asking for it."

"You mentioned God twice. Is it silly to ask if you believe in God?"

"Silly? Why? It's the only question, I should think, that is asked both by the child and the old man, the illiterate and the philosopher, the wise man and the fool and it is the only question that will remain unanswered as long as life exists – isn't is strange? But then isn't that the greatest proof that God does exist? For that reason I believe in God!"

"We have left Plato and moved on to the Sophists!"

"I don't know where you put me ... philosophically, but the way we grew up, moulded by the war, didn't leave us all that many choices. The famous commonplace words, homeland, religion – I won't mention family, because that would overwork the cliché – are the ones that show us a way, the only way which at least gives sense and spirit to our lives at this moment. We wage war. Why? Certainly not for something unknown and invisible. But to defend ourselves in our environment. So we always come back to the same things. We fashion a world in our mind, imaginary if you like, like the thousand and one nights, but it is the only one we have. As I said, we don't have many choices. What is your idea of God?"

"I don't know, but Cavafy comes to mind again:
... Because so little
is known about you from history,
I could fashion you more freely in my mind.
"You called me a polytheist! Well, I like to think of God in all the different forms of the gods of Olympus, to choose which god I want in every situation, to shape him with my mind, to take him down from the sky and put him inside us like an 'alter ego'. Does that seem arrogant to you? To have the God of Light inside you when the sun rises, the God of Love when you're in love, the God of War when you fight! To become one with your god, and, why not be another god? Like Father, like Son!"

"My God, what a man!" Ellen cried. "Or rather, my man what a god! God help us!"

"Under the circumstances God will ... help himself to a kiss!" And he gave her a kiss.

"Can't you be serious for more than a few minutes?"

"No!" he said obstinately. "But if you want me to speak seriously to you, I would say that as for that homeland you mentioned, I feel that mine, at least, betrayed me. Like a woman I loved." He stopped for moment. "And no matter how much I try to convince myself that homeland means the earth, the sea, the mountains, the trees, my home, the things I love, I can't separate them from the people who let me down. What about my friends, my fellow fighters, you'll ask? They didn't do anything to me. Why should I want to renounce the whole lot and my own country as well? I don't know, but it seems the soul works that way. Someone always has to be blamed and for me everything's to blame. At least that's how I feel now. You're not going to betray me too, are you?"

"I suggest that for the time being we dedicate ourselves to Tutankhamun," Ellen said.

Alexis wanted to see the mummies much more than the treasures of the Pharaoh. They'd always stirred his imagination, even as a child, but as he stood before the bound lumps in the showcase, his interest evaporated in a flash. The dead form left no room in his imagination for the re-shaping of history.

"Isn't is odd that I don't have any feelings about this mummy?" he told Ellen.

"Maybe you don't feel anything, but it does something to me when I reflect that this could have been a woman like me who five thousand years ago was making love. Maybe even with a Pharaoh, who knows? Have you ever wondered how often a person makes love in a lifetime?"

"No I never have. But what brought that up?"

"I don't know, it just came to me. We should count time in terms of love-making – not by the days, the weeks, the months or the years. Just think how wonderful it would be to say: 'Three loves ago, or ten loves later!'"

"And what are the impotent supposed to do?"

"Don't be banal. You're a strange person. When you go into your dreams, you become poetic, but when I have romantic fancies you cut me off like a knife!"

"Excuse me, So how would you count time with a mummy who hasn't made love in five thousand years?"

"I wouldn't. I would stop time with her last love affair."

"So History wouldn't exist?"

"History would exist, but maybe not in terms of time. And now that you mention it, when they made this woman into a mummy, wasn't that the idea ... to stop time?"

"What are you talking about? It was the guilt of the living toward the dead. 'Keep the dead happy so that we can have an easy conscience.' They filled the tombs of the Pharoahs with all this gold stuff you see, even with wooden effigies of the slaves – what does the catalogue call them, the Shawahty. To work for them, to farm for them even after death and that makes everything hunky-dory. If by any chance we treated you badly in life – in death we give you only the best."

"Why are you so negative about everything? You don't like the pyramids, the Sphinx annoys you, you ridicule the treasures of the Pharoahs. Were you always such an odd cove?"

"What's odd about me? Only that I see things through the eyes of the soul? And you, when you talk to me about the time element of love, what are you? Poetry is one thing, oddity another!"

"Whether we're talking about God or even now when the subject is death, I can never tell if you are serious or joking!"

"Do you think I know?"

"When did you first come face to face with death?"

"One afternoon, when my mother and I were having a siesta at my paternal grandmother's house, I wouldn't sit still, I was jumping up and down and my mother told me, 'Quiet down because your grandfather is watching you from up there!' 'What's grandfather doing up there?' I later asked my cousin who was six months older than me. When you're six years old, a difference of half a year is a lot. She knew too. 'Grandfather died,' she told me. 'Does everyone that dies go up there?' I asked. I don't know why but I had the impression that it would be beautiful up there! Later, when I learned Greek mythology, I didn't like the idea of Charon at all, the way he took you into the darkness of Hades. Pluto and Persephone filled me with dread, and I tried to get them out of my mind. Now, just like in the time of the Pharoahs, they hermetically seal the tombs of the dead. But instead of bringing gifts they shed tears And throw in a few flowers. What cheapskates we've become."

"But you said the gifts were out of guilt. Do we have less guilt?"

"What do you think tears are? Cheaper guilt."

"So what ought we to do with our dead?"

"You won't believe me, but as soon as my cousin told me my grandfather had died, we acted out my grandfather's funeral in the garden. Singing and dancing. When our grandmother saw us from the balcony she gave us all kinds of hell. I couldn't understand why she thought it was disrespectful. If you ask me, the cemeteries ought to be large amusement parks with lots of lights, games and bands with people strolling around, playing and dancing among the graves which would be incredible works of art and everyone would decide for himself whether he wanted to rot in the grave and be eaten by the worms, be embalmed or reduced to ashes."

"Aren't you trying to block out guilt too, by creating life around the dead?"

"You may be right, I saw death many times in the occupation and I escaped it just as often so maybe I feel guilty for being alive."

"I saw so many dead people during the London Blitz too; I told you about my fiancé. In the beginning I felt like you but not anymore."

"I can still see such vivid scenes before my mind's eye. One night I was coming down from Hymettus, a mountain east of Athens, with my friend Aris. It was winter and snowing. The road was pure white. We were coming back from scouting out a German army camp. We had to find the exact location of the ammunition dump. We had gone down through the cemetery of Kaisariani, when we met a man, all skin and bones, labouring to drag through the snow a wooden wagon covered with a blanket. He stopped us and asked us to help him drag the wagon to the cemetery. He was going to bury his mother and didn't have any money to pay for it. We looked more closely. The legs of the woman, in black stockings, were dragging in the white snow. Words were superfluous. We pulled the wagon up to the gate of the cemetery, called out to the guard, and went back down the track that had been carved in the snow by the old woman's feet. The whole picture of the occupation in one scene. The cold, the hunger, the fortitude. Her son wasn't weeping. When he asked us to help him bury his dead mother, he said it in a quite matter of fact way, as if asking for information. Not even for a favour. He had the fortitude you acquire when things don't depend on you. All the way back Aris and I walked in silence, but our melancholy wasn't despair. We too accepted the law of War, the law of Fate."

They were talking as they walked through the half-empty Museum. Every so often they stopped, glanced at the printed catalogue and went on.

"Another afternoon I went with a girl from our organisation to speak to the students of a school near Amerikis Square to lift their morale."

"On the way out of the school there were a lot of people gathered in the square. The Germans had hung two black-marketeers from the cross-bars of a lamp-post. With the noose around their necks and their tongues hanging out, they swung in the winter wind. A placard on their chest read: 'They sold olive oil at too high a profit', or something like that – I don't remember exactly. Our eyes stayed glued to them for ages and I still wonder what draws us to scenes of horror. Just like in the Middle Ages, people had gathered to enjoy the spectacle. The spectacle ... the spectacle ... no matter what it might be!"

"I can still see before my eyes the spectacle of a human sea at the cemetery in Kokkinia singing a Russian communist song in Greek. It went something like this: 'See, if you can, taratatatatata, the honourable struggle in which we died!' They sang while they were burying one of ours and another dozen or so dead from ELAS. All killed by the Germans. Ours had been shot by a German from the last car of the column which was abandoning Athens, as he tried to raise the Greek flag on the Hotel Victoria in Omonoia, our secret hang-out during the last days of the occupation. If he had just waited one minute longer ..."

"The only cemetery that still had a little free ground was in Kokkinia. I and a friend undertook the responsibility of burying him."

"Kokkinia was in the hands of ELAS. We had the coffin on the roof of a taxi which we requisitioned by force, with us lying down outside on the fenders with two machine guns. We took the Holy Way which in ancient times led to Eleusis and the Mysteries."

"Halfway along the road we were stopped by an ELAS roadblock. The civil war hadn't started yet, but relations were tense. We explained why we were going to Kokkinia. Most courteously, the ELAS lieutenant told us that at the moment their own people were being buried but there were some extra graves dug and if we didn't mind burying 'our young fellow' next to theirs, he would let us pass and would notify the head of the section who was in charge of ceremonies – as if the political convictions of the dead meant something!

"We laid our dead man next to the people of ELAS in one of the graves which had been dug in a row. Even the dead had joined hands in the ground. The people sang. Three bursts from the machine guns of the ELAS platoon sealed their reconciliation in life and in death; and with a song, not a wail.

"Three strange scenes: the old woman in the snow, the hanged black-marketeers, the grave of our comrade. Is there any way I can't feel guilty that I'm alive and they're not? What about all the others? Red-haired Charilaos who was killed by the Germans. My cousins, two brothers, the dashing Yiorgos and Angelos, who were killed by the Greeks.

"We fought side by side. Exposed ourselves to the same dangers. Now I'm enjoying life, trips, knowledge, a woman. In my amusement park, we will be all together, whether we like it or not! And who knows? Maybe their souls are taking part in our games."

They left the Museum. They had spoken of love, they had spoken of God, they had spoken of death. Once more they took the tram back to Mena House.

As they got off at the terminus, faceless figures in jelabas were gathered near the station, shouting. They squeezed in to see what was going on. Four dark-skinned soldiers were quarrelling, two against two, with drawn knives. Their uniforms were covered with blood and no-one was trying to stop them. All of a sudden, in one moment, the four of them collapsed as might happen in a modern ballet, or in the finale of an opera, while the extras in the jelabas were shouting incoherent words and making incomprehensible gestures. Alexis and Ellen gaped like spectators ready to applaud. Ellen, who knew how to distinguish uniforms, said that two were South African and the other two Egyptian.

An ambulance soon arrived. Two of the men were dead – which two didn't matter – the other two were seriously injured. The ambulance only had room for two, so it took the dead. It would return for the living. It was a tragi-comic scene.

"Honour the dead! They sacrifice the living to take care of the dead!" Alexis said in amazement.

"If I were to tell you their stupidity reaches the point where they consider the dead to be in a more ... advanced condition than the injured and therefore must go first, would you stop looking at everything so idealistically?"

"How does the French saying go: 'Talk about the dead and ... they appear before you?"

Neither the discussion they'd had nor the experience they'd shared kept them from giving themselves over completely to love-making again that night.

"What greater proof is there that we are alive?" Ellen asked him as she kissed him over his entire body. "Tonight I feel a need to make love, as a challenge to death."

Early next morning Alexis went to the rowing club to train for the race on Sunday. Later, he came back to pick up Ellen.

He found her by the hotel swimming-pool soaking up the sun. She was wearing a bright red swimsuit and he felt so proud that the girl with the long, black hair and the red swimming suit the other guests were ogling was his.

He put on his trunks and after he had had a swim, they set off for Cairo. They wandered around the city until late in the day, sometimes walking and sometimes riding trams.

One day they rented a small sail-boat and sailed on the Nile. The next day they went to a popular cinema, the Metro, and saw Ingrid Bergman in "Notorious".

Another day, in the poor Arab quarter beneath Citadella, they discovered a cinema that was showing an Egyptian film. The posters were in Arabic and they couldn't read them; only the giant image of the leading lady with large, red lips, doing a belly dance, gave them any idea of what the film was about.

"We won't understand a thing, but let's go for the fun of it," Alexis said.

"I like how we laugh together. I'd forgotten what it meant to laugh. Even when we were talking about death you found a way to make me laugh. Could it be that I'm happy?"

Ellen was game for anything. He liked that. They bought tickets, went in through one door, held their noses and went out the other. The stench was unbearable to their sensitive European noses. They just managed, lifting their eyes for a few seconds, to see the navel of the leading lady filling the screen.

It was Saturday afternoon. The races on the Nile were set for the following day. After the race they would leave. They went to the railway station to buy tickets and returned to the hotel.

That night, like every other, after eating and dancing to the sounds of the orchestra, they sauntered through the gardens of Mena House – bathed, once more, in one of the thousand and one nights!

"We only have a little time left," Ellen said.

"Won't I see you in Alexandria?"

"Yes, of course, but soon I'll be re-assigned. Perhaps to liberated Europe and perhaps to England. When the war is over we'll meet again," she said without believing it. But at that moment she only wanted to keep the hope alive, not to ruin the scenario she had imagined for the evening.

"Ellen, I only realised now that you have oriental eyes, even though they aren't black – the way you looked at me a while ago, tenderly and sadly,"

"Are tenderness and sorrow a privilege of the Orient? Your brown eyes have a greenish, melancholy cast."

"I've always pictured oriental eyes as being large like yours and oriental gazes sensuous and penetrating. It was that kind of radiance when you looked at me. Which brings another image to mind, suddenly, just like that, tonight, in this garden. A scene from a Hungarian film I saw during the occupation – 'Night Vision'. I remembered it a while back in Alexandria. The silhouette of a naked girl, standing on a rock, at the end of a dark lake by the Heuduck tower. A vision in the night watched from the distance with passionate love by Miklos Gabor, as she dived into the dark waters and vanished."

"Do you think I'm a vision in the night?"

"No, it's only the emotion arising from boundless tranquillity intermingled with erotic longing."

"Time and again I feel that I also am just a dream to you. At one moment Aisa and the next your vision in the night! You have fashioned an idol in your imagination and you worship that idol – not me as I am! Besides, you almost never ask me about myself. It's always me asking you questions. Confess it, confess it, to you I'm a dream," she said stubbornly and seemed irritable again.

"When I touch you, you are the most real thing that exists and all my senses pulsate with you. When I think about you it's true that I re-shape you in my imagination – but is it such a bad thing to want to adorn you with all the beautiful images I have in my mind? To give my fantasy flesh and bone? If I haven't asked you a lot about your life, it may be that I'm jealous of the time before I met you, or maybe I'm even afraid to know you better; at least I can take the dream with me!"

"I'm not totally convinced though I know you believe everything you're saying. What did the girl in 'Night Vision' look like?"

"She was tall with long, blond hair down to her waist. Her milk-white breasts, outlined against the back-drop of night, have become one of my most beautiful erotic fantasies."

Without a word, Ellen got up, stood in the middle of the pathway, the night and the palm trees her backdrop, put both her hands on the shoulders of her dress and pulled it down to her waist. A re-enactment of the night vision? Revenge? Erotic challenge? Ellen didn't speak, only looked proudly into the distance, showing Alexis the profile of her naked breasts.

Alexis didn't know what Ellen wanted him to do. To ask her to forgive him for mentioning his fancies or to admire her more than his night vision?

He decided not to say anything; he simply got up, stood behind her and cupped her breasts with his two hands while he kissed her neck.

"Make a wish come true!" Ellen whispered, throwing her head back, and from there on, their emotions took charge.

It was very late when they went up to their rooms. And they slept until late in the morning.

They had to be at the Club on Sunday at noon for the races. Carrying their suitcases, they took a last trip out to the pyramids, which would remain the symbol of a week of love. They had made friends with the tall servant, Mustapha, who guarded the hotel entrance.

"I'm sorry you leave," he said in broken English and accompanied them to the pyramids. "Few people like you; they all come here, go there, and no give tip, Tanks!"

"How old are you, Mustapha," Alexis asked him to find out how many years were hidden by his jet black face with all the wrinkles.

"Thirty."

"Are you married?"

"No. I know woman, I want to take but she fat and you must pay her father many cows – I no have money."

"What? You must pay the father by the weight of the bride? I mean, the fatter she is, the more she costs?"

"Yes, I like fat woman – you get much stuff"

Alexis laughed but Ellen felt offended.

"Listen to that, buying women by the pound! Which means I wouldn't be worth a brass farthing!"

"Did you hear what she said, Mustapha?"

Mustapha replied with all the politeness of the Egyptian people: "No, Miss Helen, you much money, because much heart, much beauty."

When Ellen kissed Mustapha on both cheeks, two tears ran down from his eyes. Certainly no white person had ever kissed him before and perhaps the kisses of his mother had been lost in the oblivion of time.

They came back down from the pyramids to catch the tram and embraced Mustapha, who stood waving until the tram disappeared around the first turn.

"I was thinking, Ellen, that the people of the desert, like the people of the sea and the mountains are good; their feelings arise from their primitive relationship with nature."

"Cannibals live in nature too!"

"Well then, I don't know, don't confuse me! Always the cynical Ellen."

"Just forget the philosophy for a while and concentrate on your race."

"If you want to start a quarrel, I don't mind. But after the time we spent under the palms last night ... it will be your fault if I come in last!"

"I've never met a more spiteful man than you! Or rather, you know how to defend yourself, and you always have to have the last word"

"If I'm going to have the last word I'll have to add something now and I don't know what!"

"Well, I'm not going to tell you!"

They laughed and the tension eased. This too was part of the rhythm of the erotic games they were playing by the best rules!

At the Club they were received with all the hospitality of the Egyptian Greeks, and they felt like old acquaintances. A crowd had already gathered. Ellen was given a seat next to the President, on the balcony of the floating Club, with the Nile before her eyes.

Alexis went down to the changing room to get ready for the race. He'd had a good breakfast but hadn't slept much. He stretched out on a bench in the changing room. The previous night hadn't been spent the way an athlete ought to spend the night before a race and now he might be the cause of his partner's downfall. He was tired but he had to pull himself together.

There were two other races before his. Instead of watching them he would try to take a nap. But he was so over-stimulated by the past week that he couldn't sleep. Fairly soon, instead of clapping for him, Ellen would be teasing him for finishing last; what foolishness!

The time approached. The coach called out to them to get into the boats for the run up to the starting line, as the finishing line was right in front of the Club.

He greeted his fellow rowers and the coxswain, who was shaking his head as if preparing them for the coming defeat, and the coach, who understood the motion, grabbed him by the wrist and shook him.

"The Greek Club has to win – you are better but watch out for the Egyptians."

"Philotimo – the damn Greek word for 'honour' again – Christ Almighty, what a bore!" Alexis thought.

They got into the boats and as they passed the clubs, he saw the balconies full of fans yelling for their team. Next to the Greek Club was the English, further down the French and still further, the Egyptian. Four clubs, eight boats – two from each club. The others had gone ahead, slowly and rhythmically.

Alexis raised his hand to wave to Ellen who rewarded him with Churchill's classic V-sign and beamed him a look and a smile so full of tenderness that it gave him renewed strength. He began to row, setting the pace, since he was in the first position in front with the coxswain.

His self-conviction had returned. He rowed slowly, so as not to tire himself as the starting line was a thousand metres away. He tried to concentrate but he couldn't stop looking right and left at the crowd that had gathered on the shores of the Nile, for in a while the race would start and he wouldn't be able to look at anything but his oars and the coxswain.

None of them spoke and only when they passed the two buoys marking the starting line did the cox order them to turn slowly around and get into position.

Forward a bit, backward a little bit more until the bows of the boats were in a straight line with the buoys. It was difficult to stay motionless against the current of the Nile; with small dips of the oars they tried to keep from being dragged over the invisible starting line.

The judges and the starter with the megaphone in his hand ready to give the signal, stood in a motor-boat near the right buoy.

"Take your places ..."

The sixteen rowers bent forward as far as they could, so that their first stroke would be a powerful one.

"Come on, fellows, give it all you've got from the start. It's only a mile!" the cox on their boat was shouting to whip them up.

"Ready ..."

The starting gun. The scull leapt forward as the oars bit into the water and began to move upstream.

The voice of the cox was harsh. "Eh, up, eh, up, eh, up!'

Alexis closed his eyes and pulled on the oar as hard as he could. He wanted to know what place they held, but he didn't dare look or ask, as he might lose his concentration, even if it only cost him one inch in the race.

The coxswain seemed to be in a continuous rage. "Harder, faster!" Alexis thought: "In my case I can't go harder or faster" and he began to feel tired. He was afraid he wouldn't be able to finish the race, at least not at that pace.

They had to be somewhere half way but he had lost all sense of time. He tried to find something that would perk him up and give him new strength. In a flash there passed through his mind first Ellen and then what he considered his most heroic act in the war, when he went to the offices of the SD of German Counter-Espionage under a false name to see with his own eyes the charge that had been made against him and to learn who had betrayed him. The figure of Ellen reinforced his desire to come in first but the figures of the two stool pigeons who had denounced him to the Germans gave him the hate he needed at that moment to drive his oar into the waters of the Nile with that little extra bitterness.

"Eh, up, eh, up!" the coxswain screamed.

"Those bastards, those shits, those stool pigeons," Alexis said to himself and the number two rower followed his frenzied pace.

"It can't be long now," he thought, but now he began to get really tired. Not even his fantasies were of any help. "You fool," he said to himself, "couldn't you have resisted making love to Ellen for just one night? Athletes rest for three days before the races. But what the hell, what if I do lose. Screw it."

At that moment when he had nothing left to hold onto, the voice of the coxswain came to save him. "Pull those oars, fellows, they're beating us! The Arabs have gone ahead! Pull, you carrion. Eh, up, eh, up, faster, you assholes!"

"I gave in just before the end. It's my fault," Alexis said to himself, "and I'm to blame for the others losing too."

Alexis knew that the Egyptian boat had good rowers but he had thought that at the pace they were setting they could win the race. But can you believe it, the Egyptians had pulled in front.

"The people along the banks are on their side, it's their river," he thought, looking for excuses. "Hasn't it been said that the large stones used to build the pyramids were transported by the thoughts of thousands of slaves who concentrated on matter? Maybe the Arabs have telepathic powers and all the people on the bank are transmitting energy to their people. Who knows...? Forget that nonsense and pull!" he told himself, almost ashamed.

At the orders of the coxswain, who was hoarse from yelling, he grasped the oar ever more firmly with both his hands and began to shift on the movable seat with a speed he had never reached before.

"Come on, a little more, a little more – we've almost caught them – a little more – three inches – two inches – one inch – the finishing line!"

At the sound of the finishing line Alexis let go of his oar and flopped on his back, nearly passing out in the boat. No.2 behind him caught his head so he wouldn't hurt himself. They'd lost! What a shame! He couldn't have done any more ... if he'd just had more rest ... by an inch!

"Way to go fellows!' he heard the voice of the cox, calm this time, almost tender. "We left them half a boat length behind."

Alexis didn't understand. From where he was lying he was only able to whisper to No.2 who was holding his head.

"What's he talking about? Why's he congratulating us?"

"Because we won by half a boat length!"

"How could we win when the Egyptians passed us?"

"They never passed us, we were always in front, he told us that on purpose so we wouldn't ease up."

"Why that sonofabitch!"

He lifted himself up a bit, looked the cox in the eyes, ready to swear at him, but the sly smile of satisfaction he saw there wiped away all his objections and made him smile too and maybe a tear fell from his eyes in the emotion of the moment.

These were the real highpoints of communication, that made life worthwhile. Two smiles expressing a sentiment that a thousand words wouldn't have expressed. Two transmissions from the depths of the soul, and another two receivers tuned to receive them. "If this isn't telepathy, then what is?" Alexis thought.

Still gasping for breath, but cheerful, he got up with difficulty, shook the hand of his partner and the coxswain and took up the oar again for the victory lap, passing all the clubs as the Egyptian boat went by and its rowers sent their messages of congratulation. His chest was burning and he found it hard to pull the oar.

The coxswain, facing him, turned the boat toward the Greek Club and hailed them from afar to bring Alexis a cup of tea. In a few minutes the boat pulled alongside and the Italian coach was standing there with the cup in his hand. He patted Alexis on the shoulders and had him sip slowly, while the spectators clapped.

All those who were sitting in front leaned over to watch them. Alexis didn't have the strength to even lift his eyes to see if he could spot Ellen.

The tea brought him around a little. He was ready to take up the oar again for the victory lap, when he heard the voice of Ellen from overhead. He lifted his eyes and saw her blowing him a kiss with her hand and looking at him as if saying "You did it!" Then she called out. "There's only an hour before the train leaves, don't be late, we'll miss it!"

But the lap had to be completed. At the urging of the coach they moved somewhat faster again, while the spectators at the Greek Club clapped enthusiastically and those at the other clubs with reserved politeness.

When they passed the last club, Alexis called out to the coxswain: "Let's go back quickly or I'll miss the train."

"Aren't you going to wait for the medals to be handed out?"

"Get them for me and send them to me, I don't have the time."

After showering and dressing hurriedly, still breathing hard, he embraced his colleagues, shook the coach's hand and ran upstairs to get Ellen. He had to push his way through the crowd that was trying to congratulate him to reach her, who hugged him tightly.

He took her by the hand. They had left their bags at the entrance and after they had greeted and thanked the President of the Club, they went to find a taxi to the station. They began to walk rapidly, holding hands, carrying their bags in the other, but they couldn't find a cab. They went across the bridge on the Nile, to Kasr el Nil Square – time was passing. They started to walk even faster, practically running, and Alexis began to pant again.

"This is just what you needed!" Ellen gasped as they ran. "I thought the programme for today was only rowing – not a marathon run too! Is it still a long way?"

"About ten minutes I think – but neither of us can go any faster; and you would pick this of all days to wear a tight skirt!"

"If I'd known we were going to be running clear across Cairo I would have made sure I hired a boy, who could have at least carried my luggage. I would have made sure I wore comfortable shoes or, even better, I'd have had an Arab waiting for me with two slaves!"

"You colonials want everything served on a silver platter. If you are hinting that I wasn't prudent enough to have a cab waiting! At the most you'll miss the train ... you won't get to Alexandria on time ... they'll discharge you from the Imperial Army and you'll have to come to me on bended knee begging for room and board!"

"First of all, they won't discharge me from the army; they'll slap me with ten days confinement to base and you won't see me on my last days in Alexandria. Second, an Englishwoman, subject of the Empire, as you call it, does not kneel except before the King ... and even then it is only a curtsey. And third, save your breath because I'm gasping and can't talk!"

"To save my breath I'd have to have some left – so your wish will be fulfilled!"

"Do you have to have the last word even when you're running?"

"When we get to the train, I'm going to sleep and I won't open my mouth till Alexandria."

"If we ever get there!"

The closer they got to the poor quarter near the station, the bigger the crowd on that Sunday afternoon. The clock on the station gate showed exactly six.

"I wonder if the Egyptian trains run on time," Alexis mused.

"We don't have time to wonder about it, run!"

The station looked as though it was filled with all the indigenous population of Cairo and its environs. Men in jelabas, holding baskets in their hands, women dressed in black, wearing veils and balancing bundles on their heads, children with shaven heads running every which way, the one squeezed against the other. It wasn't only that they couldn't get by, but the crowd also cut off their view of the trains. Alexis began to ask around as he tried to plough his way through.

"Eskenderegia, Eskenderegia? Alexandria? Alexandria?" All of them pointed one way but he couldn't see a train.

"I hope your Arabic accent is good, otherwise ... we might find ourselves in Ismailia or Suez!" Ellen said to him.

"It's true that when I ask for the tram and I say 'tramway' as in English and not tormai the Arabic way, no-one can understand me."

"All this is just fine but I don't see any train."

"Look, there it is, run, it's just starting."

"We'll never make it," Ellen said in despair.

"Run and jump on to the steps to the last car."

"How will we get in! The door's closed!"

"We'll think about that later, one thing at a time."

"The bags?"

"Toss them through the open window to the Arabs – they will be jammed in there like sardines. Hurry!"

Fortunately, the train was setting off very slowly and it didn't take long for them to catch up with the last car. An Arab who was hanging halfway out the window of the rear door of the car stretched out his arms and took one case and then the other.

"Now, jump!"

Alexis helped Ellen up and then he leapt up beside her. With one hand they held on to the handles and with the other the open window.

The smell that came out of the car, as the train began to pick up speed, was not all that pleasant. Two Arabs, the one who had helped them with their luggage and another one, jammed up against the door, grabbed their arms so they wouldn't fall, but obviously with a greater interest in Ellen. Using gestures and shouts they tried to make her understand that she should come through the window since the door on the train opened outward. There was no discussion about Alexis, in any case there was hardly room for more than one.

"How long are we going to be like this?" Ellen asked in a frightened voice; she didn't at all like the idea of being wedged in with the Arabs, but neither did she fancy the thought of hanging on the outside of a train which was going ninety kilometres an hour.

"Just a minute, I'll ask them," Alexis said.

"Hah, hah, hah, in what language?"

"Wait and see! Mohata feen amel maarouf?"

"Kafr el Zagiat, hamse ou arbein haouaga."

"Do you understand what he said?"

"He told me the first stop is Kafr el Zagiat and that we'll be there in forty-five minutes."

"How did you know what station is called? And where did you learn to count?'

"The first thing you learn in a language is to count and then you learn to sing."

He began to sing:

"... *Taalili yia bata – Ouana mali eh.*
Endini el sada – Ouana mali eh.
Stanini fel mahata – Ouana mali eh."
(Come so I can see you – No, I will not come.
Give me the bag – No, I will not come.
Wait at the station – No, I will not come.)

"You are mad, mad, mad! I would have been better off if I'd stayed away from the ... mahata and gone back by plane. Imagine, hanging on the outside of a train for an hour!"

When the Arabs inside heard him speaking in Arabic, they began to shout anew, this time full of enthusiasm.

"I won't be able to ... I'm getting tired ... I'm afraid I'll fall," Ellen told him.

"What about me after the race and all the running!"

"You're a man and it serves you right! It's your fault. The gentleman had to take his victory lap!"

"I'll help you climb through the window. Your two ... protectors will pull you in and as you see they've let go of me so they can use all four hands to hold you."

"I don't at all care for the way they're leering."

"You don't have any other choice! Either you hang here for forty-five minutes or you climb in!"

"I'll climb in. But I'm reserving the right to protest. And I'll push you off if they bother me. Just think, a lieutenant of His Majesty's Army in such a predicament!"

"Careful ... don't hasten the fall of the Empire! Up you go!"

He made a signal to the Arabs to pull her up, while he himself held onto both the handles to protect her from falling off and let her brace her feet on his chest, as she shoved herself in through the window.

Once Ellen had managed, after much trouble, to settle close to the window with her ... bodyguards right and left and another dozen passengers all shouting at once in delight at the unscheduled spectacle, she peered out at Alexis and started to laugh. "I'll remember this day!"

"I hope you remember a few others too ..."

She stroked his head gently as the wind ruffled his hair. "At least I never get bored with you."

"Have you ever been bored at other times in your life?"

"Often. Haven't you?"

"I don't think so. Didn't we talk about that? If there's no outside stimulation I can always find solace in dreams."

"Oh Oh! Here we go again!"

"How are you getting on in there?"

"Not so well, the fellows next to me are beginning to get a little bold."

"Pretend you're looking at the view and jam your elbows in their stomachs."

"Are you mad? They'll lynch me."

"Don't worry, they're just showing off."

"And what if they get angry and take it out on you and throw you off the train?"

"Don't worry, do what I tell you. Remember the night in the village below the pyramids? While you're doing what I told you to do I'll glower at them and swear at them in Arabic."

"You count, you sing and now you swear in Arabic!"

"A necessary adjunct to culture!"

"Is that why they helped me in, these rogues?"

"Perhaps, but if I were in their place I'd be aroused too; you're so ... sexy!"

"Oh, shut up!"

"All right. I'll shut up."

"No, don't shut up! Keep talking to me so I don't have to think about what's stirring under their dirty jelabas – I don't dare move an inch."

"Then hold on to me so I don't fall and give me a pin so I can lean in and prick them where it counts. I'll shout again like I did under the pyramids that night: 'the will of Allah'!"

"I'm not giving you a pin and I'm not doing anything else either. The whole car will jump on us. You're not going to do anything and I'll act as though I don't know what's going on and ... I'll look at the scenery ... isn't that why we went by train in the first place?"

"Then I'll be your guide. Look at the Nile with its supple palm trees against a grey-green background and the silhouettes of the women walking along the banks with jugs on their heads. Look at their stature! Their grace! It's as if they weren't walking on the ground under their long dresses. Look!"

"Oh, shut up!"

"Make up your mind, do you want me to shut up or to talk?"

"No, no, talk, talk. Tell me about the race. We didn't have a chance to talk about it. Were you afraid that you wouldn't win? In any case, you were in the lead from the start."

"To tell you the truth I didn't think I would get through it. I felt tired but ... I won't go into details!"

Ellen started to protest but he cut her off.

"But even if ... it was your fault that I was tired, you also gave me heart. I closed my eyes and saw you in front of me, sitting on the Club's reviewing stand and I said to myself: you have to come in first. It's worth dedicating a race on the Nile to this woman for all the wonderful days in Cairo."

"But you gave me the same days I gave you."

"You see! I was right. You're not a woman like the others."

"Talk, keep on talking. Oh! It feels as if I have two gun barrels turned on me, one on each side."

"Well, at least you'll have something to hold on to ... the way this train is bouncing around ..."

"Don't be coarse!"

"I'm just getting back at you. Remember when you said you got your stripe by screwing a general? I have to admit I didn't think too much of that joke."

"All right, we're even. But now do something."

"Now you want me to do something? Of course, it's a woman's right to change her mind, but not that quickly."

"Is it my fault that the Arabs are quick on the draw?"

"Hold me around the neck to keep me from falling so I can use my hands."

With his hands free, Alexis grabbed hold of the Arabs and turned them around so that they were facing away from Ellen, while he shouted at them: 'Kafr el Zagiat – bolis!' Ellen looked at him in fear.

"Don't worry, they'll be meek as lambs from here on, you'll see. They still have the slave's fear of the colonial police."

"They helped me get in the train, they took our bags. Perhaps they felt they should get something ... in exchange."

"If I didn't know your English sense of humour I'd believe you were serious."

"You've been my hero again today!"

"As I was pulling on the oar and desperately wanting you to see me come in first the craziest thing I did in the war came to my mind. It was partly the thought of you and partly that memory that gave me the strength I needed to reach the finish line ... and collapse!"

"Yes, I saw you lie down in the boat, unable to get up. The next time you take part in a race don't go with a woman the night before! Of course, I'm glad you won but I must confess I would have been very put out if you had sacrificed last night for the victory lap!"

"For us ... descendants of the Olympic victors, victory in athletics is important but ... a woman is important too! The chugging of the train and my fatigue are beginning to make me talk nonsense. But, as you can see, our friends are behaving."

"It stinks terribly in here. How far is it yet? Tell me about your craziest act in the war."

"But those are the stories we tell at night before we make love. Isn't that your love potion?"

"I've just been nearly raped by two men and you're not even willing to tell me a story to pass the time?"

"But I'm not in the most comfortable position for storytelling ..."

"You got me into this spot – the least you can do is entertain me."

"And my stories about the war entertain you?"

"Do you want me to say that I'm interested in everything about you? Alright, I'm saying it. If that puffs up your ego – well, it's already puffed up enough in any case!"

"My story is simple. I will tell it to you in simple words. As I recounted at considerable length in my previous narrative – assuming that memory remains your faithful guide – during one of the bleaker moments of that accursed occupation when I was incarcerated in an Italian prison – a deplorable situation which arose from certain disputes between the Italian occupation authorities and your humble servant with regard to who should be considered the true and proper ruler of my land ..."

"But, of course, sir, the memory remains most poignant in my mind."

"In prison I met a young guy, in prison too, not for political reasons, but because he had stolen – what else? – a package of spaghetti from an Italian army truck. It was worse than if he had stolen the Italian flag! They'd caught him and locked him up. A few months after being freed, I received a call, first thing in the morning from our 'friend', who urgently wanted to meet me. I didn't know his name, but when he mentioned the spaghetti incident I remembered him ...

"He said, 'I can't talk to you on the phone but leave your house right away and meet me on Academias Street, at EOF,' or something like that."

"What's that?" Ellen asked.

"It was an organisation that collaborated with the Germans, I'll explain it to you."

'What are you doing in such a place?' I asked him, 'and how can I walk in there – are you out of your mind?'

"Of course he knew that I was part of a resistance group.

'Trust me,' he said. 'It's something that concerns you.'

"The tone of his voice and the fact we'd known each other in captivity made me believe him, I got dressed quickly, put my Italian berretta pistol in my pocket, part of the loot following Italy's capitulation, for better or worse, and in twenty minutes on foot found myself in front of an old neo-classical building with a large sign that said: 'Greek Organisation of Friends! or something like that – I can't remember exactly. I went up a few steps, not without trepidation, and found my friend standing there, waiting for me in a large hall.

'I hardly recognised you!' he said, 'with your hair so long.'

"Without beating around the bush, with greetings and all that, he took me by the shoulder.

'Let me explain: when I got out of prison, I didn't have anything to eat, I couldn't find work so I joined this organisation that collaborates with the Germans but … I'm not doing anything bad. I try to save as many as I can, young people like you.'

"I'd heard that tale before from the translator at the Italian Carabinieri.

'There is a charge against you at the SD, German Counterespionage. They're worse than the SS and they're coming to arrest you. Don't go back home. Leave, hide!'

'Who brought the charge against me? And why?' I asked him.

'I don't know, they pass names along to us and ask us if we know them, that's our job. When I saw yours this morning, I called you. They know your address too, everything.'

'Then why didn't they come and arrest me, instead of notifying your organisation?'

'I don't know. They may have gone to your house already.'

'Do you know what I'm charged with?'

'No. But I do know there is a deposition against you made by two Greeks.'

'Greeks? Traitors, you mean?'

'That's what the paper they sent us said.'

'Why should I believe you?'

'What reason could I have for getting you out of your home?'

"He had a point.

'How can I find out who these traitors are and what they said about me?'

"He hesitated for a moment and then said:

'Should we go to the SD so you can read the deposition yourself?'

'Are you nuts? You want me to go to the SD and read the deposition against me? How will I get out of there?'

"Don't worry about that. I have free access. They know me. I'll say you're a friend of mine and that I brought you because you might know the person charged.'

'Myself, that is.'

'Yes, I'll introduce you under another name.'

'To whom?'

'To the German officer who has the deposition.'

"He was so convincing, without a trace of doubt, that what he said seemed almost reasonable to me! It's strange that at crucial moments instinct works and people can communicate more directly.

'I'm carrying a gun. What if they ask me for my identity card?'

'They won't ask and if they do just say that you don't have it with you.'

'If they ask for your identity card on the street and you don't have it, they arrest you!'

'I'm not telling you to go. You're the one who wants to know exactly what's in the deposition.'

"I could have said: 'You go and read it and tell me what it says.' What could have been simpler? But partly out of curiosity and partly because I wanted to be convinced that he was telling me the truth, I made a decision. Mad of course, but I wasn't thinking logically. At nineteen you think you can win the war all by yourself!'

'But listen. If anything goes wrong, I'll have no other choice than to pull out my gun. I'll shoot down whoever gets in my way!' I said to frighten him.

"Not that I thought for a moment that I would be able to get out of the German Counterespionage offices with a gun in my hand!

"In my mind I pictured a large building full of Germans with machine guns at the doors and on the stairs like at the SS Headquarters on Merlin Street. But instead of that, on Emmanuel Benaki Street, between Academias and Panepistimiou, a single German sentry stood at the door of an old building; he had a pistol in his belt, no helmet, and wasn't in the least daunting. I don't know why, when I think of Germans, I remember that helmet with the strange shape that gives me nightmares! The English helmets, for example, are like a turned over soup plate and they don't frighten you. In fact, they seem rather charming."

"Don't you think that it's because the Germans wore one kind of helmet and the English another that you've made up this image in your mind?" Ellen asked him.

"I don't know, maybe. But in any case I feel neutral about the Greek or American helmets."

"The guard didn't stop us when my 'friend' greeted him – it seemed he knew him only too well – and we went up two floors by an old, wooden staircase, without meeting a single soul. The stairs creaked and made the climb even more agonising.

"I began to seriously doubt if this really was German Counterespionage. Nothing was written outside, and except for the guard, there was no other trace of a German presence. But then I began to think, just what does Counterespionage mean? That no-one is supposed to know who you are, right? In any case, it was just a little late to turn back, despite the fact – I must admit – that I really felt like taking to my heels.

"On the second floor there was a round hall with worn wooden floors and three or four closed doors around it. I didn't say anything, just followed.

'Here we are!'

"My friend opened one of the doors, without knocking. I'd almost convinced myself that he'd brought me to a haunted castle and that I wasn't going to meet anyone but ghosts.

"Suddenly the two of us found ourselves in front of a German officer, sitting behind a table eating his lunch. What did he look like, what was he eating? Don't ask me, for I must confess that from that moment on my senses weren't functioning normally. I think I heard my 'friend' say in broken German that he had brought me along because I might know the young man ... blah, blah, blah ... against whom there was a deposition and would it be possible for him to give it to me to read.

"Bored, the German opened the top left-hand drawer, that I remember like it was yesterday, just like I remember the bottle of wine on his table which perhaps explained his indifference; he motioned for me to look inside.

"I bent over the drawer and immediately recognised the printed proclamations of our organisation we had handed out the previous evening behind the stadium of the Panathinaikos soccer team, two hand grenades like those I had given to the guys who took part in the 'dou' – that's how we referred to these small ventures – and a sheet of lined paper with something written on it in ink.

'Take the piece of paper and read it,' my 'friend' said.

"Up to that point I hadn't said a word. I took the piece of paper – what else could I do – and began to read, trying to control the sweat that was beginning to break out on my forehead. The deposition said, more or less, that on the previous evening there had been a meeting at my house – address, etc., of a dozen or so members of the organization National Action and that after I had passed out proclamations, hand grenades and pistols, I had told our group that we were going to slip the proclamations under the doors of as many of the houses as possible in the neighbourhood of the Panathinaikos Stadium and, if by chance we ran into any Germans (there was a German army camp near there) we would shoot at them! That was a lie, of course, because how were we going to wage a battle in Athens with two lousy hand grenades and a few pistols! We had them to defend ourselves, if by chance they got wind of us.

"The deposition was signed by two fellows who has come to our organisation that evening for the first time. They had been brought by one of the trusted ones who had said they were clean!

"It's strange how a person can pull himself together at certain moments. I put the deposition back in the drawer. I had the urge I must admit, to put it in my pocket as I saw the German was drinking wine without paying too much attention, but I thought that might be going a bit too far!

"I closed the drawer and found the courage to speak in fluent German – perhaps the only time my German saved me.

'I'm sorry, I don't know the guy, a similar name perhaps.'

"I took my leave bowing my head and clicking worn-down heels together in the German manner and without wasting time opened the door; this time my 'friend' followed me.

"I kept myself from going down the stairs ten at time but as soon as we turned the corner of the street I leaned against the first wall till my heart had regained its normal rhythm.

'Do you believe me now?' my friend asked.

'The only thing that I believe is that both you and I should be locked up and I don't mean in prison this time! Anyway, thank you, I won't go back home, I'll go into hiding right away and if you'd like a little advice, make your break with the organisation. The allies have landed in Italy and Europe and in a while they'll be in Greece.'

"I never saw him again.

"I called my mother to tell her that I wouldn't be coming home until the war was over and that I would send them a message telling them where I was. I asked her to immediately burn all of the organisation's papers and to hide the pistols, hand grenades and cartridges I had concealed in my grandmother's house, who lived nearby. Whether she liked it or not I'd mixed her up in the game the children of the resistance were playing."

"What happened to the traitors?" Ellen said.

"I reported them to the organisation and we decided that if we chanced on them we'd play dumb and lure them to a wood on Hymettus and bump them off, but none of us wanted to take the responsibility. It was only after the war I learned they had gone into EAM, the left-wing resistance organisation."

"Do you mean they were double agents?"

"Something like that. Or rather the kind of people who don't believe in anything. Thank God there were very few."

"How long did you hide?"

"Until the war ended. In the house of Pavlos, my classmate. We'd already finished High School and we were a crazy group – Pavlos, his two sisters and Alekos, who was also hiding and who slept in the same room with me."

"We waited in anguish for the war to end. We heard of the Allied victories and only went out at night for the organisation's 'dou'. All day we were shut up at 83 Patission Street, a beautiful neo-classical house with a withered garden."

"We must be nearing Kafr el Zagiat. What time is it? Can you stand to hang there just a little longer?'

"Not much longer, but I hope that as soon as the train stops we'll find our seats in first class and travel with a little dignity the rest of the way as is only fitting for a respected officer of His Majesty's Royal Forces!"

"Don't be sarcastic!"

"I can't help it. I'm a descendant of Aristophanes!"

The train slowed down as it entered Kafr el Zagiat. On the platform were hundreds of people in jelabas, just as in Cairo, coming and going with a roar he had got used to by that time; you got the idea they were shouting without reason, and that they didn't know where their feet were taking them. They moved aimlessly right, left, back and forth; it was like a ballet with hundreds of dancers but no choreographer, where everyone did as he wished.

They all had one purpose in mind, however: to get on that train. The bundles, hampers and blankets were also a part of the scene here, as well as the large, unripe, bright green bananas that the pedlars were selling outside the train windows.

Alexis and Ellen got a taste of this scene as they hustled to find their places in the forward cars. When they sat down in the comfortable seats in their compartment and the Egyptian steward in his well-pressed uniform helped them put their suitcases in the space above the seats, Alexis said:

"It's worth the suffering to get a taste of the pure pleasure of luxury."

"There is a bit of a difference, isn't there?"

"Now, that's English understatement!"

Opposite them in the compartment with its red velvet seats was sitting an English captain who didn't bear the slightest resemblance to the classic caricature with a large moustache, but was rather the Lawrence of Arabia type, tall and blond with fine features, while next to him was sitting perhaps one of the most beautiful women Alexis had ever seen; he couldn't take his eyes off her.

"You're really looking her over," Ellen told him. 'I must admit you have taste. Do you prefer her to ... me?"

"Ellen, I wouldn't trade you for the world. Don't worry!'

"At last, a tender thought!"

The captain made the first move.

"Did you board the train at Kafr el Zagiat? How did you end up in this awful place?"

Ellen was forced to tell them about their adventure. As she recounted it the atmosphere warmed up and in a while they were on first name terms. The captain's name was Tommy – what else? She, Iris. She had satiny, aristocratic skin, that of a woman who rises late in the morning, and her jet-black hair, in bangs over her forehead like something from an Egyptian fresco, compared with the finest silk of the Orient.

"Where is Iris from?" Alexis asked the captain.

The woman opposite him provoked a curious mixture of admiration and fear in him.

"My father was Irish and my mother an Egyptian Copt," she answered for herself with the calm sweet voice of the women of the Middle East.

"We only just married," the Englishman added, "and we spent our honeymoon in Upper Egypt – or I should say our honey week – I didn't have much leave."

"I wish you a long and happy life together," Ellen told them.

"Why did you choose Upper Egypt for your honeymoon?"

"I'm not a career officer. I did Classics at Oxford – and what would be more natural than to want to see Upper Egypt? We spent four days at a beautiful hotel, 'The Cataracts', in Aswan, on the Nile and the rest we spent at Luxor and Carnak."

He looked tenderly at his wife.

"One day when the war is over I want to go to Greece. Perhaps I could find employment on an archaeological excavation."

"I told Ellen, when we were standing before the pyramids the other day, that I felt overawed by the desert. Do you think the ancient Egyptians felt that awe when they built those monuments to their dead?" Alexis asked.

"It's true that the Egyptians cultivated the sense of death, just as you Greeks did the sense of life. For the Egyptians death should not be worse than life – they almost welcomed death; perhaps for them it was a confirmation of a long historical continuity. The pyramids with their endless passageways are nothing more than a form of protection so the dead could have an undisturbed after-life. Of course, we're talking about kings who put 100,000 slaves to work – they say that's how many worked on Cheops' pyramid – to prepare this after-life for them!"

"In that sense there's been a great deal of progress. Now the pashas only have a dozen servants – one to serve, one to shine shoes, another to open the door, another to drive the limousine and another to fan him!" Ellen said.

"Not only the pashas, Ellen, but some ... European colonials too, and don't try to get out of that!" Alexis interjected.

"Including the Greeks of Alexander the Great!"

Ellen wasn't going to let him get away with anything.

"I would like to be as free-spirited as Ellen, but my middle-eastern half makes me ... submissive," Iris quickly responded with a slight sense of irony in her voice on Ellen's behalf before Alexis could reply.

"Don't listen to her ... yes she used to be submissive ... before our wedding, but as soon as we got married, I discovered the other side of my wife, the rebellious Irishwoman," Tom said.

"That's not true!" Iris said. "The motive force always comes from the same side: the cunning, strong, Oriental woman."

Tom said, "You're all little Cleopatras! Enticing smiles and a heart of stone."

Ellen wasn't prepared to let the opportunity pass. "Wasn't Cleopatra a Greek?" she asked looking at Alexis out of the corner of her eye. "She has opened women's eyes ..."

"Precisely, Ellen. That's what the Greeks did, they opened everyone's eyes and they did not only teach us to perceive beauty but they also opened the eyes of thought, and, even more than that, the eyes of the soul!" Tom said seriously, as if he were lecturing.

"I didn't say it, the professor did, and he's your fellow countryman and a captain to boot! You can't talk back to him, you insignificant little Lieutenant," Alexis pointed out to Ellen.

"Do you belong to the WACS, Ellen?" Tom asked.

"Yes, to a unit in Alexandria, but I'll be transferred before long."

Tom looked at Alexis: "How old are you?"

Alexis felt uncomfortable, assuming that the question had to do with his association with Ellen.

"Twenty-one but the war years count double."

Tom said, "Don't forget that Alexander the Great was only twenty-five when he reached the site of Alexandria and ordered the capital of Egypt to be built there. Eight years later they brought him back in a glass coffin to bury him at Sharm el Daniel. But he wasn't the only Greek in Egypt. Three hundred years before Christ, Euclid founded his School of Mathematics. The geographer Eratosthenis, who correctly measured the diameter of the Earth, was also here. During Christian times, Ptolemy mapped the then-known world and in Roman times a porter in the harbour of Alexandria founded the famed neo-Platonic School which was perhaps the first cosmopolitan conception, and established Alexandria as an international centre, where Greek, Persian, Indian and even Christian art co-existed. But don't let me tire you with my pedantic long-windedness. A failing of my profession. Besides the train is slowing down. We'll be coming into Tanta."

Alexis expected to find the same bazaar as at Kafr el Zagiat, the Arabs flying around as though flocks of birds or trembling like poplar leaves in the wind or sea-spray whipped by squalls. None of that. No roar greeted them as the train screeched to a halt. He looked out the open window, and saw nothing but the tops of the palm trees which bowed politely over the low houses of Tanta, bent from the desert wind. He saw the minarets too, against the red sunset in the background, piercing the sun and the sky, and very far away he heard the evening prayer of the muezzin, like an echo of the day that had passed.

Curious, he got up to have a better look. "Why isn't there a soul in this station?"

He didn't have time to finish his sentence before he saw a rug of jelabas opening and closing like fans in the direction of Mecca.

Every person who got off the train knelt in the little space that remained in order that they too could get into the rhythm of the muezzins' prayer. The spectacle was so moving that Alexis was transfixed and for a while didn't say anything.

At last he said, "Ellen, come and look at this human sea of prayer."

"It's the time for the evening prayer," Tom said phlegmatically.

"I've seen Mohammedans praying, kneeling on rugs, but never a sight like this," Ellen said.

It was as if the invisible muezzin had a magic baton which directed the prayers and the movement of the faithful. Then suddenly, when the sun that was setting played its last note, they all rose up at once and a muffled noise grew like a volcano ready to erupt. The station at Tanta returned to its normal condition of disorder, unruliness and uproar.

"That's better," Alexis told them. "At least that is something I understand. My soul was in rapture listening to the voice of the muezzin transfixing an entire flock of people. As though it came out of the infinite."

"You're right. In the beginning my heart too would skip a beat when I heard the voice of the muezzin at twilight coming from high up on the minaret. Now, I'm used to it but it still impresses me," Tom said.

The train waited for the prayer to end and the new passengers to get on.

Alexis and Ellen sat back down as the train whistled and started up.

The moment it left the town, they entered a classic post-card scene with red sky, palm trees on the banks of the Nile, the sail of a felucca and a caravan motionless on the horizon as though in a shadow puppet theatre; this was the last, silent image before night fell.

"I think I'll try and get a little sleep," Alexis said, "sitting up in my corner here."

"That's a good idea. There's been a lot of excitement for one day," Ellen said.

Alexis was in the mood to lean on Ellen's shoulder but he thought it might compromise her in front of the captain. He leaned his head back and tried to sleep. But after a while he opened his eyes again.

"You know, it's the first time I've ever been on a train! It never occurred to me while I was hanging outside; I just thought of it, listening to the pretty music the wheels make on the tracks – what a rhythm. Clickety clack, clickety clack, clack, clack, clickety clack. Like a lullaby."

Ellen hastened to add, lest they take him for a complete innocent: "Don't mind him. He's just a tired romantic."

Tom and Iris laughed and Alexis closed his eyes again. The others stopped talking so as not to disturb him, and he suddenly felt very much alone. He would have liked to hear voices around him whispering, like when he was little and wanted to have his door open at night, so that he would have contact with the outside world.

"You can talk, you won't bother me."

He found himself drifting into that dreamy state where one catches and sifts what one hears unconsciously. In the beat of the train's wheels, he heard the satiny voice of Iris, talking about the impression that the beautiful names of the Egyptian goddesses had made on her; Herishet ... Nekhebet ... Ernuket ... Weppawet ... Anuket ... as he dozed he murmured the names to himself rhythmically.

When he awoke at the last stop at Damanhur, he again whispered the names that he had by then learned.

"And we thought you were asleep," Tom said. "I hope we didn't disturb you!"

"On the contrary. Iris' dulcet voice was like a lullaby!"

Night had fallen and the magical sensation of detachment which the dark brings had been added to the improvised ballet at the Danmanhur station.

When they once more started and the wheels returned to their music, Iris repeated the names playfully:

"Herishet, Hekhebet, Ernuket, Weppawet, Anuket!"

Tom continued: "And there is Sekhmet and Satet and Nuwet and Selket ...

Then Iris once more: "Stop before we get 'mal de tête'!"

Tom: "Don't you think Iris looks a bit like Selket? With ... a better sense of humour of course. Same face, same body. She knows it too ... but that's another story that I'll tell you sometime."

Alexis: "I know that Selket was one of the goddesses, but I must admit I don't remember which one."

"She was the most beautiful goddess! Iris looks like the gold statuette of Selket that was found in Tutankhamun's tomb."

"What Tom is reluctant to say is that Selket is connected with the scorpion," Iris added.

"I'm trying to forget it!" Tom said shaking his head.

"Deep down, Tom is afraid of women. He's always saying that only the Egyptians understood the soul of woman."

"That's how it is," Tom elaborated. "That's why Sekhmet is the lion goddess, Nekhebet, the eagle goddess, Renenutet, the snake goddess! Even Satet, the goddess of prosperity and floods, is depicted with horns! Isn't that so? You Greeks idolise women. All your goddesses are beautiful. Not only is Aphrodite sexy, but Athena and Artemis and even Hera and Demeter – they all have an erotic side to them – for me at least. Egyptians have little eroticism in their worship.

Alexis asked him: "Why did you become an Egyptologist instead of getting involved with Greek history and archaeology?"

"Out of masochism!" Iris's words of course.

"The Scorpion goddess speaks," Tom said.

It was strange, but behind the calm mask of Iris emerged words that, even though in jest, did not fit her expression.

Alexis began to feel her influence. Her resemblance to the statuette of Selket that he'd seen only in books, startled him. He began to see her more as the Scorpion goddess than a sensuous woman of the Orient.

Iris was aware of the change in Alexis' eyes.

"I'll bet you're afraid of me too."

Ellen, who hadn't spoken for some time, was becoming annoyed with all the attention Alexis was focusing on Iris.

"Alexis is easily influenced, don't take him seriously!"

"You're right, Tom, all women are the same, Lions, snakes and scorpions, they never let you get away with anything."

Tom agreed: "I must go to Greece; perhaps I'll change my ideas. Here women rule and it appears that ours have been magnetised by that fearful Queen, Hatshepsut, whose successor and nephew, Tuthmosis the Third, had all depictions of her destroyed after her death so she couldn't live in memory."

He began to recite:
"... *And only in the quietness of the crypt of a grave,*
in front of one of her gold figures,
which no base eye would see again,
did he feel the warmth of her heavenly presence.
She was dressed like a man and wore a double crown;
One was not enough for her."
"Donald Redford, dixit!"
"I've heard all this a thousand times," Iris added in irritation. "It's Tom's eternal theme! Now he'll tell us about Cleopatra, the other devil-possessed Queen. Don't tell me that she wasn't sexy at least!"
"But she was Greek!" Tom protested.
"I know one thing: whether goddesses or Queens, whether Egyptian or Greek, they toyed with men as if they were puppets. What about the fact that every Egyptian goddess took the shape of a wild animal, doesn't that mean that women are the true forces of nature?"
Iris became more and more aggressive. Her eyes gave off sparks but her smile was immobile and questioning like Nefertiti or Mona Lisa.
"Primitive forces, you mean to say," Tom said, trying to get control of the conversation. "Nearly all the great gods of Egypt are men, and human in form, and their symbols at least are domestic animals!" Both Amon, the king of the gods, anthropomorphic, and Ptah, the creator of the universe, the first identification of the Word-Universe which later entered Platonic philosophy and even later Platonic Christianity. These were the basis of the Coptic religion as well; it is said that the word "Copt" came from Ptah. Just as the word Egypt – 'Aigyptos' is Greek. Thoth, the god of learning and intellect is depicted in the elegant form of the ibis. He is holding the famous book in which all the wisdom of the world was written in a supremely moral and naturalistically logical form. Akhnaton, the husband of Nefertiti, in his Hymn to the Sun wrote: 'The sun becomes a hand, the hand is human and promises that the universe is not indifferent to human fate.' The naturalistic ethic: 'Be honest, be truthful, be in harmony with nature.' Perhaps it was this aspect of Egyptian philosophy that attracted me and got me interested in Egyptian subjects and during my research I found a goddess ... Scorpion and I captured her for my Egyptian collection!'

Iris stared at him with a severe and quizzical expression.

"Well anyway, your collection ends here. You'd like to have me in a display case, eh? I may be an oriental woman but that's only half of me and don't ever forget it!"

Again her eyes and the tone of her voice startled Alexis. It was as if she was trying through jokes to pass on a message, a threat.

Alexis glanced without a word at Ellen and their eyes met. They both had the same feeling. But the look on Iris's face quickly changed.

"Now she's wearing her sweet little face and squeezing Tom's arm," Alexis murmured to Ellen.

Tom dispelled the moment of embarrassment with his English composure, trying to show that he didn't take seriously the contradictory signals that Iris was sending out.

"We'll reach Alexandria shortly and have to say good-bye. But only nine at night – what would you say to continuing the evening and going out dancing?" he asked.

"But we'll have to get dressed," Ellen said, "and my house is a long way away."

"Let's make a date for 'Auberge Bleue' at ten-thirty – can you make it?"

"It sounds good to me!" Alexis said.

"Why don't you change at our house?" Iris offered, "We live above the Corniche. You do have your suitcases with you."

"All right, we will! It will be a delightful way to end our journey," Ellen agreed.

Soon the train reached Alexandria and the passengers poured out in new pandemonium.

Alexis, Ellen, Tom and Iris waited for the coaches to empty a bit, got out, hailed a cab and a few minutes later entered Tom and Iris's home, on the third floor of an apartment building above the famous Corniche of Alexandria, which was on a par with the Promenade des Anglais in Nice.

Tom and Iris would be living there for the first time, since after their wedding they had left immediately for Upper Egypt. The black servant they had installed in their apartment opened the door with great joy and much bowing.

Iris directed Ellen and Alexis to a room where they could change and she and Tom went into the room next door.

As soon as they were by themselves Ellen said to Alexis: "Doesn't it seem strange to you, not wanting to be alone on their first evening in their home?"

"Iris really amazes me. Either she has the oriental woman's complex very strongly and wants to express her independence in any way she can or she doesn't really love Tom. She only seems to love herself. There were moments when her look frightened me and you felt it too."

Then as if talking to himself: "Selket. The Scorpion Goddess!"

"It's true. I got a strange feeling as well, but I think that you and your overactive imagination have influenced me. I'm going to take a shower and change. Stop thinking about Selket and start thinking about changing too, so we can go out dancing."

Alexis was ready first and went into the living-room. Tom found him there admiring the beautiful English rotonda and the bahut with its silver objects which glistened in the light of a Chinese lantern. The walls were covered with paintings of English landscapes from the 19th century. In a display case, lit up by two spotlights, was a gilded statuette of an Egyptian female figure. Alexis couldn't help recognising its similarity to Iris.

"All the furniture and silver belong to Iris and now I'll tell you about the statue," Tom said. "It's the story I promised you on the train: Iris's father is the largest antique dealer in Alexandria. That's where I met Iris."

He paused as the servant entered bringing them something to drink and then went on. "One day I went into the store and was fondling a small Egyptian statue of the goddess Selket just at the moment when Iris came in to visit her father. Note that I was admiring the statue as she approached me."

'Which do you prefer – her or me?' she asked me bluntly.

'It depends on what for?' I answered.

"The similarity, of course, struck me at once, but I tried to hide my surprise."

'Don't you think she resembles me?'

'Yes, perhaps. That is, you resemble her but you don't have her divine charm.'

No one ever told me that,' she answered, and I could tell she was nettled: 'why do you say that?'

'Because you appear to be badly brought up and a goddess never is. But I forgot that Selket, as the Scorpion Goddess, is aggressive like you.'

'You mean you don't like me!'

'I didn't say that. But your qualities are human, not divine.'

'Why am I badly brought up?'

'Because obviously everyone tells you that you look like the goddess and you expected me to react by saying: what an amazing likeness! May I touch the hand of the goddess?'

Iris laughed. 'How did you guess?'

'I know human nature. I am an archaeologist and I read History.'

'Does History make you a psychologist too?'

'You meet the same human characters over and over in History.'

'Whom do I resemble in History?'

'As a form, the goddess Selket certainly. As a type I would say Cleopatra. The personification of the Egyptian woman even if she was Greek. Quick, nervous, apparently subservient, but seeking power. Intelligent but not enough to keep her from destroying herself. Like the scorpion, which is capable of stinging itself. And don't forget, Selket is connected with the Scorpion, and Cleopatra committed suicide with the help of an adder's bite.' Tom paused. "I want to confess something to you, Alexis, I'm afraid of that part of her. She is a woman with terrible conflict going on inside. She can be tender, sensuous, vivacious, but there are times when she becomes volatile with a touch of self-denigration. I don't know if you follow me: she always asks to be forgiven. And she was born under the sign of Scorpio which doesn't help matters!"

Alexis certainly didn't let on what he and Ellen had been thinking about her. Instead, he tried to reassure him. "But she appears to be so self-controlled with, one might say, an alluring tranquillity."

"But it's precisely that that frightens me. I don't know whether her outbursts are spontaneous or pre-arranged by cosmic forces that have been lost in time. Pardon me, sometimes I do speak in a rather irrational manner. I'm practically playing her game myself in believing she is a divine enigma. Cheers!"

At that moment Iris and Ellen made their appearance.

Alexis froze when he saw Iris in a gold lamé dress that rippled and slid over her supple body, a gold necklace around her neck, a replica of a piece of ancient Egyptian jewellery, and a gold belt with a large buckle. This, plus the make-up around her large eyes, that only a steady hand could have achieved, meant that she knew very well the effect she was after.

Ellen was wearing the same rose-coloured dress as on their first evening in Cairo, a little wrinkled from the trip. Next to Iris, despite her beautiful stature, she resembled an insignificant Queen's attendant.

Alexis immediately glanced toward the gold statue in the display case and knew at once that Iris was playing a part and had come to believe in that part. That's what frightened Tom and it frightened him too. Looking at the two women, the goddess and the mortal, he shivered with relief that his girl was mortal. He spoke first:

"Tom told me how you met. We got to the part where he compared you to the goddess Selket and Queen Cleopatra."

The goddess took the initiative: "Do you want me to continue his story? Well, from there on, everything got easier. I must confess that I liked Tom from the first moment I saw him and that's why I talked to him. My curiosity had been aroused; for the first time a man faced me without fawning and I said to myself: 'I must conquer him!'"

The scorpion comes out to kill, Alexis thought.

"I asked him if he wanted to flirt with the goddess or the Queen. His answer was: 'If I was a God or a King perhaps; but I do very well in the shoes of a mortal.'"

Tom interrupted. "The result is that we went out together that very evening and fifteen days later we were married. Now I'm going to get the car out of the garage. It's a Bentley you'll notice – that also belongs to Iris. I'm just the royal chauffeur! You've realised what the statue in the case symbolises. She gave it to me as a wedding gift!"

Ellen didn't understand quite what was going on except that she was caught up in a not very comfortable atmosphere.

Two forms, all in gold, one with human dimensions, alive, vibrant, in the tradition of the great women of Egypt, the other with the dimensions of a goddess, immobile, haughty, unapproachable, behind the glass of a display case, with her arms opened slightly outward, her breasts, her waist, her legs and even her navel clearly outlined under the thin dress sculpted on her.

That moment, lit by the chandelier and the spotlights, in the livingroom, after thousands of years in the dark of Tutankhamun's tomb, they faced each other as if they were competing in beauty and power. Both of them had an absolute, divine certainty. Further back was Ellen, nearly obliterated on the margin, her frightened look making her so human that Alexis suddenly loved her very much.

Is Iris afraid deep inside but doesn't show it? Does she know that she resembles a goddess but isn't one? Does this make her feel insecure? Is this what she expresses in her sudden outbursts? A dangerous game, Alexis thought. And now it's as if we are all supposed to become part of that game.

A while later the four of them were sitting on the Bentley's luxurious seats, on their way to the Auberge Bleue, which was no more than ten minutes from Tom and Iris's house.

The extremely tall doorman at the club, who wore a royal blue gold-embroidered jelaba, opened the doors of the car for them. From there on Alexis and Ellen watched the performance which was all Iris.

The doorman made a royal bow as she got out of the car. The maitre d' in a white dinner jacket, bowed even lower and kissed her hand. Everyone on the dance floor slowed and turned their heads. Every patron's eyes were fixed on her, as the maitre d' led her to their table. The other three simply followed.

The stares made Alexis uncomfortable but at the same time he was proud that this woman was part of his party or rather... that they were part of hers. Still, the uneasiness he felt didn't pass. It was as if he were waiting for something to happen. Maybe Tom had influenced him. He felt that not all was well, without being able to pinpoint what it was.

The maitre d' who seated them at the edge of the dance floor, bent down to Iris's ear and told her something that made her eyes glisten.

She suddenly turned her head and looked at the other side of the dance floor.

"Farouk is sitting exactly opposite us," she said haughtily.

It was true, King Farouk of Egypt was sitting with another man on the opposite side of the dance floor. Both of them were dressed in tuxedos with cream-coloured jackets and wine-red bow ties, obviously to match their fezzes.

For the first time Alexis was seeing the mythical figure of the corpulent Farouk with his affected moustache and dissipated face. What a night! Goddesses, Queens, Kings, the luxurious seats of the Bentley, the magic crystalline opulence of the Auberge Bleue, the intoxicating music from the twenty instruments in the orchestra, another great first in his life.

Without any pretext, Farouk fixed his eyes on Iris and said something to his friend.

Iris, who was well aware of his attention, put on even greater airs. "Imagine, a descendant of the Pharaohs, opposite me!" As if only she alone was seated at their table.

"As much a descendant of the Pharoahs as I am, the old pervert!" Tom snapped, for once having lost his composure.

To justify his outburst he said: "The ancient Egyptians didn't worship sex, as I told you on the train. There are no pictures of erotic subjects and sex was forbidden in holy places."

"The Auberge Bleue is hardly a holy place," Iris shot back.

"What's she up to?" Alexis thought and before they ordered he asked Ellen to dance. He wanted to leave the table because he felt a crisis coming on. They asked Tom and Iris to excuse them and went out onto the floor.

"Ellen, come close. I feel uncomfortable with these two. I don't know if we should have accepted their invitation."

"I feel the same way. How could we tell – there wasn't time. Hold me tight so that I feel like a human being again. I'm out of my depth in this unreal atmosphere of Gods and Pharaohs. Did you see how Farouk looked at Iris? Do you find her sexy? A sexy woman shouldn't inspire fear, but I'm afraid of Iris. I think she's the kind of woman who provokes, who arouses, but at bottom she's cold. That may be the reason she has to hide behind her divine form, to cover her lack of feminine desire."

"Cold women often need to make love more often, to prove to themselves that they're women."

"For someone your age, you know a lot about women!"

"Not from experience of course. The way Tom knows, from studying History!'

The music playing at that moment was the theme song from "As Time Goes By" the great hit of the period. It had become Alexis' and Ellen's song and it hung suspended in the wanton Egyptian nights of a dissolute Cavafian city.

The music stopped and they went back to sit down at the table. Tom had ordered food for everyone.

"I thought I'd surprise you: fried shrimp, Chateaubriand Bearnaise, Alaska flambee and a good Burgundy."

At that moment, Alexis' vague presentiment that something was going to happen, came true. Farouk's friend got up, crossed the floor, approached their table, bowed, and addressing himself to Tom and Alexis, the men at the table, said:

"The King would be very honoured to have the next dance with the lady," and turned toward Iris.

Tom, in the full glory of his British irony, answered: "His Highness honours us, but if he wants to dance he should bring his own woman. I'm sure he has a most lavish collection."

Alexis and Ellen froze. Not only had Tom refused to let his wife dance with the King, he had mocked him as well. Iris's eyes snapped with anger. "Please excuse my husband, he's had a little too much to drink. Tell his Highness that I would be delighted to dance with him."

Alexis and Ellen looked at Tom as if imploring him not to keep it up. Tom got the message. The situation was temporarily saved. Once more the music started up.

Fat-bellied Farouk circled the dance floor and in his turn bowed to Iris. Iris got up first and made a royal curtsey, and Ellen clumsily tried to imitate her.

Alexis, seeing that Tom was not disposed to stand up for the King, was confused and didn't know what to do. He very much wanted to back Tom up but felt he had overdone it. Alexis wanted to keep things from getting worse – he had no experience of kings but since the women had risen he would at least have a way of justifying himself to Tom if he stood up himself, by the time he had reached a decision Farouk had taken Iris by the hand and they began to dance a tango.

Ellen broke the ice. "That was rather daring of you, Tom, to say such things about the King – weren't you afraid?"

"He's not my King. As a Captain in the Royal Army I owe allegiance only to His Majesty the King of England. You, Ellen, can understand that. You and I keep him on his throne. If it weren't for us, Farouk would have lost his wealth, his palaces and his women."

"Do you think his friend will repeat what you said?"

"I don't know and I don't care and ... I'm not afraid; he wouldn't dare do anything."

Alexis spoke without addressing himself to anyone specifically: "Tom, the archaeologist with nothing militaristic about him, either in his demeanour or his look, suddenly becomes a Captain in the Royal Army. The intellectual who puts on a different mask to win the war."

"But this time I lost the war with Iris," Tom replied.

There was real sorrow in his voice. His fears had finally surfaced. "What did I tell you Alexis? You never know what to expect from a woman. And we're still on our honeymoon!"

"Tom, it was Iris who saved the situation! Her female intuition prompted her to accept the invitation only to cover up for you," Ellen told him reassuringly.

But Tom wasn't convinced: "You know very well what it means to Iris to dance with the King! Always the same image. The goddess, the Queen. Power and splendour!"

"Since you know that, why didn't you give her permission to dance?"

"Because Farouk disgusts me."

"When you come down to it, it would be a great honour for any woman to dance with a king – whoever he is – and I'm sorry he didn't ask me."

"She wanted to have her fun. It didn't matter to her if she was hurting me."

"She can give the excuse that this way she avoided an incident."

"There may be no incident with Farouk but ... I don't know what's going to happen with us." Then slowly and deliberately: "The scorpion ... stings ... and is stung."

"Oh, come on, Tom," Alexis broke in, "don't take everything so seriously. Iris is playing a game and we're playing it with her. When you take her to England and she's in a new environment she'll forget all this Egyptian pomp. You can't play a game if the other person doesn't play along with you!"

"Look at her on the dance floor, she's radiant with pride. Tomorrow, all of Alexandria will say that Iris, daughter of an antique dealer, Iris, the goddess Selket, danced with Farouk ... your shrimp will get cold, start eating, don't wait for Iris."

The orchestra usually played three pieces and stopped. This time it was three tangoes, obviously so the King could hold his partner more tightly. But Iris kept him at a distance. She knew how to assert her personality, even with a king. Her presence on the floor overshadowed his. The simple, rhythmic movements of her body bewitched the whole cosmopolitan crowd at the Auberge Bleue.

When Farouk brought her back to the table, Alexis and Ellen got up. Farouk bowed and moved away.

Alexis felt that somebody should say something. "Iris, after you've eaten your shrimp, I'd like to dance with you, with Tom's permission of course; I hope he won't say no."

Tom didn't answer. Several moments of silence went by before Ellen asked:

"Tell me what Farouk said to you. I saw how he was talking to you the whole time."

Tom said, "I'm sure he told her that he would send his chauffeur for her so that he could show her his Chinese collection at Montaza!"

"But, of course," Iris said provocatively: "It's only natural, isn't it?"

Then immediately making a one hundred and eighty degree turn and taking on the coaxing, cat-like look she had used on the train:

"But you're such an idiot, Tom. Don't you have any faith in me?"

With a few words she'd disarmed him.

No matter how much Alexis wanted to dance with Iris after the King, he thought he had better give Tom the opportunity of having the first dance.

"Tom, you dance with Iris. She's a real lady. I don't know if she's a goddess or a Queen, but she's one hundred percent woman."

Later on, Tom got his revenge. Dancing cheek to cheek, in an era when in the best clubs men and women still kept a certain distance, he paraded back and forth in front of Farouk with the Queen of the Ball. England always won the last battle.

Farouk and his friend got up to leave. But it was really Iris's victory. The goddess Selket, the scorpion, had vanquished the King.

As soon as they returned to the table and before they could sit down, Alexis asked if he could dance with her. "Do I get a chance to go around the floor once with the Belle of the Ball, too? Tom, you dance with Ellen."

He suddenly felt he had to take things into his own hands, even if he was the youngest in the company. Tom and Iris's 'cheek to cheek', the departure of Farouk, had not alleviated things. There was still tension. Tom had been deeply wounded, he could sense that. He took a few steps on the floor with Iris, looking her in the eyes.

"Why are you looking at me like that? I'm sure you think I was in the wrong," she said.

"No, I think Tom was wrong. Still, you have to realise that Tom doesn't see Farouk as the King of Egypt, but as a degenerate womaniser who happens to have a throne at the mercy of the English."

"Even so, he had no reason to be rude. One dance with Farouk isn't the end of the world. But when he did what he did, I had no choice."

"So you gratified your vanity and you hurt Tom. The scorpion that destroys itself."

"Now, don't you start with Tom's nonsense."

"It's important because this is what Tom believes. It's become a way of life and he's afraid of you. Tonight you'll ask his forgiveness on bended knee and you'll stop being Selket. I've only known Tom a few hours but I know he is a wonderful person. Perhaps he won't give you the life you want, but he's a good captain and he'll set you on the right course. And let me tell you, even though I don't agree with what he did I admired him for the way he stood up to the King."

"My problem is that I admire him too!" Iris confessed. "You make everything seem so easy! Anyway, thank you. Obviously you danced with me only so you could talk to me."

"Not only for that. I have human weaknesses too. You can say that you danced with Farouk and I that I danced with Selket!"

"Ellen is lucky to have you."

"She has me – but only in a manner of speaking. Soon each of us will go our own way. I'm taking my first steps in life, I don't know what I'm doing yet. Ellen and I are almost unreal to each other – part of the unreal atmosphere that is Egypt. The war passed by here but without touching it. Let's go back."

The evening ended quietly, around one in the morning. There was no more talk of Farouk, and good manners prevailed as if nothing had happened. Only Tom's heart felt the wrench. "I'll take you home," he said to the other couple.

"We'll get a taxi," Alexis replied. "You live nearby, Ellen lives in Agami, I'll take her home."

"Not a chance." Tom was adamant. No-one spoke on the way. They had surrendered themselves to the silence of the Alexandrian night.

Just before they arrived, Ellen asked Alexis: "Aren't you staying with me tonight?"

"I have to go to the house where they're putting me up in Alexandria. I need to be at the boat early in the morning, to find out when she's going to sail."

When they stopped in front of Ellen's house Tom took the suitcase out of the car boot and asked them to excuse him for ruining their evening.

"Don't even think such a thing! We had a wonderful time and I hope we see each other again soon."

Ellen squeezed both of his hands.

Tom and Iris waited as Alexis escorted Ellen to her door.

"What a day this has been!" Ellen said putting her arm around his waist; "particularly for you. A race on the Nile, the race for the train, the ride hanging outside the last car and now this evening. Pinch me, so I know I'm not dreaming!"

"You were very cool to Iris when you thanked her just now. I don't think you meant it when you said you'd see them again."

"I should think not! But apparently you've changed your mind!"

"She's a devilish woman, like a chameleon I must admit. She made me doubt everything I had felt about her. But now I must go back. I'll call you tomorrow evening when you come back from duty" (and tenderly), "it hasn't been all that long since I knocked on your door and asked for help. You gave it to me and then some."

He set her suitcase in front of the door, kissed her and went back to the Bentley.

The following evening at exactly six, Ellen ran to answer the phone. She didn't even wait for a "hello".

"I've missed you all day."

"Ellen, my boat is leaving tomorrow."

Silence.

"That's how I feel too."

"Come as quickly as you can."

Her voice could hardly be heard and she didn't wait for an answer.

Alexis got his things ready for departure and arrived at eight to ring Ellen's doorbell. The last time, he whispered, and kept his finger on the bell in order to remember the feeling.

He was surprised when the door wasn't opened by Ellen but by a WAC he didn't know.

"You must be Alexis."

"And who are you?"

"I'm Phyllis. I came the day you left. Ellen is waiting for you in her room and doesn't want to see anyone but you. Last night she came home full of joy and laughing and today she's ready to jump out of the window! You're not bad looking, I'll have to say that, but not enough for a woman to kill herself over!"

"You see, it was bad luck that I didn't meet you the night I came here. Because then I wouldn't have any problem now," he said vindictively.

"I was asking for that. I'll show you the way to her room – but you know the way, I imagine!"

"I know it. Thank you and try to keep her spirits up after I'm gone."

"What will make you forget?"

"Perhaps the sea, perhaps no one."

Ellen had set a table for them to eat in her room. She had turned out the lights and had just lit the candle in the middle when she heard his steps.

When Alexis opened the door, she was standing in silhouette at the window. A photographic cliché, he thought, and the fact that he could exercise critical judgement gave him strength.

"Why is it so dark in here, Ellen?"

"So you won't see my tear-swollen eyes. Will you do me a favour Alexis? Let's go on with our game tonight. We'll act as though you're not leaving tomorrow."

"I can try, but when I once tried to act in a student festival they kicked me out, I was such a bad actor."

"Do it for my sake. I prepared some very simple food but I hope you're not hungry because I'm not."

"The last thing I'm thinking about is food."

"What does one say when one's heart and stomach are like lumps and one is sitting at a table and isn't prepared to talk about separating?"

"Nothing. Every thought is blocked out before it is put into words and the only solution is for us to spread our two hands on the table, like the first day, since the food is going untouched."

Only their eyes could readily speak in this game which they couldn't play honestly, no matter how much they wanted to.

"When the time comes, you cannot hold it back" Alexis recited in a whisper. "But let's let our feelings work on their own. If it's tears that come out then let them."

Ellen's face, half-lit by the candle, already seemed more remote. The hands they had spread out were not to hold onto each other. It was the long touch of farewell.

But a powerful magnetism passed through the tips of their fingers, drawing them closer. With her other hand Ellen undid the buttons of her blouse one by one like the first evening at the kitchen table. The shadow of the candle flame on her breasts made them even more voluptuous.

The Alexandrian night entered the window of the room in its entirety. As they joined hands, in the same movement one tugged the other, they got up and moving almost ceremonially approached the bed for the final scene. He bent his head over her and kissed her two breasts as if he were praying before an icon. He rested his head between them for a while, as she stroked his hair, until her sobs freed their feelings and they seized each other in a wild embrace of love as the candle slowly guttered out.

Making love, Alexis tried to understand what Ellen was saying amid her sobbing as he wiped away her tears with kisses.

"It has never been so powerful. Now that you're leaving I want you even more. Isn't that strange?'

"I didn't know one could make love while crying. It makes it even sweeter!"

That night they made love without barriers and when they finally lay in one another's arms, it was Alexis' turn to speak. "Thank you."

"You are the only man who says thank you."

"You talk as if you've slept with a thousand men!"

"Don't be a fool. I thank you, I thank you for all the times we've made love and I've never said that to anyone – I swear to you. Do you think I'm really in love with you?"

"I think you are infatuated with me. In Greek, you see, we have two different words for love; erotas and agapi. Erotas is an incident in life, agapi should be forever – to the end – like Tristan and Isolde, Romeo and Juliet. I don't think you'd choose an end like that, would you?"

"You're in the mood for jokes. You don't love me or let's say you aren't infatuated with me."

"I know that I need you, that I'll miss you very much."

"But those are the very words I fear: 'I'll miss you, I need you."

"You're right, I'm talking about myself, not you. Shouldn't love be surrender? Like the love of a mother for a child?"

"Do you always analyse your emotions like that? Your philosophical legacy is a very heavy burden. I believe that you love me and you don't want to accept it. As for me, I completely lost myself in love-making tonight. My eyes were open but I didn't see either the ceiling or anything else in the room. As if the walls had opened up and we'd found ourselves suspended in the sky making love among the stars!"

"A psychologist would tell you that you wanted to drown your love in the infinite."

"If only I could ..."

In the morning her eyes were still red with tears and sleeplessness and when they said good-bye they didn't feel they were parting. They would meet again in the afternoon. Ellen would take him to the harbour. Perhaps there was that small hope that one always has at such moments, that something might occur to keep them together.

At five in the afternoon, Ellen waited for him, in her uniform, at Alakefak in Ramleh Square, groomed as never before. The uniform gave her a feeling of security she hadn't had the previous night.

They went on foot to the harbour like good friends who would be seeing each other again in a short time. They spoke their last good-byes in front of the gangway.

"I wanted to play a game last night, so let's play it now," Ellen said. "As I'm leaving, you will say: 'I'll remember you, I'll remember you, I'll remember you! And I will say 'I'll see you again, I'll see you again, I'll see you again!' They say that auto-suggestion works, well ... who knows? Perhaps one day, you with another woman, me with another man. But the scent of the desert, this small part of the thousand and one nights I spent with you, no-one will ever take that away from me."

"Nor from me either, Aisa!"

He went up the gangway without kissing her, He stood in the stern of the boat, as they lifted the gangway and loosened the cables. In the same spot, on another boat, weeks before, he had bid farewell to his family.

Ellen was motionless at the end of the pier. Only her eyes were speaking now and as the boat slowly pulled away from the pier the tears of both of them dropped into the murky waters of the harbour.

In a while they saw the wake of the propeller, like a river of tears, and they said to themselves:

"I'll see you again, I'll see you again, I'll see you again."

"I'll remember you, I'll remember you, I'll remember you."

But both of them knew this game was an illusion.

... as one long prepared and full of courage,
say good-bye to her, to Alexandria who is leaving
Above all, don't fool yourself, don't say
it was a dream, that your ears deceived you;
don't degrade yourself with empty hopes like these.
As one long prepared and full of courage,
as is right for you who were given this kind of city,
go firmly to the window
and listen with deep emotion,
but not with the whining, the pleas of a coward;
listen – your final pleasure – to the voices,
to the exquisite music of that strange procession,
and say good-bye to her, to the Alexandria you are losing.

It was the last Cavafy he would recite for her, silently, from far off, eyes brimming with tears. He had the last word. But she could not hear him.

PART TWO

THE HOUR OF EBB TIDE

Alexis closed his eyes and reminisced in the compartment of the train that was taking him from Johannesburg to Lourenco Marques through endless stretches of the African jungle.

Six months previously he had flown from London to South Africa. The plane had been an old Skymaster with the orange stag of South African Airways on its tail, a thirty-six hour flight with three stops.

His friends' last words before he left were: "Make sure you don't become a farmer and forget all about us!" He was going to get a job in a South African shipping company. But did his friends know him better than he knew himself?

He had taken off from London airport early in the afternoon, and late that first evening, around ten, they had landed in Tripoli, Libya. It was a short stop and no one got off the plane. Until then he hadn't spoken to anyone. The seat next to him was empty and he was able to stretch his legs which were hurting from lack of exercise and the change in atmospheric pressure.

He had plenty of time to build a mental bridge that would link his years in Greece, Egypt, and on the sea, with his first job in Africa.

His anticipation proved stronger than his nostalgia. Africa always means adventure. He saw himself in Livingston's sun-helmet, rifle on shoulder, leading a large safari of natives laden with boxes full of supplies, hacking a way through the lianas of the jungle to reach the source of the Nile!

He did reach the Nile, if not its source, sooner than he had dreamed. The Skymaster's next stop was Khartoum.

Five in the morning and the heat was unbearable. During the two hours it took to service the plane, the passengers had breakfast at the

Nile Palace Hotel, which they reached by bus through the dusty red dirt streets of the town.

He looked around; English officers, phlegmatic and composed, drank their tea hidden behind London newspapers which had just arrived on the same plane, ladies in straw hats, early-risers, fluttered their fans, and an army of "boys" in jelabas moved about among the sparse tables seemingly unaffected by the heat.

Only Alexis felt out of sorts, at 120 Fahrenheit. Neither the English breakfast nor the huge fans on the ceiling, which were whirling madly like plane propellers, could keep him in the high-ceilinged dining-room of the hotel.

The Nile flowed by in front of the Palace and Alexis thought it might be cooler nearer the river. He squatted down on the bank and his hanging head nearly touched the muddy water. He was completely soaked with sweat and unable to drive off the swarms of black flies attacking every exposed part of his body. He quickly changed his mind and returned to the hotel, where the screens on the windows kept the flies out at least. He sat at a table and for the first time struck up a conversation, with an English fellow passenger.

"You are used to the tropical climate, what do you do when it's this hot?"

"Are you hot?" came the reply.

Alexis wasn't sure if the question had a touch of irony or incredulity or both. He didn't persist. But when he ordered coffee the Englishman interrupted: "Tea is more thirst-quenching."

He decided he didn't have the right to question the Englishman's advice. "When you come down to it, we're in a colonial country" – and he ordered tea with eggs and bacon. He emphatically refused the kippers and sausages as well as the porridge, to which he had an aversion. Porridge and cod-liver oil – two revolting childhood experiences, worse than the bogey man.

If conditions had been better he could have dreamed to his hearts content. Khartoum! The heart of the Sudan, the beginning of the Blue Nile, the route to Lake Victoria, the slave route ... the crocodiles.

But for the moment he couldn't wait to get out of that furnace. Fortunately, two hours later he was in the aeroplane again and as soon as they took off the air cooled and so did his mind. From then on they were flying over the real Africa, black Africa, the Africa of lions, panthers and tigers.

Alexis glued his eyes to the porthole of the plane and gazed at the virgin African earth below. Early in the afternoon, as they approached Kenya, the plane flew low for quite some time before landing, and for Alexis it was like a childhood fairytale unfolding before him: ostriches, elephants, antelopes and zebras racing away at the noise of the plane over the open fields and through the thick clumps of African vegetation. They landed on a dirt runway at Kisoumou, not far from Nairobi.

Alexis, still looking out of the window, saw a very tall African standing motionless on one leg and a crutch, wearing only a white cloth over his loins. He reminded Alexis of the witch-doctors of Africa one reads about in books. For a moment, Alexis thought he was a statue. What would such a man be doing on an empty runway? They disembarked from the plane and passed in front of the strange figure, who had his eyes riveted on the great bird that had just landed. His eyes had a strange magnetism to them, even though he seemed to be blind. Was he casting spells on the plane?

Alexis tried to avoid his gaze, and hid in the crowd of other passengers, as they walked through a deserted meadow leading to another hotel, less imposing than the Nile Palace, but with more or less the same colonial decor, bamboo armchairs, ceiling fans, ladies with broad-brimmed hats now sipping afternoon rather than morning tea, while the English officers had put down their papers and were smoking their pipes.

Breakfast in Khartoum, afternoon tea in Kenya, in just a few hours. Alexis had already put in a day in colonial Africa. Here the heat was almost bearable. He felt like talking to that English major with the thick moustache or the attractive woman reading in a corner, but everything was silent and they all appeared unapproachable. "How come in Agatha Christie novels the English on hotel verandas strike up conversations so easily?" he wondered.

In any case he didn't have long to think about the problem because after tea they were taken back to the Skymaster for the final leg of their journey.

The cripple was still there, in the same spot, staring motionless at the plane. Alexis shivered. Had he entered the world of black magic? "He's blind but he can still see. I hope he hasn't put a curse on us!" he blurted out to the Englishman who was walking beside him.

It was the first time they had spoken since Khartoum.

"It wouldn't surprise me in the least," the Englishman replied laconically, which did not make Alexis feel any easier.

The figure of the black man stayed in his mind for quite some time and faded only when, two or three hours later, there appeared before him the largest and reddest sun he had ever seen. From the window of the plane it looked as though the whole sky had caught fire. It was precisely at that moment that he truly began to feel the spell of Africa.

The next image that struck him was of the millions of lights of Johannesburg in contrast with the millions of stars, the brightest he had seen anywhere. From the light of the sun to the light of the stars, to the lights of the city; it was a beautiful introduction to a new life.

He didn't like dark nights, cloudy skies, mist, or the half-light of night clubs. His thoughts came to him through his eyes. He wanted to see a clear, brightly lit world whether his eyes were open or closed, and nature at its most violent, an outburst that would bring tranquility. A squall, a deluge, a flash-flood. He didn't want a Nature of compromise, and Africa knew nothing of compromise – he could sense that. The minute he got off the plane he suddenly felt like a freed animal, or like a tree rooted in the earth that stands up to Nature's every whim, opening itself completely, and embracing the world with its branches.

But disappointment was soon to follow, at least during those first months in Johannesburg.

Instead of the two grey steeds he had imagined, he was met at the airport by Yangos, one of the directors of Southern Steamships, where he would be working, in a fancy limousine. The illuminated highway bore no relation to the jungle of his imagination, and at the bar where they stopped to have a soft drink he heard, instead of tom-toms, the same American songs that had hounded him in far-off Europe, and ordered the inevitable Coca Cola. He too, was a victim of consumerism.

Things didn't change much after that. He spent the first night in a European hotel, the Waverley, which could have been in the centre of Paris or London. He was awakened at five in the morning by a black woman with 'early morning tea' – and almost swore at her, being unaware of this British habit! Since he had been wakened, he got up and took a long walk through the colourless city with its tidy, well-planned streets and tall apartment buildings, and tried to find the offices of the company where he would be working. He did find them eventually and it wasn't long before he was seated behind a desk checking accounts of the firm's ships. If there was one thing he couldn't stand, it was accounts and accounting.

The next disappointment was his salary, which wasn't worth the 10,000 miles he'd travelled to get there, and wouldn't buy him an aeroplane ticket back either. He felt homesick and full of doubts. Had he made the wrong decision?

He would have to look for a cheap room, so he could make ends meet.

It wasn't hard to find one with a lower middle class English family – mother and daughter and their indispensable 'boy' – in Parkhurst on the north side, in an elegant area of Johannesburg; fifteen pounds a month just for the room – no breakfast. A small garden compensated for the lack of any meals. In barely twenty-four hours he had to revise his budget completely; the amount left over for extras had shrunk considerably.

The 'extras' included a sandwich during the lunch-break at work, a film now and then at one of the neighbourhood cinemas, subscriptions to a magazine and two newspapers to look for a second, part-time job. In this 'land of opportunity' he should be able to do something on the side to bolster his finances and make ends meet. In the evenings at home when he no longer could afford to go out, he had to listen to the sobbing of his widowed landlady, left with a seventeen year old daughter, who suffered from high blood pressure and was in danger of dying at any moment.

Plump, freckled, Deirdre, didn't have much to contribute during those evenings in Mrs. Wilkinson's parlour, and conversation only brightened up when Alexis tried to bring the talk around to the black boy who lived in a hut at the far end of the garden, where even a dog wouldn't have been happy. The 'boy' did all the housework, including the cooking, but was not allowed to eat the same food as he was preparing for mother and daughter. His own food was fished out of a sack of mieli-mieli, a kind of flour that he made into a paste and ate.

"He doesn't like anything else," Mrs Wilkinson would say and Dierdre would agree with a smile.

"But have you ever given him the chance to try anything else?" Alexis asked.

"It would be like giving caviar to a baby – he'd spit it out," was her answer, "And that hut he has in the garden is much better than the one he lived in, in the jungle."

The change in the environment, the different living conditions, the boy's isolation in an artificial world, were trifles to Mrs Wilkinson, and so the conversation never got anywhere.

Only once did Alexis try to speak directly to the boy. He found him in the kitchen.

"Are you happy in Johannesburg?" he asked.

He immediately bit his lip. Happy? What a stupid question? But the answer came back easily.

"Black boy must be happy."

And he went on cooking.

Alexis didn't know whether this answer came from an instinctual philosophy of life, taken from the wisdom of the earth and boundless nature, from a forbearing renunciation of the natural rights of life, or contained a hint of sorrowful irony. Whatever it was, Alexis didn't want to upset his seeming spiritual equilibrium and did not speak to him again. But he was always polite to him, more than he would have been to a white and, now and then, put a few shillings in his hand, not knowing if he was doing the right thing.

There was also a black 'boy' in the office where Alexis was working, who was there to run errands. He was more talkative, and unburdened himself more easily to Alexis. His wife and his children lived miles away, but he had neither the means nor the permission to visit them more than every two or three years. He stayed in a ghetto outside the town. Africans weren't allowed to live in the city, unless they were servants in a white house. He was not allowed to enter any place where whites went either, unless on duty, nor could he use white public transport. His monthly pay of eight pounds would not allow for lunch, so Alexis would buy him a sandwich, thereby cutting into his own extras even more.

But Alexis' greatest shock came when he heard for the first time a new word: apartheid. It had been used before the South African Parliament by the new Prime Minister, Malan, who had defeated Jan Smuts in the elections. Even members of Parliament, it seemed, pored through their dictionaries to find out exactly what it meant: 'the absolute segregation of whites and blacks'. The theories laid on the table by the white population, that South Africa was settled by the white man first, that the blacks came later from the north, that if you gave them their way they would force themselves on you, and that their brains weren't like the white man's, Alexis heard free of charge.

From the few conversations he had managed to have with Africans, he found that they had a highly developed instinct. Their efficiency at doing what they had been asked to do was surprising, if one took into account the complete lack of a logical substructure, in the white man's terms; they had to live in the society where they found themselves, whether they liked it or not, a society so different from their own. Alexis began to be annoyed by the condition of the blacks, and even more by the mentality of the whites. Twice, he almost got into a fight: once when a well-fed South African man slapped a black man on the street because he was walking on the same sidewalk as he was, and another in a tea-room when the man behind the counter threw the change on the floor for the black boy who had come in to buy some chocolates, and who had to bend to pick it up. Both times the blood had risen to his head but in the tea-room incident, without thinking about it he bent over the counter, grabbed the man by the shirt and shouted angrily: "Why did you have to do that?"

"He's just a black!" The man said, surprise in his eyes. Alexis had to drop his hands and walk out.

The longer he was in Johannesburg, the more he realised that he couldn't stand the place. He didn't like his job, he didn't like the atmosphere in the office, he didn't like the house he was staying in, and what is more he was bored to death.

His only friends were Barney Zanuck who sold bicycles on Rissick Street, and Jack, a German shepherd dog he had adopted. He had met Jack by chance outside the house where he lived. He'd patted his head and called him Jack, commonest name for dogs in his country. From then on, Jack never left his side. He would accompany him every morning to the trolley stop and was waiting for him to return in the evening; he even stood guard for him at night outside the neighbourhood cinema. Fortunately, the lady of the house had no objection to keeping him, and only the "boy" was a little jealous because Alexis' affection and goodwill were now somewhat divided.

Barney Zanuck was one of the many Jews in Johannesburg. He lived with his wife and their young children – girl and boy – in a beautiful house in Northcliff with tennis court and pool. Saturday afternoon Alexis would visit them and they would talk about the war and the brutality of the Nazis. They were the only people he could talk to about racial problems, because they felt the same way he did. Perhaps that's why they had become friends.

Occasionally, other Jews would come and dance and sing until late in the evening when energetic, plump Ruth would hold forth with "Yiddish Mamma". It was as though she'd sung the National Anthem. They all listened to it with devotion. He had a feeling that all the ghosts of Abraham, Moses, the martyrs under the Pharaohs and the Holy Inquisition and those who had died at Dachau and Auschwitz, were hovering above their heads.

The Sundays when he was alone were unbearable. He stayed in his bed until late, went out for a stroll with Jack, and returned to his room with a book in his hand. No-one invited people to their houses on Sunday. Families were shut up alone, and Alexis had no family of his own yet.

Kathy, the secretary at the office and daughter of the director, made genuine attempts to entertain him. On two or three lunch breaks she took him to neighbourhood restaurants, and on a few occasions invited him out to night clubs. Divorced from her husband, who was in America, she lived with her baby, her father and her mother.

Despite her overtures, the vivacious Kathy got no response. When all was said and done, she was the director's daughter, and if he got wind of anything Alexis would lose his job. It was not the time for complications!

One evening it appeared that Kathy had decided to become bolder. She invited him to her home for a meal and for an evening of investigation into the spirit world. The fact that those who took part each had one finger placed lightly on the glass, was irrelevant ... or should have been. The important thing was to concentrate on the spirit being called, who chose to answer them in this complicated way. They were supposed to be mere middlemen used by the spirit to move the glass as a mode of expression.

Alexis accepted because he thought that communication with the spirits would at least have some element of African magic in it. The two of them ate in the romantic half-light of two candles which didn't inspire Alexis in the least – he who always wanted either light or darkness – and after the meal they sat at a small table to call forth the spirits. Kathy had dressed for the occasion in a gold lamé dress with a high collar that concealed her neck, like a Thai priestess ready for a holy ceremony.

No matter how much he tried to avoid it, Alexis couldn't help laughing to himself; he wasn't prepared to play the game honestly. It seemed he wasn't ripe for magic yet, despite wanting to be.

They called on the spirit of Hamlet and asked it: "To be or not to be?" With much concentration and a little help from Alexis, the answer came back: "Ask Shakespeare!"

"The spirit of Shakespeare, the spirit of Shakespeare!" Kathy shouted out excitedly. "Shakespeare, I'm asking you: to be or not to be?"

Shakespeare took his own sweet time as the glass moved indecisively for several minutes and then the answer came as it practically flew over the table:

"If I knew the answer, Hamlet would too. Ask God!"

This constant referral from one spirit to another was becoming tiresome and Alexis suggested they ask something more specific since it would be a bit arrogant to call on God! Kathy was trembling all over with the idea that she had communicated with Hamlet and Shakespeare, but not to the point that she was going to miss this opportunity.

"Let's call on the spirit of Venus, the goddess of love. I have an important question to ask her."

"I thought we were supposed to call on mortal spirits; don't forget the gods are immortal. What do you want to ask of Venus?"

"If you're going to kiss me tonight or not." Alexis, trying to escape, recited to her from the last part of one of Hamlet's monologues:

Thus conscience does make cowards of us all:
and thus the native hue of resolution
is sicklied o'er with a pale cast of thought;
And enterprises of great pith and moment,
with this regard, their currents turn awry
and lose the name of action ...

"What's that supposed to mean?"

"It means that you are very attractive but ... my conscience won't let me follow my instincts and lure you into a love affair that won't go anywhere."

Kathy hadn't been soothed by the poetry, as Alexis had expected; she turned bright red and her eyes blazed. "No man has ever insulted me like that. Do you think I've fallen in love with you? All the men in Johannesburg are after me! I just wanted to play!"

At that moment the baby began to cry and Kathy hurried out to comfort it, allowing Alexis to recover from his confusion. When she came back, Alexis was standing up ready to leave. As if her anger had never been, Kathy was now wearing a transparent lace night-gown, pink of course, and over it a matching silk robe which opened below to show her legs as she walked. The fire in her eyes had gone out. In just a few moments she had changed tactics trying not to lose the game.

From youthful discussions with his friends he had formed a kind of 'rule': never flirt with a woman just to be polite. But when it comes to making love ... anything goes!

He didn't like women to be provocative, but Kathy's curves, as they stood out under the diaphanous silk, wiped away any doubt. She took him by the hand and led him upstairs. 'Why do you always have to go up or down stairs to make love?' he thought. He was thinking of the whorehouses, which were usually in basements or on an upper floor.

In the sensual atmosphere of Kathy's room, with red print bedclothes, curtains matching the wallpaper, thick pure white wool rug and red silk lampshade, he slowly began to yield, and was never really sure how it happened that he found himself naked in bed making love while Kathy whispered in his ear: "You're my first man since my divorce."

'What do I care?' he said to himself 'Why are women always trying to justify themselves?'

"I liked you from the first day you came into the office!"

'I wish I could say the same for you,' was his silent rejoinder.

Under these conditions their lovemaking was a little clumsy and Kathy was sensitive enough to realise that Alexis wasn't deeply involved with her. Just after orgasm she became meek like all women, but when the first mellowness had passed she asked him in a hurt voice: "Don't you like me at all?"

The cries of the baby in the next room saved the situation again, and gave Alexis the chance to dress quickly and, after the mother had calmed the child down, to bid her good-night and leave.

"I have to go home on foot ... it will take me over an hour and ..."

"Wouldn't you like to spend the night here? We could go to the office in the morning together. It's dangerous to be out by yourself at this hour."

"I'm always alone ... no black man has ever bothered me."

They didn't even kiss. They both knew that this had been a one night stand.

The next day relations at the office were routine again, and if Alexis had moments of embarrassment, Kathy behaved as though nothing had happened. He was a failure at his job, a failure with his free time and a failure at making love.

He had to leave that city, and the sooner the better! He would wait for his temporary residence permit to expire, and then get out. He began to look at the ads in the paper again; maybe he would find an opening.

He felt he was neither in Africa nor in Europe. Except for a few picturesque Zulus who did errands pushing carts through the streets, nothing reminded him of Africa. Where would he go? He had heard that South Africans went to Lourenco Marques, the capital of Mozambique, to whoop it up. Everybody who had been there said it was a European oasis in the middle of the jungle, and what really mattered to him was that it was right on the Indian ocean.

It all turned out to be easier than he had expected: his own company suggested he go to Mozambique and work at its agency on the harbour of Lourenco Marques. Was it a rejected Kathy that was manipulating his transfer? Or maybe 'Daddy' who had got wind of her infatuation and wanted to put an end to a hopeless love affair? He would never know.

Anyway it suited him perfectly. So that's how he came to be travelling on a train taking him to Portuguese East Africa, while reminiscing about the months he had spent in Johannesburg. An image was etched in his mind: he saw the Union of South Africa as a large gold pyramid at the base of which were millions of ant-like blacks bent over digging for the gold that grew into a mountain, steadily going higher and higher; they were trying to reach a dream cloud where there were only white people. But the cloud also rose steadily higher and higher and the pyramid never quite reached it.

He had taken a compartment on the train thinking he would be left alone. When he opened his eyes however he saw sitting opposite him a man in his forties, of medium build with a small, 'Hercules Poirot', black moustache, a round face, slicked-down hair with a parting in the middle, and a striped Mafia-style grey suit. His fellow traveller rose from his seat and, extending his hand, introduced himself.
"Sergio Donatelli, retired colonel in the Italian army."
"How do you do, sir," Alexis introduced himself in his turn.
"How do I do? Well, I do hunt crocodiles in Africa and export the hides. I always say that crocodiles, one of the most savage animals, are less dangerous than people," Donatelli said. He seemed eager to talk.
"As an officer you shouldn't be afraid of danger."

"I'm not afraid of natural danger, Sir, I'm afraid of people. Man has lost the game with man ... at least in my country, not to touch on yours. You're ...?"

"Greek."

"Ah, in that case you'll understand what I mean, seeing that you defeated us in the war."

"Yes ..." Alexis said slowly, and waited to see where Donatelli's thoughts would take him.

"We've lost our values. The men have become members of the Mafia and the women whores."

It was funny to hear him talking about the Mafia when he himself looked like a 'Mafioso'.

"We've fallen into the clutches of schizophrenics and submit to their demonic powers. That's why I fled, in order to keep my dignity – as strange as that may seem to you!"

Alexis started to ask: "Is flight a solution?", but Donatelli went on unrestrained. "I have come to preserve my essence as a human being amidst the wild beasts of the jungle and the primitive people, all children of nature. You see, I divide humanity into two: on one hand the children and those who stay children their whole life, and all the others ... all the rest who grow more corrupt with every year they bear on their shoulders. That's why I came to Africa. Here they are all children, Man and Beast."

Then, without pausing for breath: "Africa! I knew it only from the maps of our colonies: Ethiopia, Eritrea, Libya. But I would not have been welcomed in any of our former colonies. When I was a boy, I had visions of elephants in the jungle, crocodiles in the muddy rivers, caravans in the desert. I spread out the map and saw how little I knew about African geography. I got to know North Africa well during the war through the battles of Rommel and the advances of Montgomery and Eisenhower – then Eritrea and Haile Selassie's Ethiopia from our own war, French Somalia from Rimbaud – I love poetry. The Sahara is a desert, who's interested! I also considered The Congo as a berth after I first heard Danny Kaye sing: 'Bongo, bongo, bongo, it's so lovely in the Congo.' But then the song continues ... 'Oh no-no, no-no, no!', The Americans have found the way to popularise science and in this particular case, geography. Hah, hah, hah! In the Congo, as well as in other parts of West Africa there have been so many re-shufflings, one doesn't know what state belongs to whom and where its borders end. Now on the East side, Tanganyika, Kenya etc., they are definitely British – don't touch! So I went further south. I considered the Union of South Africa, the 'land of promise'. But the land of promise turned out to be the land where you fulfil promises to yourself and forget about any obligations to anybody else. It didn't suit me."

Alexis opened his mouth to ask, "Aren't you exaggerating?" But is was impossible to get a word in edgewise.

"Then, the Union of South Africa is also a part of the Commonwealth! There was nothing left but Angola and Mozambique, both Portuguese colonies, neutral in the war. The one on the Atlantic, the other on the Indian Ocean. I chose the Indian ocean – it sounded more exotic – and now I live in Lourenco Marques with my wife Dalia. How about you?"

"What about me?" Alexis said dazedly.

"Where do you live?"

"Oh! I've been living in Johannesburg, and now I'm transferring to Lourenco Marques."

"If I'm not being indiscreet ..."

Alexis beat him to it: "More for tourism than for anything else!"

He wasn't in the mood to give the man any more information, nor food for further conversation. But it wasn't easy to stop the Colonel; when he couldn't get Alexis to take up the conversation, he turned it back to himself. "I got on the train at Bloemfontein. You didn't notice me, you were sleeping."

'Who cares? What a bore!', thought Alexis to himself.

"I'd gone to visit Kruger Park – you know, the huge national park where people and animals have declared a truce. An Anglo-Saxon concept, the eternal compromise. Except that visitors go around in cars, and when things get rough they hightail it out of there. While in the jungle, my good fellow, there is no compromise. There, you are face to face with the fiercest animals. Many times, in order to reach the crocodile rivers, you must go through dense jungle with all sorts of wild animals. You'll ask me, 'so why did you go to Kruger Park?' Well, I went to see the vast variety of animals, but I couldn't stand being in a 'zoo', where in reality, man is in a cage. Hah, hah, hah!"

'Now's the time for the jokes to begin.' Alexis decided.

"My wife didn't want to accompany me. She doesn't like animals, and preferred to stay at home."

"The poor woman would probably use any excuse to get out of it," Alexis thought.

"I hope you meet her, if you stay in Lourenco Marques. Everybody there knows everybody."

"The moment's arrived to establish social contacts," Alexis muttered, more or less to himself.

"She is very beautiful, dark, the Alida Valli type – you know, the wartime Italian film star.

It was the first time that Alexis eyes showed some interest. "Alida Valli! She and Assia Norris were my favourites."

"But they are so different! The one tall, dark, a 'femme fatale', the other tiny, romantic, blonde ..."

"Why shouldn't I like more than one type of woman?"

"Of course, you're right, but that's what people say."

"Whoever says it doesn't know what he's talking about."

"Hah, hah, hah, that's very funny." The Italian burst out laughing again.

"Not in the least!" Alexis said somewhat abruptly.

They had the entire day to spend on the train, and Alexis wanted in some way to break off the conversation, to be alone. But it was Donatelli who got up, opened the window wide, took a deep breath and exclaimed: "Isn't the clean air of Africa, the free air of the jungle marvellous? Smell the aroma of the wet leaves!"

In reaction, Alexis directed his thoughts to the National Garden in Athens and the autumn scents of a certain rainy day when he was looking for a sheltered place to kiss Lillian or Nora, he couldn't remember which. Those little devils, how they awoke the most delightful desires in him. "Poor Lillian, poor Nora, this fellow sitting opposite me won't allow a few moments of sweet reminiscence!" He grew sad thinking about the distance in time and space.

But the Colonel wouldn't let him be alone with his dreams.

"Look, look at that native's hut and the little picaninnies hiding behind the bushes; they're staring at us as if they were seeing a train for the first time! But a train goes down and comes back every day. Their minds don't work like ours." Donatelli was on the attack again.

"But isn't it wonderful!" Alexis interrupted. "What makes our life so banal is that nothing surprises us. How many marvels go by our eyes without us being aware of them? These children show the same surprise every time over something that amazed them once."

He began to recite in a whisper:

"My past? I have no past.
My present? Unable to satisfy me.
The future? Is there a future for those who no longer believe in mystery?"

"What did you say?"

"I was reciting a poem. It was written by a girl I knew. A woman who didn't believe that life could take you by the hand and lead you through dream's avenues. She never opened her senses to the intoxicating aromas of the world. Her past, she said, didn't exist. Her present had already become her past. The future. We call it hope, she told me. She had no hope. Past, present and future had forced her into a blind alley. In her weakest moments she would confess that 'perhaps Death' is the only future. I'm not sure there weren't times when I didn't admire her courageous confrontation with life. She wasn't disappointed, nor was she humble. Quite the contrary! Unrepentant, she lived her life proudly with her head held high. She enjoyed it in her own way. Now that I think about it again, I think it was her way of believing that she was alive. Facing the screen of despair, in an endless comparison." He spoke slowly in the tone one uses when one has the illusion that one is saying profound things.

His words dumbfounded the Colonel who had got used to not being interrupted and wasn't really following. 'What does all that have to do with the children in the jungle?" he asked. It was obvious that he had lost the thread.

"The lack of mystery in life – can't you see? For these children, the railroad was born in the jungle, the day they saw it."

"But that's natural! We know that the steam engine was invented by Fulton, that it moves on rails of steel, and that it burns coal or oil. They don't know anything about that, and they see it as a 'deus ex... steam machina'. Hah, hah, hah!" he laughed again at his little joke. "Ignorance, my good man, ignorance!"

"Well then, ignorance is bliss, my good man, as you say", Alexis retorted.

He suddenly felt even deeper sympathy for the Africans, and told Donatelli so, giving him new food for a monologue.

"Ah, there I can agree with you. I hear that in South Africa, as well as in the British colonies, the natives are appallingly exploited. The Portuguese in Mozambique are much better colonists. You know, if there's a race I don't much care for, it's the English. Don't forget we were enemies. They hide behind the smoke-screen from their pipes and look at you with a dull eye, probing you, while intriguing behind your back."

Alexis couldn't help but remember the scene in the hotel in Khartoum where the English smoked their pipes, hidden behind *The Times*. "You're prejudiced," he told the Italian.

But he acknowledged the vehemence and passion with which the other man supported his very simplistic ideas. A real bull. And for Donatelli the British were the red cloth.

"You don't want to hear about the English aristocracy, born and bred in colonialism, about whom Lord David Cecil himself said: 'with superior immorality they apply themselves to arts and literature!' He forgot to mention golf and bridge. What a curse on the arts and literature that have nourished a Pheidias and a Vergil!"

His utterances were at one and the same time pompous and amusing – if such a combination was possible. Donatelli couldn't leave it alone: "Immobility, my good man, immobility, even in the arts. Gainsborough, Reynolds, Turner, as immobile as the sheep in the meadows! For me, art represents life, and life is movement. Nothing is static," (He was becoming excited and speaking faster and faster). "Everything is in motion, in a world of atoms and electrons which spin without mercy, which embrace, which battle each other, which make up and self-destruct without ever finding peace."

Immobility? Yes, perhaps, after self-destruction. Death the only future? Alexis thought to himself. The words of his French friend? But what kind of absurdities is this madman putting in my mind? "Is Shakespeare static?" he asked. "Was Montgomery, who kicked your asses, immobile?"

For a second time the Colonel was dumbstruck and slow in reacting. "You insult me, sir. I am an Italian officer!"

"Forgive me. I didn't mean to insult you or your countrymen. I was only reacting to your monolithic ideas. Forgive me, if I was too frank about it!"

He left the compartment to pace a bit in the corridor and to make a screen of smoke with his pipe. "And I just couldn't care less if the old colonel thinks I'm acting like an Englishman!"

They reached Lourenco Marques late at night. Before he got off the train, Donatelli gave Alexis his card: Proca Set de Mars, No. 4, first floor. "It is not far from the station to my office. Drop in whenever you like. I have nothing against you. I know I can be boring at times, my wife tells me so."

Alexis felt bad and regretted what he'd said. He suddenly realised that despite his posturing, Donatelli was a loser when it came to people. "I'll come to visit you, I promise," he said warmly.

They parted at the station exit, and Alexis took a cab to the Pensao Polana. The Head office in Johannesburg had reserved a room for him and was supposed to have someone from the agency in Lourenco Marques meet him at the station, though he hadn't seen anyone waiting for him.

He liked the town with its wide tree-lined streets, its distinctive houses with their gardens, the hotels, the main square paved with black and white pebbles before the imposing pure white neo-Gothic church. "I'm going to visit it the first chance I get," he told himself. But what he really wanted to do was walk across the square's large pebbles set in geometric designs, which struck him like some sort of exotic dream.

The Pensao Polana was perched on a rise on the side of town facing the sea, on a wide boulevard with a fringe of trees. The coastal road was one hundred metres below. A bit further on was the famous Hotel Polana where rich South Africans from Johannesburg went for weekends or holidays. The pension had the same pretentious name, but none of the luxury. He would compromise, since his finances left no room for large gestures.

He was met by a very fat, stern Portuguese woman who showed him to his room on the first floor, with a balcony facing the sea. As soon as he opened the window and saw the ocean, he knew he was going to like it in Lourenco Marques.

His room was simple; the walls were whitewashed, and the wardrobe of carved wood was painted white, as were the dresser and table. Only the Spanish style chair, varnished a dark walnut colour and upholstered in thick velvet damask with raised green floral designs, seemed out of place.

Madame 'Polana' – he didn't know her real name yet, but that's what he decided he would call her – had suggested he go down to the restaurant if he wished to eat, as it was already well past nine o'clock, but he wasn't hungry even though he hadn't eaten since the previous evening. He wanted to go down to the sea, and walk around.

He opened his only suitcase, hung up his clothes, and hurried out on the street. He had no trouble finding the path that led to the sea. He was soon on the dirt road that ran along the coast. He went north along it, under very tall trees, to where he thought the town must end. He walked parallel to the sea for about three-quarters of an hour, or maybe even an hour, without meeting a soul.

Where the road ended, in a deserted area, he saw a building and decided it had to be a club because music was coming out of its large, open windows. Five or six cars were parked in front, and there was a lighted sign above the door that was too far away from him to read. It was some distance from the beach, and even though he was curious, he preferred to move on along the vast sand beach to where neither music nor voices could be heard.

The tide was out, and he walked on the wet sand, which was faintly illuminated by a half-moon that was setting. In the background was the dense tall forest, and in front a moonlit landscape, utterly peaceful. He lifted his eyes to the sky; the Southern Cross seemed to be signalling him to stop. He lowered his eyes and noticed the outline of a man with his back to him, surveying the sea. Alexis was startled for a moment, and the image of Hamlet came to mind. Was this going to be a follow-up to his innocent game with Kathy?

But he recovered quickly, approached the man discreetly, and paused as he heard him talking to himself. He seemed to be slowly reciting something.

"Freedom … is born from the withdrawal of the soul … which remains suspended in the stupor of withdrawal. But then dreams are born in withdrawal."

The stranger turned slowly. He had heard Alexis' steps. In the dim light of the moon, they stood facing each other. Alexis made out a tall, slender, well-built young man with black, curly hair, hollow cheeks and large eyes that bored into you, but which at the same time seemed remote, beautiful, with a Latin nobility, and Alexis' fear vanished.

"Come closer. You must be new here. I've not seen you before," he said to Alexis calmly and gently.

Alexis took a few steps forward. The other man gave him his hand. "My name is Rodrigo. I often come here at night, at the hour of the ebb tide, to find peace, to put my thoughts in order, to seek inspiration. I am a poet. In Portugal I am considered perhaps the best young poet of my generation. And you?"

"My name is Alexis and I am Greek."

"Greek! How wonderful. If we were all Greeks and Latins, the world would be a much better place. But it's all right the way it is."

"Another madman," Alexis thought, but this time he didn't feel any negative reaction. On the contrary, he felt at once that he wanted to know him better. Fortunately, Rodrigo corrected himself.

"Don't take what I say seriously. They're just clichés, pyrotechnics to make me feel important. Although when you come to think of it, Goethe and Milton do have a value, but they appear so late in history! Can they be compared with Plato or Dante? I often say that to the girls I want to impress and, thank God, none has ever said to me that the

Chinese, the Egyptians, the Assyrians and the Phoenicians existed long before our peoples!"

"It's strange, your thoughts are similar to Donatelli's – a man I met on the train coming over from Johannesburg. He too has the Greek-Latin romantic syndrome! He was singing the praises of Pheidias and Vergil!"

Alexis sensed a change come over Rodrigo's calm expression.

"So you've met that ... insignificant personage? It's not by chance I use expressions that are somewhat insulting ... but this is not the moment. Stand here by me and listen to silence. Be still, don't speak. I'm certain you've never known such quiet. Let us not disturb nature; let us not disturb the sea which withdrew earlier so that the silence would not be troubled even by the lapping of its wavelets. In the morning it will come back with a roar and drown out the night dreams. Let us not disturb the stars which keep a certain distance from each other because they respect their own tranquillity, joyful in a sky of sorrow. Look at the Southern Cross, the constellation that every night stands above the earth like a heavenly protector. Peace ..."

For a few moments he gazed at the sky in silence. "I know you're in the mood to start to destroy this quiet that frightens you, to convince yourself that you are alive. You're not used to being without noise, But something paralyses you, strikes you dumb. A mere shout could never bring about such destruction. I've gone through it myself, rest assured. The sand is damp, we can't sit down. But stand here for five minutes and stop thinking. You will feel as though you are at the end of the earth, at the beginning of the universe. Now I'll stop talking as well."

Alexis did as Rodrigo said. He closed his eyes and tried to drive out every thought from his mind. First he felt his legs grow heavy, rooted in the earth, but his body was light – ready to fly off into the air, to walk on the sea, as if he was not made of flesh and blood but was a cloud, ethereal, 'Was this the soul?' He didn't know that such peace could exist; at that moment he would have liked to have been alone. He felt that without another's presence he would soar to ever more distant spheres, more spiritual planes. Why not? He couldn't express his feelings otherwise. Why should he be afraid of words?

After some five minutes, Rodrigo moved toward the sea. "Come with me."

When he reached the first wave, he leaned down and filled his cupped hands with water. He wet his face, lifted his arms into the air and took a deep breath. "The sea cleanses the soul, drives out evil spirits and leaves it virginal!"

Then he bent over and picked up a little sand in his hands. He stretched his arms out before him and let the sand slowly sift through his fingers as if falling through an hourglass. "These grains fall to mother earth where they belong, they filter all thought from the mind and leave it virginal too."

It was only the beginning of the sacred ritual. He took off his shirt and again raising his arms high, looked at the sky. "I expose my chest to cosmic energy, to the universe. All my fantasies are dissolved and concentrated into one deep reflection. The moon and the stars take me by the hand and guide me. They show me the way and I dispel any doubts that God is out there, somewhere. He is everywhere, he is inside me. And I am his child. His spitting image." Then suddenly, turning to Alexis, "You know, the young people in Portugal, who read me, think of me as their Christ. So why shouldn't I believe that I am a child of God now, at the hour of ebb tide ..."

Both of them laughed as if wanting to defuse the moment of mystery that was now over. Rodrigo put his shirt on again.

Alexis had observed the scene without question, without awe, as if it were the most natural thing in the world in this otherworldly atmosphere. One thing was certain: Alexis was at last in deepest Africa, enveloped by the magic of nature, and the magic of the magicians. Rodrigo was obviously one of those personalities who transfixed you and left no room for criticism. There was no question, he liked the fellow.

They began to slowly make their way back while Rodrigo kept up his monologue. "Before I came to Lourenco Marques I lived further north, near Beira, with my father who was separated from my mother, on his plantation, deep in the jungle. I didn't get along with him and came here. I write articles for the Lourenco Marques *Guardian* and for magazines in Lisbon, and also do a little import-export on the side.

I enjoy the good life, and journalism alone isn't enough to satisfy my greed! I'm also putting together my third collection of poetry.

"When I was on my father's plantation, going around the native villages, I met Abu. He was the witchdoctor in that region, and he taught me that the trees and the animals are brothers to me and that everything that is on earth is alive, because earth has given birth to everything. He also taught me that here one can become one with the universe. Maybe you won't believe this, but I was ready to accept the magician's words long before that; as a child in Portugal, near Coimbra where I lived after my father had abandoned us, my mother would leave me long nights alone in a hut, and rather than working on the potato harvest in our fields after school, she would catch me daydreaming. At first I was afraid during those nights, but slowly I became friends with the stars, the moon, the trees, the rocks and the stray dogs. The villagers who worked for us wanted to take me to their homes, but were afraid of my mother, who was a real Cerberus. She wanted to make a man of me, she said. She made me a poet. So I hope my earlier theatricality didn't seem ridiculous to you."

"When a man can laugh at himself, he becomes more likeable," Alexis told him.

Rodrigo accepted the compliment with natural grace. "Tell me, how did you come to be here at this hour? Are you a poet like me or ... mad like me?"

"As to the first, certainly not. Wait a minute, I did write a poem when I was fifteen years old. As to the second ... I certainly am. As soon as I arrived in Lourenco Marques, the first thing I wanted to do was to see the ocean. In Greece we have the sea all around us, and when it's not there I miss it. During the six months I was in Johannesburg, the only water I saw was in swimming pools."

"If you're not too tired, come with me; a group of my friends will be at the Costa del Sol. The night club over there – you must have passed it on the way here. Besides, it belongs to a Greek, and he'll be happy to meet you. Then I'll take you back in my car."

"Thank you. Yes, I saw the club on my way over."

"Where are you staying? Did you come all the way here on foot?"

"At Pensao Polana. Yes, I walked along the coast road with the tall trees."

"It's called Mirador. During the day it's full of little monkeys who perch on the branches of the trees or swing from them. When you see the mothers tenderly stroking the heads of their children, you'll understand how close we are to these likeable animals."

As they approached the club, the letters on the sign became clearer. *Costa del Sol,* Alexis read.

"It's a play on words," Rodrigo said. "In Portuguese it means Sun Coast but Costa (short for Constantine as you know) is also the name of the owner; he's from the island of Crete."

Costa opened the door himself, a tall, heavily-set Cretan, bald, with a small moustache.

"Costa, let me introduce you to a compatriot of yours. I just pulled him from the waves onto the sand like Nausica picked up Odysseus on the island of the Phaiakes!"

Alexis knew there were many Greeks in South Africa, and quite a few in Mozambique, which is why he wasn't annoyed when Costa's reception wasn't as warm as he might have expected.

"And where are you from?" Costa asked bluntly, deliberately using the Cretan dialect.

Alexis wasn't about to let him get away with that, and he answered him in kind, imitating the accent. "My home town, Athens; my ancestors! Cephalonia. What about you, Kyr. Costa?"

"I'm from Phodele, my friend," Costa said, warming up, and then proudly: "The birthplace of Domenicos Theotokopoulos, alias El Greco! But I've been in this place for forty years." Even though he'd switched homelands, he had kept his Cretan accent, and seemed to be proud of it.

"Come, Kyr. Rodrigo, your party is waiting – you're late tonight."

Rodrigo didn't understand Costa's Greek, but the gestures made up for the lack of comprehension. Costa led them to the table where Rodrigo's friends were sitting in a whitewashed room with a ceramic tiled floor while an orchestra of five musicians were taking a break, next to the large dance-floor, which took up the whole center of the room.

Most of the customers as they walked through the tables, turned to look their way. Alexis didn't know if they were looking at Rodrigo, the ... Young People's Christ, or at him, the new boy in town.

The reception Rodrigo got from the girls in the group left no room for doubt. Courteously, and carrying himself like an aristocrat, he bowed and kissed the three girls on the cheek, and they looked at him in admiration as he circled the table; he nodded at the three young men somewhat indifferently, and went back to where Alexis was standing and waiting. Let me introduce my friend Alexis. We've been friends for only one hour, but we returned together from the infinite!"

Alexis was flattered that Rodrigo had called him 'friend'. He had never seen a more likeable night club.

"Maga Yvonne, Maria Teresa Correia de Castro," Rodrigo made the introductions. We call Maria Teresa, 'Pi', first of all because her name is too long, second because she's as thin as the line of the diameter of a circle, but don't let her fool you – she has a round mind! Maria Teresa is the quotient of the circle and the diameter three point one four one six!"

"I don't imagine you have any doubts about who thought up my nickname?" she said addressing Alexis.

"Absolutely none. The hour I spent with our friend was enough to learn quite a lot about the workings of his mind," he replied.

"Frederico, Karl, Viriatou, all Portuguese, except for Karl, who's a Dane," Rodrigo said as he introduced the young men.

The polite, warm smiles of the girls and the young men made Alexis feel at ease. Costa brought Alexis and Rodrigo two plates of giant shrimps and a bottle of white wine.

"I don't know if you've eaten, but your friend has ordered for you," Costa said, in flawless English this time.

"No, I haven't eaten, and I must confess I was beginning to feel hungry," Alexis said.

"Only Costa has crayfish like this on the whole beach," Rodrigo added.

Then, the questions started, After his exchange with Costa, there was no doubt where Alexis was from. Where had he been before? What did he come here for? How long was he staying? Would he like to join the group? It was clear they had adopted him. Two hours in Lourenco Marques, and he had made more friends than he had been able to make in six months in Johannesburg. The lead singer, the arpeggio of his guitar full of yearning, started a sad song, drawing out the vowels with sharp modulations of pitch unlike the steadily held note found in Spanish songs.

Maria Teresa began to explain the lyrics and Alexis listened carefully, while Rodrigo rested his elbows on the table and held his sorrowful face in his hands.

"You will not have heard 'fado' before. It is sad music for the guitar that is bound to have an effect on you. Listen: She sang lightly along with the singer:

O *meu fa-ado, ama-argurada, zina minha,*
que o destino se revel

"My sad 'fado', revealing what fate awaits me," she translated for him.

When the song ended they all remained silent as if they were still waiting for something. The voice of the singer came again, powerful, full of passion:

Coimbra eh una licao – de sonho e tradicao ...
e aprende-se a dizer, saudade.

"Coimbra is a lesson in dreams and tradition which teaches you to say saudade.' Maria Teresa repeated dreamily. "The most beautiful word in the world. A greeting full of terrible nostalgia ... the greatest hit of a young, but already well-known singer, Amalia Rodriguez."

For the first time Alexis looked at her carefully. Her thin face had taken on a glow it hadn't had when he entered. The other two girls were perhaps more beautiful. Maga with her shiny long hair and rosy, silken skin and enigmatic look; Yvonne was of the same medium height as Maga, but with less emphatic Mediterranean features, with kindness, tenderness and submission written on her angelic face; but neither had the magnetism of Maria Teresa.

He turned to look at the young men. Viriatou, a romantic type who didn't talk much, with large eyes that revealed simple, pure, earthly thoughts; Frederico, tall with chestnut brown hair, delicate features – he could have been English – looked like a practical man with the kind of mind used to solve problems; Karl, a typical Scandinavian with a round face and rosy cheeks, the only one with Viking origins, though he didn't have a beard, was not at all grim, and was always laughing and seemed full of life.

Alexis took a better look at Rodrigo in the light. He had a romantically melancholy face, and you couldn't tell if he was play-acting or if indeed the 'fado' had transported him to other worlds. When the song ended, there were again a few moments of silence – and then the orchestra broke into a wild rhythm. Rodrigo jumped up as if he'd suddenly awoken from a nightmare, grabbed Yvonne by the hand and began to dance like a professional, the two of them alone on the dance floor. After he had done a few turns, he called out to Alexis as he passed the table: "Get up and dance the samba! Take Pi and dance!"

Alexis would come to learn these sudden changes of mood were a characteristic of the Portuguese which affected the poet Rodrigo with an especial intensity.

"I don't know how to Samba."

"She will teach you while I and Yvonne ... will demonstrate."

She looked at him sweetly and Alexis decided to give it a whirl, trying to imitate, albeit clumsily, Maria Teresa in the beginning and later Rodrigo, somewhat more tolerably. As they danced, Rodrigo called out loudly to him in order to be heard. "The Samba started out in Africa, now it comes back to us from Brazil! Your feet are caressing the earth that gave it birth!"

"You're really very good," Maria Teresa said encouragingly to Alexis.

"You're a good teacher," he replied.

She squeezed his hand as they danced. A first spark between them.

The movements of the 'samba' don't leave much room for talking, especially if one isn't very sure of one's steps, but he felt strange dancing in silence, so he made an effort. "Who is Rodrigo's girl?" he asked.

"All of us, except for Maga, and none of us!" Maria Teresa immediately answered to the beat of the 'samba'. "I was his girl too. I loved him ..." she continued, panting from the dance. "But I told him that I wanted to have a child by him, and the next day it was over. Yvonne was also his girl, for three months. Only Maga – never mind how sensual she looks – hasn't fallen into his clutches; in fact she is a little cool to him. Besides, she is engaged to the Governor's son."

She did another few steps in the dance.

"She is a very beautiful girl," Alexis said.

"Do you prefer her to me?"

Alexis drew a little closer to Maria Teresa while she went on, satisfied by Alexis' response. "Rodrigo himself says that he's madly in love, but then he flees like a frightened bird before he's bound hand and foot. He has a magic formula for leaving women. He says it was given to him by a witch doctor! He disappears at night and talks to spirits, the stars, God – who knows! And they tell him the course he must follow. He told me that the answer he got from whatever oracle was clear: 'If you have any feeling for this girl at all, leave her, you're relationship won't go well, you'll be bad for her.' Some feel cheated, others like me, don't – but none of us have anything against him. As you see, he is worthy of our love."

"What if he really believes what he says?" He didn't want to betray his meeting with Rodrigo on the beach, but he felt he had to take his side.

"For a while he was disappearing every so often with a mysterious woman from Johannesburg, who came to see him at least once a month for two or three days at a time, and sometimes he'd go to Johannesburg to visit her. Sooner or later you'll meet her. Now she's become part of our group too."

"Aren't you in love with him any more?"

"No. We stayed good friends because I believe I know him better than anyone else and … he knows I know him."

"And who's your boyfriend now – Frederico, Viriatou or Karl?"

"At the moment … I'm trying to flirt with you. No-one is sleeping with anyone else in this group, if you don't count Rodrigo of course, who holds us under his magical powers. That does not mean that we have all slept with him. Yvonne for example, is a virgin. Girls here are very cautious and want to get married. That's why boys either go to whorehouses or to the cabarets, which are not first rate. It must seem strange to you that I'm talking so bluntly since I've only just met you – but your eyes make me trust you."

"You're making me blush."

"Your blushes give me even more confidence!"

"You mean that you, who aren't shy, trust me, the shy one? Maybe then I shouldn't have confidence in you?"

"Only for my frankness, nothing more."

The conversation turned back to Rodrigo.

"He says he is like Christ to the youth of Portugal. Is that true? Is he a good poet?" Alexis asked.

"He's good, and young people do read him. Up till now he has called himself an Apostle. Now it appears he has promoted himself to Christ! One thing is certain: he is a wizard and bewitches both women and men."

Later that evening Rodrigo offered to take Alexis back. Despite Alexis' objections, Rodrigo picked up the cheque. No-one said where or when they would see each other again, but it was obvious that you couldn't lose touch in a town like Lourenco Marques. Besides, Alexis felt he already belonged to the group.

While driving Alexis home in his four year-old American Ford, Rodrigo told him:

"You will be making other friends as well. You will find that Lourenco Marques is a pleasant town. I'll enrol you in the Naval Club – since you come from Greece, a land bathed in the sea, I imagine that you like sailing or rowing; we'll take excursions to beautiful beaches on the coast and you can dance every night, that is, if you wish; at the Girassol, the round tower you couldn't have missed seeing on your way in from the station, or at the Roof Garden of the Hotel Aviz, or at the Night Club of the Cardozo. There are three excellent movie houses and fine restaurants – if you come to the office tomorrow morning well go for a coffee at the Scala pastry shop which belongs to another compatriot of yours, Menelaos, or to a small coffee shop on the corner of the street where you live."

"I think that tomorrow I should make an appearance at the office where I am supposed to work. What time do the offices open?" Alexis retorted.

"Six in the morning."

"You must be joking!"

"No, not at all. It gets so hot during the day that the offices are open from six to ten in the morning and then six to ten in the evening. In the middle of the day, if you can take the sun, you go to the beach, otherwise you shut yourself up in your house for a long siesta. That is why life begins at night, as soon as it cools off. It is late now, but tomorrow I will call the owner of your pension to make sure she takes care of you, and I'll send you a 'boy' to be private servant – the brother of the girl I have in my house. She'll arrange it with Madame Mendoza, your landlady, and he'll do everything for you. He'll do your washing, tidy up and cook if you want. He will eat and sleep in front of your door, and you can give him whatever suits you."

Alexis' finances couldn't support such extravagance, but the idea that he would have a boy, like an English officer in the colonies or the explorers in Africa, tempted him so much that he couldn't refuse.

"There isn't much work at this time of year, and if there is one thing that Africa has in abundance, it's servants. Let's enjoy them at least. Not that I am a racist in any way: I love the blacks, they are my brothers, I lived with them on my father's plantation. You'll see that we live in harmony here," Rodrigo went on, trying to put him at his ease.

No longer surprised, Alexis accepted Rodrigo's continual offers as an example of Portuguese hospitality.

"No matter what time you finish at your office, or if you decide not to go the first day, I will be at Praca Set de Mars, No. 4, first floor."

"But that's where Donatelli is too."

Rodrigo grimaced and went on hurriedly.

"You go up the stairs to a long corridor, like a balcony. The last door is Donatelli's and mine is two doors before that. It's an office building with offices and unfortunately one can't choose one's neighbours. Good night."

"Thank you," Alexis said simply as he got out of the car.

He was flattered by all that Rodrigo had offered and for the friendship he had shown him – but wasn't it all a bit extravagant? Wasn't he overdoing it?

He slept well that night.

He opened the shutters before the sun had risen, but the sky was already pink and the moist, intense fragrances of the morning coolness pulled him ever deeper into the atmosphere of Africa. He had become a captive of this part of the earth.

He looked at the sea as Rodrigo had done the night before and at the tall trees of the Mirador that drew a line between himself and the ocean. He took deep breaths to fill his lungs, and opened his ears to the chirping of birds and to some high-pitched sounds that he took to be small monkeys – if the memory of visits to zoos weren't deceiving him. He began to feel a vast sensual pleasure, as if he were making love to nature and was becoming one with her. He was in the mood to write a poem to nature, and even more than a poem, a prayer in rhyme; to sing of the awakening of the day and to shout out to the ocean that he, Alexis, who had come from so far away, from a continent where the eye wasn't drawn to the infinite the way it was here, was embracing the rosy dawn, just as the rosy dawn was embracing him. He couldn't handle it, he became confused. He couldn't find either the right words or the right rhymes. Why did he have to make a poem at all costs? Had he been influenced by his meeting with Rodrigo?

Slowly, the first rays of the sun began to glitter on the ocean, like on the mirror of his soul that had suddenly awoken with nature.

It was early. He had seen the dawning of the day. Now he wanted to see the awakening of the town. He got dressed swiftly and went in the opposite direction from the night before, toward the centre of town. As the colours on the roofs and the trees changed with the dawn, the town took on a joyful, festive look to receive the sun that would stay with it till evening. He had always admired peoples who worshipped natural phenomena; and now, more than ever.

There were only Africans in the street at that early hour, going to their work. If you're black, you have to get up earlier. I hope their souls are as full of dreams as mine, he thought. Do I say it to comfort myself? To keep my white conscience easy?

The doors of the coffeeshops had opened, and black "boys" swept the trash from the preceding evening off the sidewalks. He paused by a park with a sign that said, *Vasco da Gama Garden*, and felt like picking a branch of bougainvillaea. He had always been dazzled by the colour of its flowers.

His desire was nipped in the bud when he caught the suspicious look of the guard. Guards and policemen are always suspicious of anybody out walking very early or very late in the day, he thought. They don't acknowledge romantic souls who walk in the streets like ghosts at an hour when the ... honest people are sleeping!

He paused at the Lisboa Cinema and looked at the posters and studio shots of *Les Miserables* which was on that week, and thought; If Victor Hugo had lived in Africa, then no Jean Valjean would ever have been conceived. No black, not even a slave, can be a 'misérable' in such an environment.

His thoughts stayed with Victor Hugo till the corner of the street, where a young black man was selling newspapers. To complete the sacred morning ritual, he had to buy a newspaper, go to church, and have a cup of coffee in a coffee-house. The sesame covered bread ring you had in Greece was missing, but you couldn't have everything.

He began with the newspaper. For one and a half escudos he bought the Lourenco Marques *Guardian* which had an English section, patted the head of the small, black newsboy, and went to the Scala coffee-house on the opposite corner of the street. Hadn't Rodrigo said it was owned by a Greek named Menelaos? He sat at a small pavement table and scanned the headlines. A newspaper always gives you the pulse of life and is the barometer of the interests of a city where the publisher sits shoulder to shoulder with the Governor and is on familiar terms with the Chief of Police.

On the first page of the English section the lead article read as follows: *The Governor of Mozambique, General Fernandos Gomez, receives accredited ambassadors and consuls in the garden of Government House.* Then in smaller letters: *An evening straight from the Thousand and One Nights, bathed in moonlight. One hundred guests, one hundred candles, one hundred waiters, and the Governor and Lady Gomez, the perfect hosts.*

On the second page, in small headlines, and even smaller letters, was the news from the rest of the world: *War continues in China. Hostilities in Palestine. Guerrillas in Greece Suffer Casualties.*

How odd that news was so dependent on geography. The small type in Lourenco Marques would be an inch-high headlines in Greece, Alexis thought.

On the third page, in bold type, the news from Portugal: *Salazar receives Franco in Lisbon. The Iberian Peninsula in Firm Hands*, etc.

The fourth page had news from the Union of South Africa. A few words about these neighbours, the local gossip, then art and sports news and the indispensable lottery.

The lottery! To gamble, to hope, the only connecting link between all the newspapers in the world.

After he had drunk a thick, medium sweet (at last) cup of coffee in the Greek coffee-house of Lourenco Marques, served by a black waiter (Menelaos hadn't appeared yet), he went to the imposing church he had seen the previous evening.

When he walked through the square toward the church, he felt the large black and white pebbles massaging his feet through the rubber soles of his shoes, sending a mysterious pulse through his entire body, from head to toe. It was like a pilgrimage. Had these stones, with their geometrical patterns, acquired divine properties for him? Was he, too, beginning to feel a metaphysical connection with the material elements?

There were only a few black Christians in the church who were listening devoutly to the morning liturgy. Alexis tried to understand from their expression if the contact they had with the Christian religion was an idolatrous one, and he wondered how missionaries overcame the sacred communion the natives had with the phenomena of nature. Maybe Rodrigo would know.

He didn't stay in the church long. Time was passing and he had to go and present himself at his new job. He found the agency where he was supposed to work, but it was closed. He looked at his watch; it was eight. Did they work different hours than what he had been told by Rodrigo? Was it vacation time? Was that the reason no-one had shown up at the station to greet him?

He walked around the harbour looking at the boats which were loading and unloading, then turned back and passed by the one-storey building on the pier, which was now open. On the outside a sign said:

"Africa Shipping Agency." There were only two rooms facing a corridor, one was empty, and the door to the other was closed. He knocked, went in without waiting for a reply, and met the severe expression on the round, swarthy face of the grey-haired Indian director of the office who didn't appear to want to be bothered during his morning idleness.

The Indian asked him who he was in a bored voice. Irritated, but also amused by the Indian's expression, Alexis said: "I hope I didn't knock on the wrong door ... literally. No-one came to meet me at the train yesterday."

"Really! What did you expect, a guard of honour?" said the Indian sarcastically, though seemingly without malice.

"A full guard of honour and a brass band!"

"Prrrrr." The Indian gave him the raspberry. "There's your music. And since you like honours: 'Present arms!'" and he made a rude gesture which left Alexis dumbstruck.

Such a reception didn't exactly bode well for a fruitful relationship, but in the environment of this African harbour, and the heat that must have been beating on his head, the Indian's manners didn't surprise him. He was like a character out of some novel set in an exotic and primitive place where there is always a fat merchant in a white suit who has become cynical after many years of a hard life, who endlessly wipes sweat from his forehead with a dirty handkerchief and who treats every newcomer as if he were some greenhorn who didn't know which way was up.

Alexis decided that the only thing to do was to play his game.

"I accept the honours, be they ever so late and hereby ... answer them in kind" (he made the same rude gesture). "Now tell me – what kind of crap am I supposed to do around here?"

Confronting rudeness with rudeness usually works, and the Indian was one of those people who appreciates you standing up to him. Instead of being annoyed he answered: "If you came here to work, you'll be disappointed. There are already two of us, and not much to do. Your firm in Johannesburg told me to pay you 1,000 escudos a month, and to use you as I saw fit. I think the best thing would be for you to come once a month and collect your wages instead of standing around and getting on my nerves day after day. I have nothing against you, but everybody gets on my nerves. Stay long enough in Africa – I've lived in this wretched place for thirty years – and you'll see ..." he said as he wiped his forehead with a dirty handkerchief "If there is any work for you to do at any time, I'll inform you – I know where you're staying. Good day!"

Taken aback by this, Alexis asked, "But don't the ships that you represent ever call here?"

"I have one colleague – much younger than me – he's the one that goes to the harbour – and, believe it or not, he enjoys it! The three or four boats a month that we represent, he can handle perfectly well by himself. I spend half of the day in the office, bored, and the other half at my home, bored."

"Don't you have a family? Where are you from?"

"From Marmagoa – and don't ask how I ended up here! As for my family, I have an Indian wife – she bores me too – and two boys who are sailors."

"With only three or four boats a month, do you and your colleagues earn enough to live on?"

"After thirty years in Africa, if you don't have pots of money you're a total fool. It appears that you don't know how one makes money from an agency. Maybe you ought to drop in now and then, after all, and learn the ropes, because you seem to be all right, even though you are trying to be clever."

Though Alexis had begun rather to like this man, he felt, once more, annoyed.

"Listen to me boss" (the word 'boss' said ironically). "I don't mind in the least accepting your first proposal and never setting foot in here again since you'll be paying me, even if I don't learn the secrets of the job. I'm sure I can find a second job and so have twice as much money. If you want me, you know where to find me. See you!"

He left satisfied that he had kept his end up. He wasn't sure he hadn't slammed the door somewhat too hard on leaving.

"If I weren't a disciple of Ghandi, and if I believed in the use of violence, I would get up and knock your block off. In any case, it's too hot to move!" the Indian shouted behind him, and his voice could be heard through the closed door.

Now Alexis felt free. He had ensured himself a salary and apparently without having to lift a finger, or at least only once in a while. He had not been expecting such a windfall, He had no definite plan in mind, but he felt at that moment that all options were open to him. It was as if Africa itself had suddenly opened up before him, to be explored, its secrets to be discovered, to be enjoyed. Back on the street, he felt like a bird. Giving his boss a lesson had made him expansive.

The money would come month in, month out, and he would be able to do something on the side without anxiety. But what could he do? Why not be a poet or a writer? Like Rodrigo. And there was no reason why he too, couldn't enjoy the same success with the girls. He would have time at his disposal, relative financial security, plus the aura of a man of letters!

Poetry or prose? Probably prose, otherwise his imitation of Rodrigo would be too obvious. What would he write about? His experiences in Africa? He'd come up with something – that wasn't the problem. One thing at a time: where to go for the moment?

He had two addresses, Donatelli's and Rodrigo's, both in the same building. He would go to Rodrigo. He had no particular desire to see Donatelli, even though Rodrigo's negative reaction to the Italian's name had whetted his curiosity. He had the feeling that there was something personal between them.

By asking, he found Praca Set de Mars, No. 4, and the outside staircase that led up to the corridor on the first floor. He looked at all the door signs. The last door was Donatelli's. The second door was Rodrigo's. When he got there he changed his mind and knocked on Donatelli's door.

"Avanti!" a voice called out.

The moment Alexis entered, an awful, indefinable stench struck him. Sergio Donatelli was standing on a chair and, with his back to the door, was attaching to the wall, on the left as one entered, the skin of an enormous crocodile. It must have been two and a half metres long because it stretched from the ceiling to the floor. On the same wall was hanging the head of a lion, the head of a wild animal unknown to Alexis – maybe a tiger, panther, hyena? There was also another, smaller crocodile. All were stuffed.

Four rifles and a map of Mozambique hung on the wall opposite. Under a large window, there were stacks of more crocodile skins. On top of a messy table, Alexis could see two open account books with pages in blue and red vertical and horizontal lines, several cardboard containers of shells, and a table fan. In an open drawer, he couldn't help noticing an Italian beretta pistol and a dirty, yellow feather duster. One other chair and a warped wooden wardrobe completed the furnishings.

The Colonel turned his head and appeared delighted at the unexpected visit. "Oh! che sorpresa! I didn't expect you so soon. Come in, close the door."

Alexis hesitated – the smell was overpowering – and Donatelli understood.

"I know. The hide of the crocodile has a powerful odour before it is processed, but one gets used to it quickly. Close the door, otherwise it becomes too hot in here. I'll turn the fan on."

He got down from the chair and told Alexis to take a seat.

"I won't sit down, I only passed by to say 'good morning'. I also passed before Rodrigo's office, who seems to be a neighbour of yours – I met him last night."

"Ah! My wife's great love! Fortunately, I am not a jealous man. He's a good fellow, but his mind tends to run away with itself. He's always off in the clouds, in his own enchanted world. Now my wife, after spending some time with him, is beginning to come under his influence and brings black magic home!"

Alexis didn't know if Donatelli was an 'innocent' content to close his eyes. With Rodrigo's fame – at least from what Maria Teresa had told him – he had no doubts that the woman Donatelli had described on the train was Rodrigo's mistress. This would also explain Rodrigo's irritation when he heard him mention the name Donatelli, unless Donatelli didn't give a damn, and the only thing that interested him was the jungle, where he could live 'without compromise', as he himself had said.

But if his wife was deceiving him and he knew it, wasn't this a compromise? So what? People's theories and convictions aren't always that straightforward. But not Donatelli's, Alexis thought. The

Colonel is too one-sided to have a flexible conscience on matters that touch his ego. If there was something going on between Rodrigo and his wife, he would probably be ignorant of it. Besides, didn't he say that Rodrigo was a good fellow? The matter began to intrigue him. In twenty-four hours he had met two people who were connected by a special relationship. The first African mystery for him to delve into! He turned toward the map of Mozambique and examined the long, narrow country with its extensive coast on the Indian Ocean, opposite Madagascar. "I've always liked to look at maps" he said, "They make you dream. I imagine you use this one for your safaris in the jungle. Where do you hunt crocodiles?"

"On the Limpopo river. From the border of Transvaal to here." (The Italian put his finger on an area a bit inland from the coast). "From there on, the river is too near the sea and there aren't any crocodiles. I'm usually gone three or four days a week, and I have two boys with me as helpers. If you're not a dolce vita type, you can come along one day."

"I'd like that a lot. But I have to be going now, we'll talk about it again."

By the time he'd gone from one door to the other he had made another rapid review of his new circumstances. Apart from the group of friends he had made, he had learned to dance the samba, he had heard 'fado' music, and now he had been invited on a safari! How different from the time in Johannesburg, where nothing ever happened.

His sense of well-being continued to grow. He walked smiling into Rodrigo's office.

"This is the third door I've knocked on this morning. At the first, my Indian boss told me in no uncertain terms to get lost, that he didn't want to see me, that people got on his nerves, and that I should come in order to get paid on the first of every month. How does that strike you?"

"Who's your boss?" Rodrigo asked, not at all surprised by Alexis' morning visit.

"Adi Munjab."

"Did you find him sitting in the lotus position?"

"A yogi, him? He seems more like a crook from Bombay without a pinch of conscience!"

"Well, all his years in Africa have got to him, and he's trying to escape to other spheres of consciousness through yoga. He seems to manage very well however, having decided that all contact with human beings is an attack on his peace of mind."

"Attack! Nonsense! He's bored with life, he told me so himself, he's even bored with his wife – and as for peace of mind, you should have heard him shouting that he would knock my block off."

"Everyone knows him around here and they try to avoid him. Don't pay too much attention to what he says. If you had told me last night you were going to go to see Adi, I would have warned you. You must have really annoyed him because he seldom has such outbursts."

"Anyway, it's fortunate for me things worked out this way, and it looks as though I won't be having too many dealings with him. Just think, I'll have free time to do whatever suits me!"

"And what does suit you?"

Alexis hesitated and then said: "I didn't talk about it yesterday, but I've always had it in mind to do some writing myself. I'm not a … Christ to the youth of my homeland, nor have I published anything yet; but maybe now I'll have time to do some scribbling! I also thought of putting an ad. in the newspaper offering lessons in Modern Greek, There must be Greek children here, and there doesn't appear to be any Greek school. In any case, one comes to Africa to make money, isn't that so?"

"That reminds me of the Jewish joke where a certain Malamed, a teacher, said: 'If I was Rockefeller, I would be even richer than he is; because I would do a little teaching on the side!'"

"The only trouble is I'm not a Rockefeller!"

They both laughed while still standing in the doorway and Alexis hadn't had a chance yet to look around. He became curious when he saw all around the room shelves with dozens of bottles of different sizes, some full of dry leaves, others with roots, and still others with multi-coloured seeds – the room was the same size as Donatelli's office but empty of furniture. An open door led to a second room.

"By the way, the second door I knocked on was your neighbour's; my traveling companion, Donatelli," Alexis said suddenly and turned to see if Rodrigo would react the but immediately changed the subject.

"The bottles you see are samples of various items I export to Portugal." As if trying to justify himself, he continued, "But, as you already know, I'm a poet-merchant or merchant-poet, whichever you prefer. Every leaf, every root, every seed you see contains poetry, energy, consciousness and soul. Nothing is without soul. Everything lives, dies and is re-born, without ever reaching the Nirvana that is sought. And I speak to my seeds just as they speak to me. Everything around me sends me messages."

Two completely different people, Donatelli and Rodrigo, the one unrefined and simple, the other cultured and romantic, had told him nearly the same thing in different words. Was it Africa that had left its mark on them?

Alexis wanted to talk about his own emotions, what he'd felt that morning walking on the pebbles in the square in front of the church, but it would have shown a lack of modesty, he thought. When you got down to it, he was still a novice.

"Here in Africa you will learn to value matter, to live in harmony with it, to worship it," Rodrigo told him. "Believe me, the Africans opened my eyes. What attracts a native is not what an object looks like but its meaning, its symbolism if you like. It is not only its utility, but the secret behind its existence, the reason for its being. The African is moved by water because whether it flows in the river or the sea or out of a spring, it has movement, energy, it loosens, cleanses, purifies. The seeds that he plants come alive, become plants, are cut down, become food and give life again. The Africans have a metaphysical relationship with matter. Not on a conscious level, but in the springs of the unconscious, in the deepest of roots."

"When you talked about the water that purifies," Alexis said "there came to my mind an inscription by Justinian on a fountain in front of Aghia Sophia church in Constantinople:

'Νιψον ανομηματα, μη μονοναν οψιν'*

---

*Wash your sins, not just your face!

"Perhaps here lies the answer to a question I had this morning watching the Africans in Church. How can they combine an idolatrous rapture for the objects of nature with an abstract conception of God?"

"You're right. This is the difficulty the missionaries had when they came face to face with the shamans of Africa. I believe that if there was a conversion, it happened not because of the theories of Christian religion, but through the objects they brought with them, and the tangible results from treatments by drugs, which were more effective than the alchemy of the witch doctors. Matter had led them to accept the dictates of the Christian religion – and this doesn't mean that just because they go to church they stop worshipping the rocks and the rivers. They know better than we do that heaven, in its religious sense, is not fenced around, and that it also belongs to those who worship idols and symbols. I'll recite for you the prayer of someone who was lost at sea, so that you can see how beautifully they wed God and Christ with nature:

I am blind.
I don't know which is North, which is South.
I don't recognise the sky or the underworld.
I am lost on the ocean and drink its water.
You God, you Christ, are earth and ocean.
All the wind that blows.
Calm the wind and put the ocean back in place.

"In my own land, during certain religious ceremonies, the priest blesses the water, and then we drink it. Perhaps that is why I also have a predisposition toward idolatry," Alexis cut in before the Rodrigo went on, "The blessing of the Catholic priest, for the natives, takes on a materialistic meaning. It means security, good health, prosperity but, (and this above all), protection from evil spirits! The priest is nothing more than a magician who drives out the evil spirits that exist in each thing on earth. And the witch doctor is nothing more than the 'Lord' of the spirits. You don't love the witch doctor. You venerate him. The same holds true for the priest and for your ancestors. Because the spirits of the dead also influence your life, as do the phenomena of nature, and you must placate them all through your deeds if you want their protection. Before I eat, I lift the bread in my two hands and pray: 'I consecrate this to my ancestors. I am without sin, I have not committed incest, I have not harmed the creatures of nature. I am transcendent. I touch the Sun. I embrace the Moon. I turn back the spirits of evil, the spirits of death. I am not lost. The blessing is mine!"

At that moment the door opened and a tall, imposing woman entered; she had long, black hair which reached her shoulders, deep red, sensual lips and jet black eyes which sought out their target without being distracted

The target at that moment was Rodrigo; he seemed somewhat irritated and confused by the arrival of this beautiful woman. Her dress perfectly set off her hair and the colour of her eyes. She was wearing a pure white silk blouse which left no doubt as to the dimensions and rise and fall of her breasts, a black skirt, black shoes, a black handbag hanging from her left shoulder and a red belt which matched the colour of her red lips.

Alexis had no trouble recognising her. 'Alida Valli'! He had now met the third corner of the triangle.

"May I introduce you to my friend Alexis. He's from Greece. He arrived yesterday. Mrs Dalia … Donatelli." He said the 'Donatelli' hesitantly.

"You must be the Greek who travelled with my husband on the train" she said to Alexis. "He spoke to me about you enthusiastically and is hoping to see you again."

"I visited him a while ago."

"You see how small the world is?"

"Much smaller than it seems," Alexis replied with a smile, wondering if Mrs. Donatelli had understood the innuendo.

"Alexis, would you wait for me in the next room for a couple of minutes," Rodrigo said politely, although it was clearly not a request.

He led him next door, where there was a makeshift bookcase, table and chair and two leather armchairs. "Sit down, I'll be right back."

After a moment Alexis returned to the other room on a pretext. "I'd like to say good-bye to Mrs Donatelli in case I don't see her again before she leaves."

He shook her hand feeling the same spark he had felt when they'd met two minutes before, and then went back and sat in the armchair in the next room.

Rodrigo half-closed the door and Alexis didn't know if he'd left it half-open out of politeness or on purpose, since he made no effort to lower the tone of his voice.

"Didn't I tell you not to come here? You're playing with fire. What if your husband saw you? He wouldn't take it kindly."

That, Alexis suspected, was for his benefit.

"My husband knows very well that we are friends and you know equally well that he lives in his own world. I came because lately you've been avoiding me."

"I've had a lot of work to do. I had to finish some articles for a magazine in Portugal and ..."

"And ... you couldn't even talk to me on the phone? Don't tell me that the black enchantress you have in your house is keeping you all to herself Your relations with her seem suspicious to me anyway! She's quite beautiful, even if she is black."

Dalia was trying to speak in a whisper but her voice came through the open door clearly enough. The mystery was no longer an enigma. The enigma was no longer a mystery.

"Listen, just go now and I'll phone you later. I'm very busy at the moment, I have all kinds of problems, including ... existential ones. I have to sort out a number of things in my mind, which is why I'm thinking of going back to my father's plantation for a while, to my friend the witch doctor."

"I understand. In other words, you want to get rid of me."

"I told you before, it's all very confused. Things are never black and white like that blouse and skirt you're wearing ... can't you understand?"

"I understand simple truth. Farewell. When it's clear in your mind what you want, if you ever do sort it out, let me know!"

A proud woman, Alexis thought. I could really go for her. Perhaps, if ...?

The outside door closed and Rodrigo returned without any comment.

"A beautiful woman!" Alexis told him with discreet irony. "Donatelli is a lucky man!"

Rodrigo had enough sensitivity to express his feelings while keeping the forms. For the first time, he spoke somewhat more openly. "Donatelli is a man wearing blinkers, a soldier without imagination, without the sensitivity that a woman like Dalia needs. You'll have to get to know her better. Since you already know her husband, it will be easy. The first contact has been made, and I had the impression that she was looking at you with interest. Dalia and I are good friends."

What game is Rodrigo playing? Alexis wondered. The half-open door had done its job. It had let through the egotistical tone that every man uses when preening himself over his conquest.

But when the door opened Rodrigo again kept up appearances. "I offer her what her husband isn't able to give her: the poetry of life. I'm certain that you, too, can become her good friend."

Did Rodrigo want to foist Donatelli's wife off on him now? Did he want to break it off and think that he'd conveniently found someone who contained the elements that Dalia's restless soul was after? Because she must be a restless soul, that was obvious from the start. A woman to the core who also wanted to live without compromise.

Alexis turned these confused thoughts over in his mind. He was flattered that Rodrigo had chosen him as his successor if indeed his suspicious were true. But he didn't want to reach the point where he believed that the friendship and attention shown him since the previous night was some sort of deliberate plot, with Donatelli's wife the last move! Time would tell, and he changed the subject. "Life seems to go by at cinematic speed in this town. I've met a 'sui generis' hunter, his stunning wife, a paranoid Indian, my compatriot Costa, the owner of the Costa del Sol, that gang of young men and women whom you introduced me to last night, and of course you. But on top of everything else, this is the first time I've felt so close to nature. It seems as if I, too, am slowly being drawn into a magical atmosphere."

"You're wrong. Nothing runs at cinematic speed. You are running, you are seeking, and along the way you meet people in their environment. Because you seem to have a restless spirit, like me. If you hadn't taken the road along the beach as soon as you arrived last night and walked to where the town ends and imagination begins, you wouldn't have met me. You go after life, it doesn't go after you. Otherwise, Africa would be tedium and isolation. Perhaps that is why every stimulation is a form of escape.

The loneliness is great.
You call out and no-one hears.
Nature is boundless and without sound.
No barrier there to send back you voice
which heads for the infinite, with silent souls.
Only they return, ceaselessly,
definitive, guides
in prayers and magic.
Thus your voice finds resonance
against an immaterial fence which rises up
beyond the horizon of the earth,
where there is neither hope nor despair,
neither geography nor history
neither patience nor haste.

"I wrote that poem a few months after I came to Africa. When I was still in the north and the days were endless, like my father's plantations."

Alexis found the opportunity to bring up the subject that was on his mind. "When did you decide to come to Lourenco Marques to pursue life and girls? From what I've heard you're a renowned lady killer!"

"So that's what that little gossip Pi calls me? Not that it isn't true. It is only natural that women like me. They always try to find in a man the signs of their own sensitivity. And I, in turn, am completed by a woman. Each of them is a unique world that opens one's eyes. The closer you get to a woman, the more your sensitivities are polished and the more fulfilled you become. Each time, your antennae are more finely tuned, and you feel you become a better person, while trying to reach the final image of perfection. Women are my own Pygmalion. I'm going to tell you a secret I've never told anyone before."

"Why me?"

"I don't know, but I felt from the first moment I met you that I had found a kindred spirit. Someone who wouldn't misunderstand a person like me, who isn't confined by the moulds of established thought and behaviour. That is why I can speak openly."

He seemed to be sincere, and Alexis' fears that Rodrigo was using him faded. Rodrigo went on: "When I was fifteen years old, the time when you begin to have visions of women and love, I stumbled on a large book in the library, at home. I had leafed through it and gazed at it many times before but only then did I really become aware of it. The book was an old anthology from 1880 with the title *A Vision of Beautiful Women*. I can still remember the green leather cover with the gold and red flowers in relief. On each of the pages on the right there was an etching in black and white, of a woman of the romantic period who had weathered time, protected by a piece of silk paper, while on the page on the left there was a poem about Woman. Poems by Shakespeare, Shelley, Byron, Keats, Wordsworth and other less important poets. And the names of the women: Samela ... Rosalind ... Anthea ... – Celia ... Lucasta ... Amanda ... Diaphenia ... Fienore ... Juliet ... Thalia ... all very poetic, romantic, sensual! Through the years I made a composite of these poems, the figures and the names, and fashioned the ideal woman as I imagined her."

"Do you remember the poems?"

"I'll recite it for you, but not here. The atmosphere of the office does not inspire me.

We'll go to the little coffee-house I told you about yesterday, the Café Polana. We'll talk about poetry in a more romantic setting. It's cooler out there and you can watch the sea, near the Pensao Polana, on the Avenida Polana."

They took Rodrigo's car and in a few minutes were sitting in a corner of the Café Polana with two iced coffees on the table in front of them. Without preamble Rodrigo said "I gave the composition the name of the woman of my dreams: Amaranthea! Aunar, in Latin to love, the element of eros. Mar, from the Latin, the open sea and Anthea, from the Greek, the blossoms, the flowers. Two things from nature. Then, *Theà* the Goddess in the language of your homeland, the divine element, but also *théa* – the view, the glance, the presence, the surprise, the wonder showing through the eyes of the face and the soul. And one more word: Anti, from a west African language, the spirit contained by each object on earth. Then from Greek once more: *maraino* to wither, to decay ... the end which is never final, because there is always the negation: Amarando! The never fading, the new beginning, the cycle of life."

"Amaranthea!" Alexis repeated, staring out at the view, trying to envisage an image through the veil that the morning mist was creating on the horizon. Rodrigo respected Alexis' musings, and after a few moments had passed, continued.

"I have taken verses from each poem, but not always in order, and sometimes I switch from first to third person." In a quiet, calm and distant voice Rodrigo began to recite:

The fountains mingle with the river
and the rivers with the ocean.
The winds of heaven mix for ever with a sweet emotion.
Nothing in the world is single.
All in pairs by divine law.
See the mountain kiss high Heaven;
and the waves clasp one another.
No sister flower would be forgiven
if it disdained its brother:
And sun-light embraces the earth
and the inbeams moon kiss the sea.
What is all this sweet work worth
if thou kiss not me?"

From the Philosophy of Love by Shelley.

How fair the maiden?
Ask the mariner who sails
over the joyous sea,
if wave or friendly gales
are half as fair as she.

Portuguese poem from my homeland.

"*A dancing shape*
an image gay

to *haunt, to startle.*
A spirit yet a woman too."
                              Wordsworth ...

Her tresses gold,
her eyes like glassy streams.
Her teeth are pearls,
the breasts are ivory.
Her cheeks like rose and lily.
Her brows' arches framed of ebony.
Like to Diana
in her summer weed
girt with crimson robe
of brightest dye.
Whiter than be the flocks
when washed by Aretûsa
As fair Aurora
decked with ruddy glister.
Passeth fair Venus in her bravest hue,
and Juno in the show of majesty.
Pallas in wit
and matchless dignity."
                              Robert Greene ...

"Her lips like cherries.
Her snowy neck like to a marble tower;
and all her body like a palace fair."
                              Spenser ...

There be none of Beauty's daughters
With a magic like hers;
And like music on the waters
Is her sweet voice to me,
When its sound makes the waves to pause
And the lulled winds seem dreaming."
                              Lord Byron ...

And each motion
of that warm, lithesome,
dainty soft-curved form,
so unconstrained, so free,
Blends like some ethereal choir
In one sweet harmony.
       Lamartine ...

One in whose gentle bosom I
Could pour my secret heart of woes,
Like the care-burthen honey-fly
That hides his murmurs in the rose,
– My earthly Comforter!"
       Anonymous ...

I think nature has lost the mould
Where she her shape did take.
       John Heywood ...

All that in woman I adored
In thy dear self I find.
Why should I seek further store
and still make love anew?"
       Sir Charles Sedley ...

Such if thou wert in all men's view,
A universal show,
What would my fancy have to do
My feelings to bestow?
       Wordsworth ...

Yes! I hope may with my strong desire keep pace
And I be undeluded, unbetrayed,
For if of our affections none find grace
In sight of Heaven, then wherefore hath God made
The world which we inhabit?
       Michaelangelo ...

Honour to women! entwining and braiding,
Life's garland with roses for ever unfading.
As nature's true daughters, how sweetly they dwell.
Schiller ...

How could we love if women were not?
From an Andalusian poem.

Therefore Heaven Nature charged
That one body should be filled
With all graces, wide enlarged?
Shakespeare!

He had recited the last verses slowly, and when he finished, he took two sips of coffee, and smiled.

Alexis was impressed that the last line had ended with a question. "Well done! What a memory!" he cried out.

"You have memorised the Creed, haven't you? I have my own 'Credo', my Love Gospels, the jigsaw puzzles of my imagination."

"From what I've seen however you also stage an erotic play in real life by seeking the perfect woman. First you mould her with your imagination and slowly fill in the puzzle, as you call it, one experience after another."

"I told you, first I mould myself, and perhaps, somewhere along the way I might encounter the ideal woman," Rodrigo said somewhat pompously. "I don't know if I really want to. I'm afraid of the perfect love. The perfect love is also the last one ..."

Then in a whisper: "The Flying Dutchman and Senta, Tannhauser and Elizabeth, Tristan and Isolde, Parsifal and Kundry!"

Then out loud again: "But fate is preordained, and you try to skirt the pitfalls, drawing strength from wherever you find it, in nature, in people, through supplication, through compromise, through sacrifices to the living and the dead. An eternal struggle which sooner or later you always lose."

"Fortunately, your method has a theatrical touch to it," Alexis said, "and I know that what you say does not necessarily dictate your way of life. Your words may be pessimistic, but your acts are full of longing for life. I saw that last night when you were dancing the samba!"

"When you are sensitive, you can feel great sorrow, but great joy as well, both at the same time, as strange as that may seem to you."

"It doesn't seem strange to me."

"I knew you would understand me. That's why I have spoken openly to you."

But Alexis had the feeling that the soul of Rodrigo held other secrets, deeply hidden, which did not come to the surface of his serene yet sombre features. Perhaps Maria Theresa would know more, perhaps Dalia!

It couldn't have been a coincidence that at that very moment Maria Teresa Correia de Castro walked by. She was wearing a colourful dress with a Cuban flounce, white sandals and large, red bone earrings.

Rodrigo called to her through the shrubbery that separated the garden of the coffee-house from the street, and she skipped up and stood before the table.

"I was going for a swim," she said brightly, "who's coming with me?"

"I have to go home," Rodrigo said. "Why don't you go, Alexis?"

"If we can go to my apartment, I can get my trunks. Then I'll be ready for my first dip in the Indian Ocean!"

"It will be like a baptism," Rodrigo said, – "you even have the godmother!"

"A godmother who wasn't good enough for you," Maria Teresa shot back.

While Rodrigo smiled maliciously at her comment she turned to Alexis and said: "Let's go."

"I'll come for you at the Pensao Polana around ten this evening," Rodrigo told Alexis, without asking if he was free or wanted him to. "I'll bring along Fernando, the boy I promised you. You go ahead, I'm going to sit here for a while longer."

As though it were the most natural thing in the world, Maria Teresa took Alexis's arm.

"I feel as though I've known you since childhood, I'm going to call you just Teresa. Maria Teresa is too long and Pi is too short. It robs you of your dignity." Alexis said.

They arrived at Pensao Polana in silence and went up the few steps that led to the hall. The fat owner looked at Alexis curiously when she saw him with a woman. It was clear that she was collecting material for gossip.

"Good morning. Are you the friend of Senhor Rodrigo? He called to tell us to take good care of you, but I see that you are handling things perfectly well on your own."

That was the beginning of a mutual dislike, and Alexis realised that the fewer conversations he had with this woman, the better.

"He is sending you your own servant boy too!" she said ironically.

Alexis did not reply.

"I'll be down in a couple of minutes," he told Teresa, and went up the stairs to his room, leaving her exposed to the critical eye of the fat woman.

"I have a strange feeling that you won't be getting along all that well with that Varina. Where on earth did you find this pension?" Teresa asked him as soon as they were on the street again, going down the path to the beach.

"My office in Johannesburg found it for me, but I like it. I have a room with a view of the ocean, and it's very convenient – near the sea, near the centre of town and near the coffee-house where you found us, where I have a feeling I will be spending many hours."

"Aren't you going to work?"

"Fortunately, I have a boss who will pay me to stay away. It seems I'm an undesirable both at my job and in my temporary home, if I can judge from your mention of ... what did you call her?"

"Her name is Eliz Mendoza but everyone here calls her Varina, because she resembles one of those fish wives along the coasts of Portugal: if they ever start talking about you, you're better off miles away!"

They came to the beach, above which the pier formed a large terrace. At high tide the water nearly reached the level of the terrace, which was strewn with sand. To get to the sea, you went down five or six steps. In the distance, a net fenced in the swimmers.

"What's the net for?" Alexis asked.

"For sharks. Don't ever swim outside that net, not even for fun. We'll swim here, but let's go to the Naval Club first and change. If you like, I'll register you as a member. You can sail then – but be careful, the sea can be dangerous here."

"Thanks," Alexis said, "Rodrigo already suggested it. I'm ready for anything that has to do with the sea."

Each went to their own changing room and when Teresa came out she saw admiration in Alexis' eyes. She had a shapely body crowned by a pretty head and a face from which sparkled two lively eyes. In the dress, she had seemed less shapely than she really was.

The Naval Club was a beautiful old building with a tiled roof and hanging gardens which reached down to a little sandy beach. Small boats with their sails unfurled were pulled up on the sand, while others bobbed on the sea. Beyond the sand, there was a slip for launching boats.

There weren't many people at the club at that hour, but still enough to make Teresa stop and greet acquaintances and friends and introduce them to Alexis. Then she said, "Let's swim out to the net, and afterwards we can and sit under an umbrella."

"As long as it isn't in the sun," Alexis said. "Now I understand what they mean by tropical heat!"

They went down the steps and the water came up to their waists.

"At ebb-tide, the water goes out all the way, well beyond the net. That's why I prefer to be here at high tide," Teresa said.

The sea was calm and the water clear, although Alexis thought it lacked the crystal transparency of the Mediterranean.

They swam out to the platform. Teresa climbed up on to it and dived off two or three times while Alexis took the opportunity to swim out to the net, go over it and swim in the open sea, in the forbidden zone. Teresa shouted at him from afar that he was insane. But that was precisely his aim, to frighten her. Fortunately, no shark made its appearance, though he had it in mind to return quickly if by chance he saw the water start to churn. Teresa's reaction when he returned to the platform was the reaction of an intelligent woman not impressed by show-offs. She had warned him, she had called to him from afar, she would not give him the satisfaction of girlishly admiring him. The "Oh, how you frightened me!" he expected to hear was not part of Teresa's style – he would have to get used to it. Even when he dived deep and disappeared for two minutes beneath the surface of the water, or when he swam crawl in his best form, Teresa was a woman with a head on her shoulders. If I want to impress her I'll have to use my own head ... if I have one, and not just exhibit my bodily accomplishments! he thought to himself.

But did he really want to? He liked Teresa as a person, he was flattered by her intelligence, by the interest she showed in him, but he didn't feel the same attraction to her as for Dalia. Dalia had got to him. He had all but been given the green light by Rodrigo. But from what he could see, Dalia was in love with Rodrigo.

For the time being let's be happy with what we have, Alexis thought. When all is said and done, Teresa is acceptable in every way, and when you have the chance to find a girl on the very first day, in a place you hardly know, you can't just throw away such an opportunity.

The burning sun dried them off almost immediately, and they sat down on two deck-chairs under a green umbrella.

"Tell me about Rodrigo," Alexis asked her. "I've known him for only a few hours, and he's practically adopted me, but despite the feeling that he had talked more to me about himself than to any other person, I feel that the more I listen to him the more the veil of mystery around him grows."

"But he holds on to that veil – don't you see?" Teresa replied with wisdom in her voice.

"To a point, yes. I always have the feeling that he himself confesses his real nature through the games he plays, and that under his serene expression lies a tormented soul."

"You're right. He has many personalities and masks. But he has found a 'modus vivendi' in which his various sides have signed a treaty of friendship and co-operation, and he gets along just fine with all of them, without them causing him as many problems as you would think. He has completely orchestrated himself and is fully aware of the 'mixage' (to use a cinematic word) he is making of the parts that spring from his soul, and the others which he conceives with his imagination."

"Tell me about your time with him."

"I was his first girl in Lourenco Marques. My father, who is a friend of the Governor, introduced me to him, at a dance at the Governor's Mansion. Rodrigo had just arrived from northern Mozambique and had already managed to be invited to the Governor's Mansion. I caught my breath when I first saw him. He reminded me of a portrait by a Spanish painter I had hanging in my room. For me, he was always the embodiment of the man of my dreams. And when he talked to me about his life, about love, about poetry, about music, it didn't take long for me to convince myself that he was the man in the portrait, and he looked at me and spoke words I didn't understand. I still remember them: 'Senta,' he said 'you appeared before me to free me from the demons that have haunted me since childhood, from my unfulfilled desires, from the unfulfilled dreams I had when I roamed in a daze through my mother's fields in Portugal, at night on my father's plantations in Beira.'"

She paused. "I was almost engaged to a young officer who had served in Mozambique and had been transferred to Angola. It was not a difficult choice. The same evening I wrote a letter to my fiancé and told him the truth. From that day on, and for the next three months Rodrigo and I saw each other practically every day, but while my love burgeoned there was always something that startled and frightened me. He told me: 'In you, I find the paradise that every man is seeking: to return to his previous life, to go from birth to the moist peace of his mother's womb. To save my troubled soul, I called on the Devil, the Great Witch of Beira. He exorcised me of my fears so I could face life, till at last I decided to come to Lourenco Marques; away from my father, away from my mother; to become a man.'"

Another pause, then she said, "He often talked about his mother. Seldom about his father. But his big escape was from her, despite the fact that in me he was still seeking the ideal mother, the pure, the faithful, the true one. But when I swore eternal devotion he got angry: 'You also made an oath to the man you were engaged to, and you betrayed him!' he said. Three months went by without him trying to make love to me. He was testing me. Testing my innocence. I didn't dare be more assertive. I went along with him, not wanting to disturb the serenity, so much cherished. One day we were at his house. The presence of Samia, the black Venus-like maid that serves him, didn't appear to bother him. She went in and out of the living room, but to Rodrigo seemed not to exist; she also had a peculiar remoteness, as if her large, black eyes didn't see us sitting side by side on the foam cushions on the floor, not even when she brought us tea. She was like a robot.

"Every time we were at his house the record player would be playing the *Flying Dutchman*, non-stop, and he would talk to me about Wagner, the man with a rootless soul, the man who sought Eros without finding it, the man who chased a chimera in the quest of a new ideal in life; but also a man who touched the masses, the creator, the visionary of consciousness beyond simple reason, in the most composite form of the spirit, where the symbolic images contest, accuse and condemn the scandal of existence! When he spoke about Wagner, it was the only time he seemed impassioned, otherwise he was as you know him, thoughtful, calm, and a little unapproachable.

"I don't know why, but that afternoon I remembered that he had called me Senta on the first day we met. I had nearly forgotten it, and never asked him about it. Had I not understood him properly? Had he perhaps said 'senta', the Italian word for listen? I decided to ask him. He didn't reply immediately. He got up, went over to the record player that was playing the *Flying Dutchman,* as usual, and took out a booklet from the box that held the twelve records of Wagner's opera. 'Read it,' he said, and so I did. The more I read, the clearer in my mind became the scenario that was being staged, and in which without being aware, I had been given one of the leading roles. Rodrigo had identified with Wagner's hero who wandered about the world, trying to break the bonds of the curse which tied him to his mother forever and would not let him become a man. In the story, Dalland, a sailor like my own father, introduces the Dutchman to his daughter Senta! Coincidence? And in Senta, the Dutchman looks for that paradise he had lost, eternal faith. And when Senta offers eternal faith – the terrible misunderstanding! Or perhaps only a justification? I felt at that moment that Rodrigo didn't really want me, and I was seized by terror. Who was this person opposite me? Who was this

Rodrigo? I plucked up courage and looked at him carefully. He had the same serene expression and for the first time I noticed an appeal in his look, like an appeal for salvation, and I called out to him: 'I want a child by you.' It was my way of saying that I wanted to make love to him. But it was more the mother speaking, trying to save her child, rather than the woman.

"His eyes filled with tears. He stroked my head, lifted the needle from the record, and the *Flying Dutchman* stopped forever. He took me by the hand, led me home on foot, and I knew that I had disappointed him. I cried a lot, but I felt at peace. As if I had escaped from a bad experience, from an uneasy, complex spirit who would have lured me to catastrophe, like Wagner's heroine. He had me playing a role without me knowing it. He deliberately used the Wagnerian heroes for the embodiment of his own unconscious. Just as Wagner did."

"Except that Rodrigo has a double metamorphosis. He enters the skin of Wagner through the Wagnerian heroes." Alexis said. The vivid way she had told the story had almost made him shudder.

Teresa understood, and stroked his cheek. Suddenly she jumped up playfully.

"Do you want to go out sailing?"

"It looks like you want to continue with me the story of the *Flying Dutchman* you started with Rodrigo. With a happy ending I hope. O.K. let's sail out onto the ocean! Don't be afraid, the weather is good, and I was raised on the sea," Alexis replied.

"Still, your look frightens me. You have the same look Rodrigo had that evening. Only he wasn't smiling. Let's go!"

They put towels over their shoulders and went down the stone ramp to the sand. Two young men had just returned in a Sniper with the name *Rosa* on its bow, and Alexis and Teresa took it over. Teresa borrowed a sailor's cap for Alexis, to protect him from the sun. She herself was wearing a straw gondolier's hat with a ribbon under her chin so the wind wouldn't blow it off. They walked a couple of steps into the shallows, turned the prow of the *Rosa* seaward, and then jumped in.

Teresa grabbed the rudder and the main-sheet in her hand.

"Let's sail further out to sea, so they won't notice, if they're watching from the club, that you're not a member yet."

When they had moved off, she turned the skippering over to Alexis. "You didn't tell me that you were such a good sailor." Alexis said.

"How much did you expect to know about me in just few hours?"

"You're right, I keep forgetting that this is my first day here. But is it my fault if everybody took me by the hand as soon as I arrived and spread the red carpet? I feel so much at home here because of you, Rodrigo, your friends, and even that eccentric Donatelli. The only discordant notes have come from my boss and Madame Polana, but I'm in such a good mood that even they seem likeable in their own way."

A light, steady breeze was blowing. When they had gone out about half a mile, they turned north, parallel with the coast. Small waves splashed and cooled them.

"It's like flying over the waves. As though the final recollections of the past are being washed away, wave by wave, and that the foam striking our faces is filtering the soul, turning it into a dry, fluffy new sponge, ready to soak up new sensations, new experiences. I don't know if you realise than I am flirting with you," Teresa told him, playfully.

Alexis looked straight ahead and felt all the sensual pleasure of the wind blowing on his face and his body. "What I do realise is that you are passing over a bridge from Rodrigo to me, that you are making an arch over the waves."

"Am I not playing the game the way it should be played?"

Alexis smiled. The wind blew stronger and the waves began to thud against the moving boat. Teresa looked around a bit uneasily.

"We haven't been paying attention, and we're too far out. You know that squalls can spring up here from one moment to the next. I see all the other boats are turning back; we're the only ones on the open sea, and the weather is getting worse. Turn back."

"We're not so far from land, at the most a mile from the club, but since you want to, we'll sail back."

"You don't know the weather around here. Look at the sky. Two minutes ago there wasn't a cloud. Look out into the ocean; it's turned black – soon we'll have a storm."

"Don't worry, the weather is coming from the sea. With the wind aft, we're bound to reach land quickly."

He loosened the main sail a bit, to take the wind which steadily grew stronger, but the waves were becoming threatening, and as the *Rosa* plunged into the troughs of the waves it was in danger of taking in water.

"This boat doesn't sail well with the wind aft in this kind of weather," Teresa told him.

"What am I supposed to do about it? Thanks a lot, weather!"

"You're the captain now!" she said in a frightened, cold voice. "The Flying Dutchman! You cursed the weather, and now we're in the clutches of the Devil!"

Alexis looked at her to see if she was joking, but there wasn't a trace of a smile on her face, and he began to feel odd himself. "Are we playing with fire? Are we tempting fate here where everything is moved by supernatural forces?" he suddenly thought, and looked around for a silver lining.

He grabbed hold of the chromium plated ring that held the fair leader of the main mast, the way men grabbed their balls when they met a priest in his homeland, and counted from one to thirteen and a half, to drive out all evil spirits, all evil influences, wherever they might be from – one more superstition he had carried all the way from Greece. "What if the storm is caused by the vibrations from the Flying Dutchman or … Wagner himself? Had he fallen into a trap? Who was Teresa? Was all this story about the Flying Dutchman' her own invention? What if she was a witch? Hadn't Senta lured the Flying Dutchman to a shipwreck, to death?"

"Come on, you idiot!" he told himself "Are you becoming superstitious now? Do a couple of waves a thousand metres from shore scare you?"

Teresa didn't speak; she stared into the distance as if she'd departed for another world. Meanwhile, the wind got stronger and stronger and Alexis had to strain to keep the Rosa on its course, with the wind broadside, since she wouldn't travel with the wind aft.

They were now nearly level with the Naval Club but getting no closer to dry land. To reach land they would have to turn.

He tried, by tacking, to get a little closer, but every time he turned the sail, the waves dumped water into the boat. It was getting hard to control the *Rosa*, which was in danger of capsizing at every turn as the waves sloshed about in the scuppers.

He looked in the direction of the Naval Club, to see how much distance still separated them, and saw people on the shore watching his struggles. "Any more of this and we'll be a laughing stock," he told himself. The *Rosa* had now taken on so much water that Alexis was afraid to make another turn.

"Teresa," he shouted, "it's still about two hundred metres to the shore. I'm going to take the wind aft, come what may. Be ready to jump into the sea. Sit as far back as you can for ballast."

Teresa did as she was told and started to mumble as if in a delirium, but sympathetically, as if she'd accepted her fate. Every so often Alexis could make out her words in the roar of the wind.

"This wretched man, this man who has never grown up, I love him and I have to rescue him."

But he didn't know who she was talking about. Rodrigo? Himself? The Flying Dutchman? It was a nightmarish scene. "But it takes a storm to tell a Captain."

"Teresa, get hold of yourself," he shouted, "and do what I tell you."

Teresa still had a glassy stare.

"He'll be swept away before he's able to take his place in life. He'll be lost in the water of his mother before he is born, and I with him. It's too late, I can't rescue him."

"Teresa, you're raving! Haven't you got Rodrigo out of your system yet? I'll go mad myself in a minute."

"If we capsize here, the water's full of sharks," Teresa said simply.

"We're going to capsize, that's for sure, but we should get a hundred yards closer before we get swamped."

He embraced her, to give her heart, but he knew that Rodrigo still had a great deal of influence over her. He let the sail unfurl in the wind while the *Rosa* plunged ahead into the waves and took on more and more water.

Just as Alexis had calculated, after they had covered a hundred yards and there was still another hundred to the shore, the *Rosa* plunged for the last time, turned over, and they were both in the sea. Teresa started swimming toward her hat that the sea had snatched away, but Alexis pulled her back,

"Stay close to the boat. The waves will carry us to dry land if no-one comes to pull us out."

The *Rosa* was on its side and stayed that way for a while until the sail became soaked, and then it turned over completely, mast down. The waves crashed furiously against her hull and while they were holding on in the sea, Teresa had come around and was once more the logical, practical, composed woman.

"Dive underneath, into the hollow of the boat," she told Alexis. 'We'll be safer from sharks."

In a while their two heads were outside the water, in the hollow of the boat's hull which pitched and tossed in the waves, with just a little reflection of light from underneath the surface of the sea. Now smiling again, Teresa put her arms around Alexis and said: "Here we are, the Flying Dutchman and Senta, embracing and transformed, in the Great Beyond, but more alive than ever, in the sea up to our necks!"

"Listen," Alexis replied, "to the voices of the crowd on the beach – they are singing the final notes of the Flying Dutchman, like a chorus."

"Now you're becoming delirious," Teresa said and kissed him passionately.

Her kiss, in the hollow of the boat, sounded like a bell in a belfry, while at the same moment their ears caught the chugging of the gasoline engine of a boat coming to pick them up. They dived down again, to get their heads outside the boat, only to hear the voice of the driver launch shouting:

"Get in quickly, there's a huge shark just a few metres away!"

They clambered into the launch, with some difficulty, tied a line onto the *Rosa* and slowly towed her to the shore. Both of them felt embarrassed at having capsized before so many people, but the reception they received revived their good spirits. Young men and women shook their hands and congratulated them on having managed to get so close.

"Don't congratulate me, congratulate the ... Flying Dutchman," Teresa said modestly, but the others didn't of course know what she was talking about.

Only the President of the Club, a tall, stern, curly-headed man with a small moustache, in a white suit, straw hat and sporting the badge of the Club on the top pocket of his jacket, addressed himself to Teresa, snubbing Alexis.

"I don't know who this young man is you had with you, but you at least ought to know the regulations. You didn't consult the weather report, which is posted in the Club, before you got into the boat, and you gave the helm to someone who is not a member of our Club."

Before Teresa was able to reply or introduce Alexis, he left.

"Let's get out of here," Teresa said to Alexis, angrily. "I apologise for the way he treated you."

"Don't let it bother you. I'm beginning to get used to it. Here everything is wonderful one minute and awful the next. Some embrace you, others ignore you. There is no middle road. Everything seems to be extremes and antitheses. Like nature, like the winds, which one minute caress you tenderly and then suddenly, without warning, give you a slap and dump you in the sea ... Africa! – whatever you are, you're exciting!"

The President had two beautiful daughters, friends of Teresa's, who as soon as they learned of their father's behaviour, came to ask for forgiveness on his behalf.

"Teresa, don't take him seriously, you know how stern he always tries to be! Aren't you going to introduce us to your friend?"

The introductions were made and the two girls took hold of Alexis, one on each arm, ostensibly to give him support, but in reality because in a small city like Lourenco Marques each new person is a source of interest.

"Are you planning to steal him away from me?" Teresa teased.

"He's an adult and dry behind the ears; let him decide for himself.' one of the two girls said languidly while the other added archly: "By the way, Teresa, where's Rodrigo?"

"As if you didn't know that we haven't been together for months," Teresa replied. Alexis had abandoned himself to the girls' attentions and was floating in a sea of happiness this time, looking from one to the other with an innocent smile, saying nothing.

Teresa intervened: "Excuse me for spoiling this beautiful ensemble, but I have to go. If you wish to stay, Alexis, please do, you don't have to take me home."

Alexis politely bid farewell to the girls, and they moved off.

"You're close to becoming a second Rodrigo, and you've only just arrived," Teresa told him, sounding a little cross.

"Yes, but only second best – you said it!" How strange! Why hadn't it occurred to him that he was identified with the personality of his friend? For the time being, at least, it was as if he had become his shadow. Teresa was using him as an extension of Rodrigo, even if she didn't realise it herself.

He took her home. They said little on the way back. Both seemed to be concentrated on their own thoughts. Teresa lived in a one-storey house with a small garden like most of the houses in Lourenco Marques. They parted without any warm embrace. In the evening the group would meet again anyway, Rodrigo had said.

Alexis returned to the Pensao Polana where he found the boy that Rodrigo had sent, waiting on the first floor landing, He was sitting in a chair, and when he saw Alexis unlocking his door, he got up and approached.

"Me Fernando. Senhor Rodrigo send me."

"Ah! Fernando. How do you do?"

He put out his hand. The other fellow wasn't used to handshakes and didn't understand. Alexis was forced to take his limp hand and shake it. Fernando was of medium height, wore clean, white clothes, and had a clear, innocent face.

"How old are you?"

"Me don't know, sir."

Alexis judged him to be around eighteen but it was difficult to tell an African's age.

"Look, Fernando, I'm going to lie down for a while" (he made the sign for sleep, inclining his head sideways on his hands). "You do whatever you want and wake me at six in the afternoon with tea."

"Me sit here sir, cadeira."

"Cadeira?"

"Chair, sir."

"As you wish!"

Then he thought he'd have some fun. Since he had a boy, why not act like a European colonial?

"Listen, Fernando. Don't call me sir. Call me, my Lord, my Great Master – you understand?"

"Of course, my Lord, Great Master, me cadeira."

"So we're back at the cadeira again!"

Tired after his adventure, Alexis lay down to sleep and slept deeply.

At precisely six in the afternoon, he was dreaming that he was being rocked on his back by the waves. He awoke with a start, and realised it was just Fernando shaking him. He woke easily and wasn't angry at the way his alarm clock worked. He got up, showed Fernando the open door, knocked on the outside several times and told him.

"Fernando, when you wake my Lord, Great Master, you knock on the door like this, no shake, shake – understand?"

"Si, Senhor ... my Lord, Great Master, cadeira."

"Boy, I'm talking about the door, why do you keep telling me about the chair?"

Fernando looked at him blankly and didn't answer.

"Did you bring the tea?"

"Fernando cadeiro, My Lord, Great Master,"

"Tea, Fernando, tea, tea!"

He mimicked drinking out of a cup. The boy continued to stare blankly so Alexis gave up the struggle. "Leave it, forget it, make up my bed" – and he pointed at it.

Had Rodrigo played a trick on him by sending him Fernando, or had he wanted to unload him as a favour to his sister, the black beauty? He would make one more try and then he would talk to Rodrigo. He took a pair of white shoes, a bottle of white polish and a small sponge, and gave them to Fernando. "Fernando, polish my shoes."

Fernando took the shoes and left the room, leaving the door open. Alexis secretly watched and saw him sit down on the chair and start polishing the shoes. He sighed.

How did he understand about the polishing but not the tea? And this mania about the chair? Oh, well, Africa has a lot of mysteries to look into!

He would go for tea to the coffee-house, to pass his time before the evening meal in the pension. Rodrigo would call for him about ten – hadn't he said so? He would take some paper and a pen and start writing. The coffee-house would be his bolt-hole.

He had to go and get his shoes from Fernando. "Why didn't you bring in my shoes?"

"Fernando cadeira, my Lord, Great Master."

"I'm going to wrap that cadeira around your head," he said laughing. Fernando's answer had seemed ludicrous and incomprehensible to him.

At the coffee-house he sat in the same corner where he and Rodrigo had sat that morning, and after he had drunk his tea, took out a pencil and paper and tried to think of a subject. It wasn't difficult. The morning's adventure, combined with the story of the Flying Dutchman, had possibilities. Rodrigo, the main character, the central hero – what name should he give him?

He couldn't find one. For the time being he would use his real name, and maybe change it later. But above all, there was Africa. What did he know about Africa? Very little. A place takes on sense only through the human element, or in this case, the natives. What did he know about black people? Almost nothing. His contacts had been mainly limited to the boy in the house where he had stayed in Johannesburg, the fellow at his office, and now a few scraps of conversation with Fernando, which were not all that illuminating.

He remembered a phrase from the book by Alan Patton which had just been published and which he had started to read: *Cry, the Beloved Country*, a novel about the parallel lives of two families, a white preacher and a black one. The son of the black preacher kills the son of the white one only because he has nothing to look forward to in life. Even prison is better. The white preacher understands, and forgives him.

"And now, for all the people of Africa, the beloved country. Nkosi Sikelel Afrika, God save Africa. That men should walk upright in the land where they were born, and be free to use the fruits of the earth? What was evil in it? Yet men are afraid, with a fear that is deep, deep in the heart, a fear so deep, that they hide their kindness. Such fear could not be cast out but by love."

That would be the theme of the book he was going to write. Yes, he would write about people. Through the story of Rodrigo he would try to call out to the black person who lived hidden in the African night, the mystical, magical night, where he could dream without fear as long as he was free, as long as he wasn't 'emancipated'. What did emancipation mean? To become just another European? To remove his spirit from the rock? His breath from the tree? To be deaf to the babbling water? To be blind to the messages of the wave-tossed sea? To become immune to the light of the stars?

He looked at his watch. It was time to return for the evening meal.

The few guests at the Pensao Polana were all on time. He was the last to arrive.

"Bacalao, cod-fish, tonight," the black waiter told him.

Cod was the one food he hadn't been able to stand since he was a child. An English family sat at the next table. Father, mother and a son, about twelve years old. The father, seeing that Alexis had left the fish untouched, told him, with the ease the English have in striking up a conversation:

"I see you don't care for the national food of the Portuguese."

"It's the only thing I've never been able to eat. As much as I like the sea, I can't stand the smell of the salt on cod-fish."

"Maybe that's the reason. We don't want to eat something we really like," the Englishman said laughing.

"It depends on what that something is," Alexis said, "perhaps not to eat it, but just nibble at it!"

They introduced themselves, and Alexis ended up at their table holding the glass of wine they offered him. Soup and a banana were his food that evening. He hadn't eaten at all in the middle of the day, but in the heat of Lourenco Marques that was no problem.

Rodrigo arrived at that moment, He had met the Englishman, who worked at a bank in town. He sat down at the table, too. Alexis immediately brought up the subject of Fernando.

"Thank you for the boy, but you didn't tell me he had an obsession about a chair!"

"Chair? What chair?"

"Whatever I tell him he answers: Me, Fernando, cadeira. And he's stuck a chair in front of my door and sits there. I asked him for tea and he didn't bring it, but when I gave him my shoes to polish he polished them."

Rodrigo burst out laughing. "You don't understand the natives yet! They can only have one thought at a time. Complex thoughts are outside their ken. You put the shoes in his hand and he did them. For the tea he has to go to the kitchen and ask them to make it for him and then bring it to you. Their minds can't analyse a complicated series of acts."

Alexis let that pass and asked: "But what about the chair?"

Rodrigo laughed again. "I told him: You'll take a chair and you'll sit all day in front of Senhor Alexis' front door, waiting to serve him! And he, like a faithful pet, wants you to know that he is performing his duty!"

"What you're talking about is fear, the age-old fear that if he doesn't do as you tell him, he'll be in trouble!"

"It's not just that. It's that the African doesn't think, he just remembers. He has great observational and powerful imitative abilities, but to conceive of a plan with his own mind is beyond his capabilities. His reason lies in his habits, in his instinct. He doesn't specify concepts, which is why he isn't surprised about something that to us would be laughable or absurd."

"Rodrigo is right," added the Englishman, who had seemed a person with an open mind, different from anyone he had met up till then in Africa. "Their ideas are more abstract than ours, and if two images aren't connected by logic, it does not create a problem for them. The explanation is in the instinct, and instinct is much more flexible than the mind. That is why knowledge is always tempered by their emotions, by what moves them."

"And that is why you must always show Fernando what you want," Rodrigo added, "like the shoes. So for tea, the first time go down with him to the kitchen and be patient, and show him how to make the tea, in every detail. And now and then, show him that you appreciate him. He doesn't understand love in our sense. Pat his head. That is an instinctual gesture. If you walk in the forest by the beach, as I told you last night, you'll see the monkey mothers holding their children in their arms and stroking their heads."

The Englishman continued: "The tribal African, you see, as soon as he is born enters into a state of symbiosis with his mother. But the moment she feels he is standing on his own two feet, she lets him loose in the world. From that point on, he is in psychological limbo. No emotional development, except with his brothers and sisters, and other relatives for as long as he stays in the tribe. If he is put into a European family, he acts like a domesticated animal, a dog that will catch the ball you throw or will lower its head for you to pat it."

"And we accept – you and I – this situation. We've created an unnatural environment for these people because it's to our advantage," Alexis objected.

"The worst thing is that it suits them, too, because they don't have the same consciousness as ours or the same existential problems – which doesn't mean of course that they won't acquire them. If you have strong instincts, logic will follow, and it may be a thousand times more powerful than ours," Rodrigo added with a note of finality in his voice, and started to get up. "Let's go Alexis, they'll be waiting for us."

They bade goodnight to the others and left.

"Where to, tonight?" Alexis asked.

"Girassol. From the roof garden you can see all of Africa and the ocean spread out around you."

"Is it the same group as last night?"

"I don't know if anyone else is joining us. I told you, the groups in Lourenco Marques are like a samba during Carnival in Rio – everyone enters, dances for as long as he wishes with whomever he wants to, and exits when he chooses to."

Yvonne, Maga, Viriatou, Frederico, Karl and Teresa were already there. They had learned from Teresa about the morning's adventure and now the whole town would be talking about it. A new person had been added to the group, another one of Rodrigo's girlfriends, according to Radio-Pi: Kiarka, a Greek dancer – looking the way one would imagine a Mediterranean ballerina might – tall, with an athletic body, black eyes and a shock of hair gathered in a bun at the back of her neck. She was wearing a light blue evening gown with one bare, tanned shoulder exposed; firm, tan calves could be glimpsed through her split skirt. There was a vitality in her face and in her movements.

It was natural, as compatriots, for Alexis and her to embrace each other and spend nearly the entire evening talking to each other. Teresa seemed piqued that Alexis didn't pay more attention to her. She said as much after asking him to dance.

"Maybe you kissed me in the boat, or for that matter, under the boat, but your heart is still with Rodrigo, and you know it," Alexis told her defensively. "Don't expect me to become another Rodrigo."

"Why not?" And with that question she left him in the middle of the dance floor. Without hesitation, Alexis asked Kiarka for a dance. Kiarka had danced in Italy after the war, and was now spending the winter season dancing for the Johannesburg Opera Company, (she was both the lead dancer and the choreographer). She spent the summer in Lourenco Marques.

As he danced with her, the conversation unavoidably came round to Rodrigo. Kiarka slowly began tell a story. "That evening the Johannesburg Opera put on *Tannhauser*".

Alexis began to have suspicions about the outcome. *The Flying Dutchman* was not, it appeared, a unique performance in the world of Rodrigo's imagination "I was dancing in the first scene where Venus, surrounded by the nymphs, the Bacches and the Satyrs, holds in her power the knight and poet, Tannhauser." Kiarka went on: "I had choreographed it, using black female dancers, trying to wed on stage the ceremonial expression of the Roman worship of idols with African idolatry. During the first interval a beautiful young man appeared in my dressing room. He stood in the doorway and looked at me. I was still wearing Venus' costume and getting ready to be made up for the second act and I saw him in the mirror, but I didn't turn around immediately. His eyes had a sorrowful, melancholy look that touched my heart. I only heard his voice: 'I am Tannhauser and I have come to sing you the songs of love.' We became lovers that same evening. He came to Johannesburg from Lourenco Marques every so often and stayed with me. I should say, with us. Because I was living with the other girls in the company in a large house surrounded by luxuriant panoramic gardens, on top of a hill in the suburbs."

"So you are Rodrigo's mystery woman from Johannesburg!"

Kiarka acted as if she didn't understand and went on. "That is where we all slept, ate and had our rehearsals – and in the evening we sat on the lawns in the gardens, singing. Rodrigo made believe he was in Venusberg, the mountain of Venus in Wagner's opera. For him, I was Venus. He often stayed for two or three days, sometimes a whole week. He would often lay his head on my knees, listen to our songs, and at times he recited his poems to us, just like Tannhauser, who had become part of his being, and he played the role like the best of actors. It was an ideal role for Rodrigo! The knight and the poet! But something was troubling him. He tasted the delights of love, but it didn't free him. I had the feeling that he was bound to me sexually, and that was precisely the reason he hated me. In a corner of his soul lurked the image of a woman different from me, less liberated in her love-making, of a woman who had more of the spirit and less of the flesh."

"The slavery of the mother again. He burrows into the warmth of your embrace and yet he hates you, because we want our mothers to be pure – the old cliché!" Alexis said.

"What do you mean 'again'?"

"I mean, the classic complex." He didn't know if he should reveal the secret of the 'Flying Dutchman' and divulge all he knew of Rodrigo's relationship with Teresa.

Kiarka resolved his dilemma. "The story has a follow-up. Look at Viriatou and Yvonne sitting at our table. Viriatou loves Yvonne. Yvonne loved Rodrigo, and perhaps still does. No-one can resist him! All women yearn for a man like him. Handsome, athletic, a poet, tender. Strong enough to give you orders and weak enough so you have to protect him.

"And you, the goddess Venus, do you have maternal feelings?"

"More than other women. Men come to me to be suckled."

"I'm a mammal too – will you adopt me?"

Kiarka smiled and went on. "Viriatou, as I said, loves Yvonne, but knew that she loved Rodrigo. As a perfect knight and a man with a heart, Viriatou, like Wolfram, Tannhauser's best friend, revealed to Rodrigo Yvonne's love for him which she wouldn't confess herself. Everyone in Lourenco Marques knew that Rodrigo disappeared every so often, and they gossiped about the mysterious woman who kept him away. The mysterious woman, as you know, was me. For Rodrigo this was a unique chance to carry on the role of Tannhauser. He asked me to throw him out of my life because he didn't have the courage to leave on his own. He spoke to me of 'Elizabeth' who loved him and was patiently waiting for him. She was none other than Yvonne. I tried to hold on to him. I told him that in me he had found a world of laughter and joy that he would never find in the arms of any 'Elizabeth', who would be a boring bourgeoisie. But he persisted, and in the end I got angry and told him to leave."

They danced silently for a while, and then Kiarka said: "The follow-up I learned from Rodrigo who now, completely at a loss and unable to accept the sensual peace that Yvonne gave him, the complete love he had always yearned for, called on me to save him from his terrible anguish. That evening, various friends had gathered in the garden of Yvonne's house. I met the group for the first time. We talked about love. Viriatou spoke of love as something ethereal. Rodrigo always wanted to shock. He defended, with a passion, sensual and idolatrous love and confessed to everyone that he had spent moments with me of great carnal delight and passion. It was the only time they all rebelled, ready to tear me to pieces. Only the good Viriatou told Rodrigo in a calm voice, 'If you don't stand up to the Devil, how can you expect the angels to protect you?' Despite the fact that I felt insulted by the reactions of Rodrigo's friends and Viriatou's words, I must confess that, on second thoughts, their outburst was moving. They only wanted to protect Yvonne's feelings. I left, so as not to put them in an even more awkward situation. 'When you solve your problems, call me again,' I told Rodrigo. The same evening I took the train back to Johannesburg. We became good friends again, six months later, when the whole story was over. Rodrigo told me he had gone to the witch doctor of Beira to have the knot in his soul untied by magic. The witch doctor quarelled with Rodrigo, scolded him, and made him feel even more persecuted, more accursed. After the way he'd insulted Yvonne, she fell ill, and Rodrigo felt that, like Tannhauser, he had to pay for all his sins. He had reached the point of wanting to commit suicide. One evening, at his house, sitting in an armchair with Samia, the black girl, kneeling next to him, he listened to *Tannhauser*. As he had reached the second scene, he visualised 'Elizabeth', or should I say 'Yvonne', dead, and decided he was responsible. He took a pistol out of a drawer and put it to his temple. Samia looked him in the eyes, put her hand out calmly, and took the gun away. Did he really mean to kill himself? Was he playing the part? No-one will ever know."

"What did he tell you?"

"He told me that he would have killed himself – but you know Rodrigo! He himself doesn't know where truth begins and dreams end."

For the second time he had heard Teresa's very words; and for the second time he had listened to a Wagnerian scenario. "The deliverance of death," Alexis told her, "or rather the return to non-existence. The failure to pass the tests, to become a man."

"Perhaps, but no man has ever spoken to me of love like Rodrigo. He told me that with me he had discovered true love. He gave me the impression that he was reborn. He told me that he reached orgasm with his whole being, with a dual dimension – with his body and his spirit – and we became one, woman and man, human and god together in a supreme cosmic convulsion. But then, at other times he'd say: 'Why is this mechanical motion of love needed to reach supreme pleasure? Why do you have to *make* love when you *are* love?' The question was directed to Venus and I, the goddess, didn't know how to answer him. Then again he'd say: 'You are aware of love on three levels – the body, the heart and the spirit. In your body you feel the celebration, in your heart the love and in your spirit the divinity. Through the spirit you achieve transfiguration, the final ecstasy!"

"In fantasy is what I'd say," Alexis said. "The Flying Dutchman and Senta in the Great Beyond, Elizabeth dead! The purification that comes with death."

"Why are you talking about the Flying Dutchman?"

"I was making a Wagnerian extension."

Teresa had her story, Kiarka had her own. They both had entrusted their secrets to him. He didn't have the right to embroider them.

"But Tannhauser died to be redeemed, while Rodrigo hasn't ceased being tormented. The circle still hasn't closed," Alexis said.

"First of all, Yvonne didn't die like 'Tannhauser's' Elizabeth. As you can see, she is dancing over there cheek to cheek with Viriatou. Rodrigo and I remain friends, and we go out together with Teresa. Why should I hide it? A piece of my heart belongs to him!" How strange! A boy who can't find a way to be a mature man, can get so much out of women!

"But just as you men are seeking your mother, so are we mothers – whether we want to be or not. And one cannot be set free from oneself all that easily, perhaps never! I'm afraid, from the little I know about Rodrigo, that he still hasn't been freed of Yvonne."

"Don't worry. He didn't play the role of Tannhauser to the end, nor is he going to. He will find some justification that will serve his other side, the eager optimist, the person thirsty for life. Rodrigo is two people. You don't have to do more than look at his two profiles: the left one shows the melancholy, the poetry, the child-like innocence, the intense presence of the unconscious, the narcissism, the attraction to non-existence; and the right courage, joy, the brilliance of conscious action; life in full eruption."

"Perhaps you're right. Rodrigo often said to me: 'You have to have passed through the worst, to know the best!'"

"Do you know how long we've been dancing? It's a good thing they're playing slow, romantic music."

"We lost track of time, should we sit down? They'll think you're flirting with mc."

"Would you mind?"

"Not at all!"

Back at the table they were teased by Karl, Frederico and Viriatou, in the courteous, gentle manner characteristic of them. These three men, Alexis believed, offered the group comfort and certainty. Without much talk, but with tenderness in their expressions which one would think came straight from their souls. He trusted them, perhaps more than he did Rodrigo.

Soon after they were seated, Alexis asked Teresa to a dance, so as to make up for his former aloofness. She had after all been very supportive of him and they had shared quite an adventure, so he couldn't ignore her. The orchestra played a fast samba that left little time for conversation, which he preferred to avoid. At the end of the dance, Alexis declared that he felt tired and would go home.

"Shall I come with you?" Teresa whispered in his ear. "I give you my word I won't talk about Rodrigo."

"It's not a question of not talking but rather not thinking about him."

"You underrate yourself. Try me."

Alexis didn't turn her down. Before they said goodnight to the others, they agreed that the next day, which was Sunday, they would go on an excursion to Namaacha.

They went out on the street, and Alexis felt the need to put a little order in his thoughts. It's easier to clarify things if you have someone next to you. He trusted Teresa. He would talk to her after all. He couldn't keep everything locked up inside.

"I've been in Lourenco Marques nearly twenty-four hours, and I feel as if I've been riding carousel horses, one by one. And they keep shouting at me, 'Rodrigo is a better rider, Rodrigo is a better rider!'"

He told her Kiarka's tale.

"It doesn't seem strange to me," Teresa said, in a low voice. "Tannhauser, after the Flying Dutchman. But always the same scenario. We are friends with Kiarka and go out together, but to tell you the truth, her chemistry and mine don't match all that well. I think she's afraid of me. Now, let's forget about Kiarka, and I don't want you to talk to me about Rodrigo either, Put your arm around my waist as we walk."

"In Rodrigo's stead."

"You're incorrigible!"

It was late, and the pension was dark.

"Fortunately, Madam Polana is frugal with her lighting, so we can go in without anyone seeing us. Anyway, everyone is asleep by this time," Alexis told Teresa.

They went slowly up the stairs, and to Alexis great surprise Fernando was still on his chair.

"Watchful guard!" Teresa said.

"Watchful ... in a manner of speaking. He's sleeping like a log. What can I do? Should I wake him up or let him sleep?"

"I think you should wake him up."

He let Teresa into his room and rested his hand gently on Fernando's shoulder so he wouldn't wake up suddenly, but he leapt up terrified, shaking like jelly and blurted out: "Fernando wait, my Lord, Great Master."

"Fernando, please, I want you to try and understand that in the evening you will go and sleep in a bed. Didn't Madam give you a room?"

"Fernando sleep good cadeira!"

"Fernando, go sleep bed, now, immediately, I order you!"

"Yes, my Lord, Great Master, Fernando go bed!"

He went downstairs silently and Alexis didn't know if he'd pleased or displeased him. He went into his room and closed the door. Teresa was sitting on the bed laughing.

"I heard that sparkling dialogue with Fernando. I saw him once at Rodrigo's. He's Samia's brother, isn't he?"

"Tell me, Teresa, what part does Samia play in Rogdrigo's life?"

"Ah! That is the greatest mystery about Rodrigo. The truth is, I don't know. But she must have a strong influence on him if, as Kiarka told you, she took the pistol from him, which doesn't mean he was going to kill himself."

"Don't you believe it either?"

"Are you joking? Rodrigo adores life; that's why he plays with it. He isn't playing with death; he's playing with life. He uses death like a wall to bounce his ball against. Deep down, he dreams of immortality, and every time he plays the death game, he's doing nothing but prove to himself that is he winning the game of life. But here we are talking about Rodrigo all over again, instead of you kissing me and us talking about ourselves."

"Who started it this time?"

"What does it matter? I want to make love with you. I assure you that I'm not caught up in the fantasies of the Flying Dutchman, and when you get down to it, the last scene of the play is already behind us. So let's say that we've been transformed, and let's see how lovemaking is in the world ... beyond. It may be the only place we can get away from Rodrigo! Where there is no link to the world we know. To be alone, aware of our isolation, to give ourselves absolutely to each other, without pre-conceived scenarios."

Alexis was swayed by Teresa's words. He pushed her gently down on the bed, lay next to her, and after undressing each other, their naked bodies came together into an ecstasy which could not be found in this world.

When they awoke, he told her: "You know I was terrified of you saying to me: 'I want a child by you!' Because then I would have been certain that you were continuing your affair with Rodrigo through me."

"You're not only crazy, but stupid! And I thought Greeks were smart."

"They used to be!"

He took her home before dawn to avoid gossip; at ten in the morning the group had an appointment at the Scala pastry shop for their expedition.

Teresa and Alexis (though they didn't get much sleep), Viriatou, Yvonne and Kiarka were all on time. Rodrigo was late. He always liked to make a theatrical entrance.

They all sat round a table inside the shop, trying to keep cool from the breeze of a wall fan. Outside, the heat and humidity were unbearable. The owner of Scala, Menelaos, came and sat down with them. A quiet, modest man, the antithesis of Costa the Cretan, who filled Costa del Sol with his presence, Menelaos treated them all to morning coffee. He was introduced to Alexis.

"Look here my friend, you're crazy to go off to Namaacha in such heat. Why don't you wait until afternoon?"

At that moment the undisputed head of the party, the organiser of the expedition and the possessor of the automobile, arrived. At the sight of Rodrigo, Teresa touched Alexis' arm and looked him tenderly in the eyes: out of female coquettishness? Female revenge?

Rodrigo's sharp eye caught the movement, but having an even quicker brain, he smiled to show he wasn't annoyed. He turned to Menelaos. "Good morning, Menelaos, I see you've met your compatriot. You Greeks, from the time of Homer, have conquered worlds and ... hearts."

The allusion was also undoubtedly a barbed comment.

It was already eleven by the time they set off – Rodrigo, Kiarka and Yvonne sitting in the front, Teresa, Alexis and Viriatou in the back of the car. Until that moment, Alexis hadn't realised that all the Wagnerian characters of the *Flying Dutchman* and *Tannhauser* were in the car. Senta, Venus, Elizabeth, Wolfram and, of course, the Flying Dutchman and Tannhauser in one figure, that of Rodrigo. Alexis was only a spectator. Or was he?

Was the composition of the group deliberate or by chance? A slight shiver ran through him at the idea that Rodrigo had again used him in some obscure game of his soul. But the African landscape was new, and as they drove along the dirt road through the tropical plantations, raising clouds of dust Alexis quickly forgot about all that and became absorbed in the beauty of surrounding nature.

Rodrigo, who was driving, at some point began to hum a song. Kiarka was the first to catch the melody and suddenly turned around and faced Alexis. The introduction to *Tannhauser*! The Wagnerian drama was continuing, there was no doubt about it. Teresa caught on and curled up next to Alexis. But Rodrigo appeared to be cheerful, carefree even, and every so often made jokes or recited a poem such as the following:

"I was born before the lion, before the lioness,
But the lion and the lioness are my parents.
I come from another cold, another heat,
But grow cold and hot with them."

"Maybe you're cold, but I just get hotter and hotter!" Viriatou interrupted. "Menelaos was right: we should have left either early in the morning or late in the afternoon."

Irritated, Rodrigo stopped reciting. Various animals, mainly monkeys, jumped from tree to tree, and their cries, together with the cries of the birds, made up the background music of the African jungle.

After two hours of driving, the jungle thinned out and now they were passing through an expanse of planted fields with an occasional cow. To the left, a village could just be made out in the distance, with low earth-coloured houses daubed with mud.

"We'll soon be in Namaacha," Rodrigo announced. "There is a stream near the village, and we'll cool off in the water."

When they reached the stream, and got out of the car, they saw stark naked black women washing their clothes and bathing. Teresa pinched Alexis' arm when she saw that his eye had come to rest contentedly on the most beautiful bosom he had ever seen. It belonged to a statuesque, jet black body.

"Call me perverse, if you like, but we Greeks are accustomed to admiring female beauty."

"We Portuguese are the same," Teresa answered, "but we do it in a more discreet manner!"

Rodrigo, who was listening to the exchange, broke in: "Teresa is right. We Portuguese live for beauty. I will tell you a true story that happened in Portugal. At a bullfight in Lisbon, a very good looking couple, a very handsome man and a very lovely woman, entered the official boxes. As soon as the crowd noticed them, they rose up from their seats and began to applaud them, for their beauty alone!"

Alexis began to clap his hands. "This is exactly what I am doing! I applaud the beauty of the black woman washing her hair, and even better, I applaud her breasts! You'd think they had a life of their own. Proud, joyful, provocative, optimistic!"

"I'll pinch you again!" Teresa told him.

"No problem! Punish me so I won't have to feel guilty!" Alexis answered.

"If black nakedness isn't shameful, then why should we whites be bashful about our bodies?" Rodrigo asked.

"So why don't we have a swim in this crystal clear water?"

Viriatou, the prim Wolfram, was embarrassed for a moment. Neither Kiarka – wasn't she the Venus after all? – nor Teresa, who was spiritually more liberated, gave it a second thought. Rodrigo, who understood the wavering Viriatou, said to him:

"Viriatou, nature was born like that woman who is enjoying the breeze, the water and the sun on her body, even the eyes of men."

Viriatou looked around for Yvonne, who could just be seen undressing behind a bush. He watched startled as she slipped discreetly into the water.

"Come on, Viriatou, it's like a baptism!" she called out to him.

All eyes turned to watch the angelic Yvonne, the only one they hadn't imagined would go naked. Was this a last try to attract Rodrigo with the fresh virginity of her body?

"The running river water quenches each and every desire," Rodrigo said, without the others understanding what he meant. He urged Viriatou to plunge into the river with everybody else, who were now wallowing in it.

Viriatou had no choice but to follow suit. They played for quite some time in the water, which ran over slippery rocks and formed small waterfalls between broad-leaved bushes and thick-leaved trees, while the black women watched them curiously, and giggled. They weren't used to seeing naked whites.

"It must have been something like this at Venusburg," Alexis whispered to Kiarka.

"Here, in the heart of nature, the environment is even more Dionysian. We didn't go around naked in our garden!"

Viriatou wasn't participating wholeheartedly and clearly appeared out of his depth. At the first opportunity he suggested they get dressed and go for a bite.

"In Namaacha, about a kilometre from here, I have a friend who has the only restaurant in the village and he makes the best 'piri-piri' chicken you've ever eaten," Rodrigo said.

"What's that?" Alexis asked.

"Chicken with peppers," Teresa explained.

Set on the riverbank, the small village of Namaacha, with a handful of one-storey whitewashed multi-coloured houses, contained only a few white inhabitants. The whites had plantations in the area, where they grew corn, sugar cane, cashews or copra. On the other bank was the small native village, with its round, straw huts, shaded by very tall trees.

The six of them went straight to Carlo's restaurant, whose owner embraced Rodrigo before he took the order for the 'piri-piri'!

"I was together with Carlos in the North," Rodrigo explained. "He was working in my father's plantation."

After quite a wait, Carlos returned holding a large pot out of which he served the chicken broth in plates. Small pieces of red pepper floated on the surface.

"It is very spicy, be careful! " Teresa warned Alexis. "Just take very little at the beginning. You too, Kiarka, if you've never tried it before."

Alexis and Kiarka looked at each other and made a show of each ceremoniously lifting a spoon of chicken broth to their mouths in unison, and then swallowing it. Kiarka turned bright red and her eyes blazed, but she was able to control herself. Alexis jumped up and began to run around the table asking for a bottle of lemon soda pop to put out the fire, while all the others roared with laughter.

"You Portuguese must have another kind of palate if you can laugh about it," he shouted at them.

When he sat down again, he began to fish out the bits of pepper one by one and sprinkle the chicken bits with the lemon drink to cool it off, before each mouthful.

Kiarka, more daring, managed slowly to come to terms with the 'piri-piri', tears streaming down her face.

"I didn't know that goddesses could weep!" Alexis said in Greek, so the others wouldn't understand.

"Goddesses weep for the sorry state of mankind!" Kiarka replied.

Carlos sat with them and announced that in the afternoon the native village was having an initiation rite for the young men, with dancing and singing.

After lunch, they walked for a while under the dense trees and then over a bridge to the native side of the river where the festival was being prepared.

They seemed to be the only visitors. As soon as they were seen, a tall, bare-chested black man, who must have been the chief, approached them and gave them to understand that they could sit next to him in front of his hut in order watch the festival.

Alexis' head whirled with images of cannibals with bows and arrows, cauldrons where they boiled whites, long poles on which they bound them hand and foot like sheep before roasting them over the fire. Here, no bows and arrows, only pleasant black people, men and women, without masks, without clothes, except for a white loin cloth, sitting peacefully in a circle on the ground. A large fire in the middle was more reminiscent of a boy-scout campfire than the African jungle.

The celebration was begun by three men who were sitting opposite the chief. Each one held a tom-tom between his knees. Rodrigo explained that with this rite, which he had experienced before in northern Mozambique, the young men were initiated into manhood. "It is the moment when they are separated from their mothers. The moment they become adolescents, and can even marry and carry on the race. The elders sitting around the Chief show by their presence, their respect for the order of things, that the old are a bridge between the ancestors and the young. They carry on the wisdom of the ancestors and are ready to pass it on to the young.

"The young men approach and stand silently around the fire. This silence is an obligation, as the spirits of the ancestors send them messages from everywhere in nature. Despite the fact that many have been converted to the Christian religion, they do not abandon their customs and in rites such as this, use protective idols that have magic powers," Rodrigo explained as the feast went on. "The mothers, in the circle, are the ones that hold the idols. Then the young men have their first test, wrestling. This is followed by running, jumping and finally a dialogue between the young men through tom-toms. The tom-toms are symbols of masculinity and only men use them to communicate and be heard, even far away. They are symbolic of power. The young men call out words that have ceremonial significance and the tom-toms reply to them. It is a symbolic dialogue fraught with meaning which weds the fantasy element with reality. It is the last rite, when instinct and reason are harmoniously reconciled.

I sow – boom boom, boom boom.
I sprout – boom boom, boom boom, boom boom.
I harvest – boom boom, boom boom, boom boom, boom boom.

I wait – boom boom, boom boom, boom boom.
I sow– boom boom, boom boom.

"In the intoxicating atmosphere created by the dance of the young men and the sound made by the taut hide of the tom-toms, the whole cycle of life, which does not cease with death, is recreated simply in a few words. The celebrations continue well into the night with a dance around the fire, and is completed by the final rite, the final liberation from the mother: a Dionysian orgy where the girls enter the dance and the newly formed couples go off in the woods for their first lovemaking as the tom-toms beat slowly through the night while the chief, the elders and the parents, the living and the dead, wait in silence and devotion, united and embraced by nature, concentrating on the lovemaking of their children, sending them positive vibrations."

Rodrigo, as if he felt a need to take part in the sacred rite again, began to recite in a whisper so as not to disturb the quiet.

"The spirits of our ancestors are near us.
Listen to the trees, the fire, the sea;
listen to the river weeping, the wind, the sighs of the dead.
Listen to your shadow, your image in the mirror,
the sun-split rock, the spasm of the moon.
Listen to nature rather than to people."

There were a few moments of silence and then Rodrigo continued:
My mother told me:
"Run behind the light of the sun and the moon
Warm your hands in the warm sand.
Cool your hands in the transparent sea.
Wash your hands in the blood of the lion.
Spread your hands on my face
and love your very self."

Alexis and Teresa looked at each other: was it only by chance that they were present at the African version of Wagnerian symbolism? Was Rodrigo just pretending he didn't know about the festival when Carlos mentioned it? And his poems? Had he prepared them beforehand? Or had the inspiration come now? Without saying a word to each other, they both had the same questions.

Kiarka and the others appeared not to have drawn any such parallels.

The tom-toms slowly slackened their pace and as soon as it was quiet, Rodrigo got up and then was followed by the others; they thanked the Chief and walked back in the darkness to their car. Carlos followed them to the car. Rodrigo went to open the door on the driver's side, paused, and gave the keys to Alexis. "You must drive."

"Must? Why must?" Alexis didn't understand. But it was all so strange that one more unanswered question made little difference.

This time Alexis took the wheel with Kiarka and Teresa in front, while Rodrigo, Yvonne and Viriatou sat in the back. Rodrigo had arranged it that way.

It must have been about an hour before midnight when they set off on the moon-drenched dirt road back to town.

Alexis was the first to make a comment. "The politeness, the dignity, of these primitive black people really made an impression on me."

"Politeness is not an attribute of skin colour,' didn't your Meandros say that? And much earlier, someone else, one of yours as well said: 'Zeus left Mount Olympus to take part in a festival of innocent blacks on the ocean. And all the gods followed,' Rodrigo answered. He waited for a few seconds to see if Alexis would know the lines, but as no-one spoke, he murmured with a modesty that contained a note of triumph: 'Homer!' Then, an endless source of surprise, he went on:

"*The colour of human beings is, like nature,*
white and black, like the day and the night.
African night.
Black, sweet, pure.
Rest, for you belong to the earth,
for you are the earth and the words of harmony.

* * * * * *

Oh! Classic beauty, cornerless, elegant, supple, courteous
Oh! Sweet curve, melodic form.
Oh! My verse, my black beauty, my black night – my nakedness."

"That is neither Homer's, nor ... mine," Rodrigo said laughing. "It is by the Senegalese, Senhor. What a great poem!"

Alexis had been driving for about an hour when he suddenly saw in front of the car a herd of large animals – he couldn't tell what they were – crossing the road. He was going about one hundred kilometres an hour and knew he couldn't avoid them. All he could do was slam on the brakes, and swerve right, toward an open field. His eyes just caught the eyes of a cow, gleaming with the reflection of the moon, before he smashed head on into it with a terrible thud. He hit three cows, hurling them right and left, before the car stopped at the edge of the carnage. The rest of the cows first paused inquiringly over their fallen companions, then crossed the road and disappeared on the other side into the field, accepting fate's consequences.

None of the passengers in the car had spoken, nor cried out, when they ran into the herd. They all got out of the car and noticed that the front end of the car had been completely wrecked by the collision.

Alexis stood motionless, full of remorse, not able to understand why he hadn't seen the cows sooner. Was it their colour, barely distinguishable from the earth, in the light of the moon which camouflaged them? "But no-one else in the car could have seen them either," he said to himself, "Otherwise they would have cried out." Teresa squeezed his arm, trying to comfort him, while Viriatou, having struck a match, then another, tried to see if all three cows were dead, moving the light of the match over the bodies.

Suddenly, he cried out: "The large cow is pregnant!" And a bit later: "Who closed her eyes?"

It was becoming a tragic-comic scene and the others, fortunately none of them injured, began to laugh, but only because the accident could have been much worse. All of them, that is, except for Alexis who didn't know what to say and Rodrigo, who stood like a block of marble in front of the cows, as if he wasn't present.

Finally, he spoke: "This Vacanal provided the solution."

Then, to comfort Alexis: "Don't worry, it had to happen. It was me who told you to drive the car. The final sacrifice, the solution! It was destined to happen."

And he began to sing the final notes of *Tannhauser*. In his paranoid mind, Rodrigo had conceived this riddle through a far-fetched pun, substituting the word 'vaca' (cow in Portuguese) for 'Bacha' and thereby coming up with 'Vacanal' instead of Bacchanal, the Dionysian, Bacchic orgy! From the Mountain of Venusburg to the Dionysian African festival and now, the final act, a sacrifice!

He would not have to die to receive divine forgiveness. Through the sacrifice of the sacred cattle, he had received a deferment on eternity. Everything is slowly falling into place, Alexis said to himself; but was Rodrigo responsible for these events? Did he invoke them through his fantasy?

He himself, as in the mishap on the ocean the day before, was living the end of the second Wagnerian scenario. Had he entered Rodrigo's skin for the final sacrifice? And how much was this solution his own responsibility? It was the second time he had identified with Rodrigo and he was filled with dread.

There was no way for them to get away from where they were, on this flat land in the middle of the African bush. It was highly unlikely that another car would pass at that hour. When they had recovered a bit, they turned to practical questions.

"What were the cows doing in the middle of nowhere?" Alexis asked.

"Wherever there are fields like this one, even in the middle of the jungle, the animals move about freely, which is why one has to be very careful – there are many accidents; I should have told you," Rodrigo said. "But it wasn't by chance that I didn't tell you. It's not your fault, one cannot distinguish a cow from the dirt road, by moonlight."

"I'm going to walk down the road to see if I can find a house – someplace where we can spend the night. Or at least to notify someone," Viriatou suggested.

"I'll come with you," Alexis said.

"I wouldn't do it if I were you," Rodrigo cried out, but they didn't listen to him and walked away in the direction of Lourenco Marques, past where the field ended and the bush grew dense again.

At first they saw no sign of life, not even a light. The only sounds were their own footsteps and the voices of indistinct animals, far enough away not to alarm them. But then they suddenly heard the roaring of lions that couldn't have been more than two or three hundred yards away.

"This is where the scouting party ends!' Viriatou said and Alexis agreed without the slightest objection.

It only took half as long to get back and Rodrigo was gentleman enough to say "I told you so!" They spent the night in the car, their heads on the girls' shoulders. Alexis on Teresa's shoulder and Viriatou on Yvonne's, while Rodrigo nestled in the arms of Venus! They were awoken now and then by the bites of huge mosquitoes and when it got light they caught the first morning bus, full of Africans on their way to work in the town.

"I feel as though a cycle in my life has come to a close: it started the moment I arrived in this town. I seem to be seeing the sun rise for the first time," Alexis said to Teresa who was sitting next to him on the bus. "It's as if a new cycle were beginning, a more peaceful cycle, without adventures, centred on you and me for the time being, without impediments."

"When we first met, you asked me: 'Who is Rodrigo?' Now you know."

"I only know that I was playing a role where someone else was the protagonist and I was the stand-in, the one who undertakes the risky ventures on his behalf. But from here on I plan to be a spectator. I'm afraid of Rodrigo. His contact with shamans and spirits, his thoughts which lead you into a maze in which he seems to revel. I am afraid of becoming involved in fetishes, becoming superstitious. I don't know if you've noticed, but I've started leaning against the straight-backed trees to aquire their vitality and their breath. I tread on pebbles which seem ugly and crooked to me to drive out their evil influence, in case any evil spirit is hidden in them – don't laugh! – and caress the pretty ones, so they will send me good vibrations, to get their blessing. Touching iron, I drive out all the negative energy from me – and just think, when I was small and my mother burned cloves to keep the evil eye away from me, I mocked her. When the burning clove cracked open, I told her that she was concentrating on her best friend, to confuse her! Am I beginning to go mad?"

"Let me tell you," Teresa said, "if you really feel that way you must have some predisposition towards madness. Three days in Lourenco Marques couldn't have possibly addled you! On the other hand maybe you like me because you're crazy!"

"The sick man's consolation. And if you love me after three days, you are crazy too!"

"Because you don't love me, you mean? Haven't you ever heard of love striking like lightning?"

"First I see the lightning which tells me to protect myself from the thunder."

"You're awful, but I don't care, because I know you do love me!"

"Say it, keep on saying it and I may be convinced," Alexis told her jokingly and they squeezed hands.

That evening, after all the emotion of the previous night, Alexis and Teresa decided to remain quietly at the pension and not meet up with the group. Fernando set a table for them and discreetly brought food for two from the restaurant under the interrogative eye of Madame Polana – he could never remember her real name. Teresa came up to the first floor by an exterior stairway, which led to the front veranda, so she wouldn't be seen, and only Fernando was a witness to their meeting.

"Fernando, tonight you cadeira. Look, how it comes in handy once in a while! Don't let anyone in – understand?"

"So, my Lord, Great Master, Fernando cadeira."

Teresa rolled about laughing.

Alexis locked the door and they sat down to eat before the balcony, facing the sea and the slowly darkening sky.

"It looks as though we'll be having another storm," Teresa said, "but luckily we won't be travelling this time!'

"Cheers! " Alexis said to her, emptying the last glass of wine.

"Cheers!" she replied, at the moment the first flash of lightning came, and it was as if it had flashed right before their eyes, as if they could touch it.

"Take care!" Teresa called out to him. "Now Eros will strike!"

The thunder that followed rattled the windows, even the glasses on the table, and was immediately followed by a downpour. A great cataclysm! It was the heaviest, most intense rain Alexis had ever seen. He stood at the balcony door, pulling Teresa next to him – and suddenly he had an idea. First he kissed her and then began to undress her.

"Eros has struck but Eros must be naked!"

Soon both of them were standing naked on the balcony in the black night, under black clouds, in front of the black ocean, as the wind lashed their bare bodies, which by now they knew intimately.

Teresa curled around him. "Now I'm afraid, and I'm cold."

Alexis took her to the small shower in the rear and opened the narrow window facing the ocean. They made love under the hot water of the shower as the terrible flashes of lightning tore over the sky and the thunder shook nature to its roots.

"I've never seen lightning so close and so intense, or heard such terrible thunder," Alexis almost shouted to be heard in the pandemonium of nature, as he held Teresa tightly. "With your hair wet, you look like a native!"

He was in the mood to shout, to embrace not only Teresa but all of nature and to become one with the sea, the clouds, with the lightning, with all that gave him energy, which through their lovemaking, he transmitted to the woman he was holding in his arms. Teresa had surrendered herself completely, like a frightened child, into his hands. Both of them were intoxicated, breathing in the wind till a sweet sensual thrill, like an electrical discharge, ran through their bodies in an eruption of absolute union, in the ecstasy of orgasm. "Don't be afraid!" he said to her at the final moment. "You must drive fear away to feel the total grandeur of love."

They stayed under the hot water of the shower for a long time.

"It could rain all night", Teresa said.

Soon they were dry, and between dry sheets, with the lights off; they lay in bed for a long time, silently, with their heads propped on the pillow watching the rain which didn't want to stop.

"Now that the rain is slackening off and the first rush of sexual desire is past, I'm beginning to feel afraid again," Alexis said to Teresa.

"What are you afraid of?"

"A boat wreck in a raging sea and a collision in the jungle all within three days – does that seem like nothing to you? Who or what has been directing my life since I first set foot here?"

They both knew the answer. Alexis continued with his thoughts. "However, I have never felt myself living so intensely and in so much harmony with my environment. Isn't that strange?"

"But you're afraid …"

"Wouldn't you be afraid, if you felt you were living the life of someone else, wearing his shoes? When Rodrigo talks he says things that I think I could have said myself. When he is melancholy, I think it is my own melancholy; and the women he loved, I love as well."

"The women?" Teresa shot back.

"A figure of speech … the woman!"

"Truth lies behind slips of the tongue. The women, you're right. Kiarka made an impression on you too. And I'm sure you wouldn't say no to Yvonne either!"

Alexis was actually thinking about Dalia, Donatelli's wife, but Teresa didn't know about her.

"It's as if you and Rodrigo had parallel lives and by chance your paths crossed on the beach one night, or rather it wasn't by chance. The same forces influence you both and if you stay in Lourenco Marques long enough, you'll live through other scenarios where Rodrigo will have the leading role. And what will be your part? It depends on how cleverly you defend yourself. I am a form of security for you, protection. For your own good I warn you, stick close to me, let me hold your hand."

"Now you are talking oddly as well and it makes me even more frightened. As if you know the next move and can't reveal it to me."

"No, I don't know the next move. But I feel that there will be a next move!"

"I know there will be one. Now I remember! The day I met Rodrigo at his office, when he told me he was seeking the ideal woman, the perfect love, which would also be the final one, these are the words he whispered: 'The Flying Dutchman and Senta, Tannhauser and

Elizabeth, Tristan and Isolde, Parsifal and Kundry!' Everything is slowly falling into place."

"Do you mean to say everything has been pre-arranged?"

"Perhaps not pre-arranged. Moreover, how can one predict the actions of the others? He is not playing the game by himself, but manoevres along the way and makes the necessary adjustments until life resembles his fantasies."

"I wonder who Isolde might be?" Teresa asked anxiously.

"You'd know better than I would. Tell me about Maga. She is the only woman in your group who hasn't become part of Rodrigo's charmed circle yet. You told me that she was going to marry the son of the Governor of Mozambique."

"That's true. She came from Lisbon the first time on the same boat Rodrigo was travelling on; he had gone back to Portugal a few months before to see his mother. Maga met the Governor's son while her father was still serving in Portugal. She came here to marry him."

Alexis' mind went to work immediately. He whispered to her: "Scene one: on the bridge of the ship which is taking the Princess of Ireland, Isolde, to the shores of Cornwall where she is to marry King Marke..."

"Now you're beginning to have fantasies. Couldn't it have been a simple coincidence?"

"Coincidence yes, but in Rodrigo's mind, if my hunch is correct, it becomes part of a fantasy – his not mine! What I can't understand is why Rodrigo and Maga haven't fallen in love yet."

"You talk as if you're sure it will happen ... how should I know? Maybe ... they didn't drink the love potion! Besides, Maga is the only one who snubs Rodrigo, even though she doesn't seem to be in any hurry to marry the Governor's son. To tell you the truth, I don't think she really loves him."

"Where is the Governor's son?"

"He's an officer in the Navy, like my father. He is based here, but right now he's on a training exercise in the Indian Ocean, going to Australia, New Zealand and the Pacific Islands for three months. The night I met Rodrigo at the Governor's mansion, Maga and her fiancé were there."

"I don't know if you agree with me, but I feel a tension between Maga and Rodrigo. When she was in the group the other evening, even when she was dancing with him, she seemed to be keeping him at a distance. Perhaps I sensed a coldness on her part that wasn't natural. You'll see, the sequel will come any time now. I somehow feel that Maga loves Rodrigo, even though she won't admit it."

"You're making up a scenario on someone else's behalf, now, when you're in bed with me and should be devoting yourself to me!"

They didn't say another word till dawn.

The days in Lourenco Marques went steadily by for Alexis, one dawn followed by the next. On most of them he awoke in Teresa's arms. The mornings and afternoons he spent writing in the garden of the Cafe Polana or swimming in the ocean.

Often Rodrigo would drop in to the coffee-house and they would talk for hours, without touching on the subject of women, which for some reason, despite their friendship, had become taboo. When day ended and night began, Alexis joined the group and every night was a party.

On the few days he was required to work at the shipping agency, he plucked up his courage to face his boss, the Indian, whom he had grown more fond of as time passed, despite all his eccentricities – perhaps because of them. One time when they were together on a boat that was loading tea plants and Alexis saw the skeletal blacks swarming like ants as they carried sacks on their shoulders, he asked: "How much are they paid for this work?"

Adi Munjab gave him a strange reply: "Does it bother you to see the bones under their black skin? If you were a yogi you would know that when you are able to see yourself as a skeleton you have overcome your profane human existence and have begun the road to salvation. When you can free yourself from flesh and blood, which are expendable and ephemeral, as Knud Rasmussen said, you are more than halfway to metempsychosis, and even more so, if you are a skeleton!"

This cynical outlook, festooned with theories from the East, at least had a dose of creative fantasy.

"If you can salve your conscience that way and think you don't have to feed them any more, good for you boss," Alexis told him.

"The dead live much longer than the living and since the Negroes believe that their spirits enter into all things on earth, those sacks they are carrying on their shoulders may even be full of stowaways spirits, who will make the trip to Europe, free of charge. You laugh, but both you and all the rest of the world are eternal and if you could reach psychic catharsis, the spiritual innocence that I have reached, you could see your former lives, one after the other."

"I always knew you were impudent, boss, but if it was the evolution from one life to the other that brought you here, that means you have a lot of sins to pay for! Furthermore, you would be in better harmony with those around you and not be so bored at being alive."

"Perhaps I'm bored because I'm in a hurry to get to my next life which I hope will at least be in a place with a better climate!"

"I pray that in the next life you go to Norway so that, if nothing else, you'll be able from your two lives to average at least one good one."

"You are not an ascetic like I am, able to set free your latent unconscious forces and find the real cosmic pleasures. You carouse with women, dancing every night – nothing is secret in Lourenco Marques – and mock things you don't understand!"

"The only thing I know is that you aren't an ascetic either."

"An ascetic in spirit, my good man. Now, get out of here. I don't need you any more."

Their meetings ended more or less in the same manner each time.

That particular day, Alexis thought he'd again call at Donatelli's office. He hadn't seen him since the first day in Lourenco Marques as he was caught up with another group and the apparent jealousy between Rodrigo and Donatelli made things more difficult.

In reality, he longed to see Donatelli's wife, whom he couldn't get out of his mind.

Dalia wasn't there, but Donatelli received him with typical Latin profuseness and a barrage of questions. "Hah! The beautiful girls of Lourenco Marques have made you forget your old friends. Nothing stays secret here."

"Same old story. Maybe gossip is the only meeting point for all the races who live in this town – Portuguese, Greeks, Italians, English and Indians. Only the poor Negroes glide like black, silent, discreet ghosts among us." Alexis spoke in a low voice.

"I'm pleased you came. Your friend Rodrigo was here and we have decided you will all join me on a crocodile hunt."

"What do you mean by all?"

"Your whole group of friends. I have a small truck that will hold us all and then some."

"Whose idea was it for all of us to go?" Alexis asked.

"My wife has been telling me for some time that Rodrigo wants to go on a crocodile hunt. I told you that she was a very close friend of ... the descendant of Vergil! Doesn't he call himself a poet? I just met him a while ago in the corridor, as he was leaving to go home. I asked him in for a coffee and whether he was still interested in the crocodile hunt?

"What did he say?"

"He accepted and suggested that he bring his whole group of friends along; I hope you're coming."

"I belong to the group, so, I suppose have no choice! Not that I am not delighted with the idea!"

"Marvellous! Work out the where and when with Rodrigo. You'll meet my wife too." Alexis didn't tell him of course that he'd already met her in Rodrigo's office. "We won't be away for long. We'll leave Friday morning and return Sunday evening. Bring blankets because we'll be sleeping outdoors."

Alexis was anxious to find Rodrigo and learn more about the project. Why had he accepted when he was trying to avoid Dalia? Unless he was still seeing her on the sly? He'd go to Rodrigo's house to get some answers. Strange!, he thought. All this time Rodrigo had never asked him to his house. Did this have anything to do with the presence of the black beauty, Fernando's sister?

He would risk being an intruder. Soon he was knocking on Rodrigo's door and almost fainted when the door was opened by a creature from a world he had no knowledge of, a figure that contained Africa entire, the grace of a palm tree, the eye of an antelope, the walk of a tiger, the skin of a banana leaf, wet from tropical rain. Her breasts, inside the light red skin-tight dress, were like burning suns, her hands like the caress of the wind.

He couldn't look her in the eye. He seldom felt the need to lower his eyes, but this time he focused on her elegant bare toes, as he asked the woman if Rodrigo was in. She didn't have to answer because at that moment Rodrigo appeared, having heard his knock on the door.

Alexis wasn't sure if Rodrigo was glad to see him or not, but he treated him courteously, as always. "What a surprise! What brought you here? You've never been in my house, come in. Have you met Samia, Fernando's sister?"

Samia made a small bow and stepped aside so Alexis could pass. My god, what a beautiful motion, Alexis thought. It seemed to him like he'd entered Rodrigo's hiding-place, as though he'd violated some unwritten law. Rodrigo seemed to take pride in Samia, just as he had with Dalia, and it was clear that, forgetting pretexts, he wanted to show off.

Rodrigo's home, like most 'fricato' houses in Lourenco Marques, was detached with two floors, a relatively large garden, the rooms perhaps a little extravagant for a bachelor. But was he a bachelor? What was Samia's role in the house?

The hall and living-room were furnished with Spanish furniture, Persian rugs and comfortable armchairs of real leather and, despite the warm climate of Lourenco Marques, the curtains were of heavy velvet, with raised floral patterns. It could very well have been the living room in a Spanish tower. The only picture was a large portrait of a woman, his mother, Rodrigo explained, when she was young. She was wearing a snow-white evening dress. The picture was set in a heavy gold frame. Alexis examined her carefully. She had a severe, imposing bearing; a powerful woman, without a doubt, just as Rodrigo had described her. In the living-room there was a desk also in Spanish style, and in the book case, between a jumble of books and records, a record player, a radio, some glasses, a bottle of gin, a bottle of whisky and a bottle of port.

It was eleven in the morning and, without asking, Samia brought in a tray with tomato juice. She drifted in and out like a nymph with a tender smile on her face, and Alexis' eyes followed her until she closed the living-room door, then turned to Rodrigo.

"I would really like you to show me the book you talked about: A Vision of Beautiful Woman. Since I believe all you do in life is transform real women of flesh and blood into the poems you recited to me when we first met. What's more, thanks to you, I now find myself surrounded by a bouquet of girls, each one more beautiful and interesting than the last!"

Rodrigo took the book out of a shelf and Alexis looked through it's pages. He stopped every so often to read but it was obvious that Rodrigo, as he had said himself, was writing the poems in the book to fulfil his own fantasies about women. Alexis put the book aside and without wanting to make any comment, asked:

"So, Donatelli tells me you've arranged for the whole group to go on a safari?"

"Yes, indeed, on Friday," Rodrigo answered.

"I thought you didn't particularly care for Donatelli ..."

"I must go," Rodrigo said in exactly the same way as he had spoken on their excursion to Namaacha when he said, "You must drive."

His tone of voice was also the same and did not allow for any opposition. "Why 'must'?" Rodrigo got up, went to the record player and put on a record. It was the first act of *Parsifal*. He then came back and sat in an armchair opposite Alexis, who suddenly felt that the whole atmosphere was becoming eerie.

Rodrigo spoke loudly so his voice could be heard clearly over the music which he had put on at nearly full volume. "Donatelli is a magician, an enemy of wild animals which are, like every living thing, whether trees or beast, the knights of nature, the knights of the Grail. Our rivers are the blood of Christ. All nature is Christ. Donatelli kills, injures. He kills the knights one by one with the spear that pierced Christ's side. He is worse than Klingsor. A voice tells me that I must go on the hunt."

As he spoke his gaze was lost in space and his eyes had a mad gleam in them.

Alexis vaguely remembered the libretto to *Parsifal* but it was difficult for him to follow Rodrigo's galloping fantasy and to combine the scenes of the Wagnerian opera with Rodrigo's delirium. The only thing that he could think of was that Tristan and Isolde had been put to one side and that Rodrigo, after being the Flying Dutchman and Tannhauser, had now become Parsifal, the innocent young knight who knows nothing of his history, who doesn't know that his mother died of heartbreak when he deserted her. "Here, in this tower of isolation are where the myths are re-moulded," Alexis shuddered. Then he took courage and suddenly asked Rodrigo: "So what is Dalia's role?"

Rodrigo, lost in his dream, had no difficulty in answering. "Dalia as Kundry, is in the service of evil, held by Klingsor's spell. She is a devil in the flesh! Whoever approaches her is lost. In African nature there is a balance between spirit and body – in man and in woman. The Grail is a female symbol. The spear a symbol of masculinity. These two are always united. Klingsor and Kundry have come to destroy the balance. And Parsifal succumbed when Kundry told him: 'Only the love of a woman can replace motherly love.'"

Rodrigo's words had a deep, serene resonance, the confession at last, of this drama which was repeated in each of his Wagnerian mythic creations. When Samia had opened the door to Alexis earlier, it was as if she had given him permission to enter Rodrigo's inaccessible unconscious, to visit the tower where magic forces moved the strings.

Alexis tried to think of how the libretto unfolded, to foresee the development he feared. Parsifal is the only one who can heal the King of the Knights, Amfortas, wounded by Klingsor with a 'sacred spear'. The Knights are the wild animals, Rodrigo had said. Who among them would be the King that Parsifal would heal? He wasn't in a position to give an answer, and he could swear that, at this stage, not even Rodrigo would have the answer. A voice had told Rodrigo to go on the safari. A voice like all the others that guided him, like the voice he had heard at the seaside weaving its magic. It was as if he had received an order from another world, that directed him, through his imagination. He shuddered at the idea that a simple crocodile hunt could have other, metaphysical possibilities and consequences.

"Who else is coming?" he asked, in the hope that the presence of ordinary mortals would act as a safety valve so that he wouldn't lose control of himself completely.

Rodrigo pronounced the names slowly, with a pause between each one, as if he were reciting a cast of characters. "Karl. Frederico. Viriatou. You. Me. Teresa. Kiarka. Yvonne. Maga. Donatelli. Dalia."

That is, the entire cast on stage. The Grand Finale! Alexis thought to himself. And not being able to stand any more of the Wagnerian musical intensity, which was becoming unbearable, he said goodbye to Rodrigo and left without seeing Samia again. He went to the sea, to cool his mind and to shake off the strange thoughts to which, involuntarily, he was led. The sea always cleared his mind – it was his solace.

When he met Teresa in the evening, they discussed his meeting with Rodrigo.

"Rodrigo is now playing his game openly," he told her. "We are in the first act of *Parsifal*, but something doesn't fit."

"What doesn't fit"

"The story of Tristan and Isolde hasn't reached a conclusion yet and he's already jumped to another drama."

"What if he simply can't carry it on because Maga, who you see as being Isolde, won't play his game?"

"No. Something tells me that Tristan hasn't said the last word yet. Don't forget, Parsifal did not fall in love with Kundry. He succumbed in the beginning, but then he resisted. The love that Kundry offers him is incomplete, false, inhuman. Rodrigo is searching and searching for the perfect love, which he will only come to when he is finally emancipated by the love of the woman he has not yet found. I think that the developments on the safari will be dramatic and I'm afraid of becoming, against my will, once more, one of the characters."

"Let's not go on the safari," Teresa said. They were walking along the seaside holding hands and the dark of the night frightened her even more.

"We must go," Alexis told her and was frightened when he realised that he had repeated Rodrigo's words.

"All the cast on stage, isn't that what you said?" Teresa asked him.

"Yes, that is what I said. You have played your part in the *Flying Dutchman* so you don't have anything to be afraid of. I can't imagine that he would re-use the characters that exhausted their roles. Perhaps he wants everyone present as part of a supreme endeavour of his imagination to cut the umbilical cord," He paused for a moment, then went on: "One thing is certain. As Parsifal he will come into conflict with Kundry, wanting to support the beasts of nature, the Knights of the Holy Grail, as he says. At that point, we will have to keep our wits about us!"

They walked for a long time until they reached the beach where Alexis had met Rodrigo for the first time. They lay down on the damp sand.

"I felt very lonely before I met you," Teresa told him. "My time with Rodrigo had left me desperately alone. Do you love me?"

"Love is not a way to save yourself from loneliness. Many times it makes you feel even more alone. You acquire an awareness of your loneliness by giving your whole self to the other person."

"Meaning what?"

"Meaning you can only find companionship within yourself and then your love is more correct, more balanced."

"You didn't say whether you loved me?"

"I love your presence. Isn't that a great thing?"

"Is it enough?"

"What does enough mean? When and what is enough? Aren't you happy at this moment? Without worrying that you will lose me? What could be more beautiful?"

"The truth is that for the first time I am living day by day, without thinking about the future. I wanted a child by Rodrigo, with you I only want the pleasure of the moment."

"What if we make love here, right this minute?"

And they made love right there, right that minute, as the flood tide surged against their feet and it was the water of the Indian ocean that they felt brought them together with the entire world, with India, New Guinea and Thailand.

The small, green Chevrolet truck was travelling north. Its wheels ran on two narrow cement strips which had been laid down through the jungle in the middle of the dirt road, muddy from the frequent tropical rains.

When they set off, Frederico was driving the truck, and Donatelli sat next to him giving him directions; next to Donatelli sat his wife Dalia, the only married woman in the group. In the back of the truck were Rodrigo, Maga, Alexis, Teresa, Karl, Viriatou, Yvonne, Kiarka and, to everyone's surprise, Samia, who had never been seen before leaving Rodrigo's house. Some were lying down, some sitting and others standing up.

They started out at daybreak, while it was cool, and they greeted each other like an excited high-spirited excursion party, except for Samia who maintained the low profile of her social standing but also the genuine discretion and modesty of her race.

They carried enough food for three days, as well as two of Donatelli's guns. They would spend the first night at Sao Martino de Bilene, Donatelli had explained, a salt-water lake framed by a wide, sandy beach with a dense forest of very high trees beyond. To reach it they would cross the Limpopo river and the next day they would go back to the river, higher up, to the land of the crocodiles.

It was a long way and all the men in the group shared the driving. There was no tension, everyone was relaxed, perhaps helped by the fact that Donatelli, Dalia and Rodrigo sat apart. When Rodrigo took the wheel, Donatelli and Dalia moved into the back of the truck so the others would take their seats in front.

When Dalia settled down in the back it made Alexis feel uncomfortable. Her eyes were so provocative that he kept losing track of the conversation he was having with the rest of the group. But not wanting her to see how flustered he was, he tried to appear indifferent to her.

They reached the river crossing early in the afternoon. They got out and while the truck was being put on, entered the ferry on foot. At that point the river was quite wide and the current was mixing the shallow waters with the sand on the bottom, turning the Limpopo into the colour of mud. Two hippos were swimming heedlessly against the current. Like all primitive ferries this one was attached to a cable stretching from bank to bank. Six Africans pulled on a rope, tied to the pier ahead.

"Do you remember the poem by Kipling about the Limpopo?" Karl said. "The one about the crocodile that pulled the elephant into the river by his proboscis?"

Rodrigo was the only one who knew the poem.

As they pulled the rope, the black men chanted. Alexis seemed to hear the names of the girls in the party among unintelligible words:

"Maga, Teresa ... Zgounda! Kiarka, Yvonne ... Zgounda!"

Alexis asked Donatelli if he was really hearing what he thought he was.

"You certainly are," he replied. "Their ears caught the names of the girls in the party as we were calling each other and now they are repeating them and adding lewd words. Zgounda means 'fuck' – and they believe no-one will understand! For the blacks, sex is the driving force from adolescence and on and they lose no opportunity to demonstrate it. The words they add now for example give them the strength to pull the rope. They age suddenly if they no longer experience sexual desire. From then on they adopt a passive role in life."

Why did he ask Donatelli and not Rodrigo or someone else? Maybe since he made the trip regularly when he went hunting? Or maybe in order to find the opportunity to approach Dalia? To his delight she entered the discussion.

"Sex is not the driving force for the blacks only!" she said coyly.

Kundry playing her role, Alexis thought. Ready to seduce the knights. So what if the knights of the Grail were wild animals, beasts or proud trees as Rodrigo said? Here nature is a blender for all things alive. But where did Rodrigo put mankind?

It was the first indication that the Grande Finale had begun, and one by one the members of the troupe were coming on the stage to play their parts, directed by the director's fantasy, holding the conductor's baton. Donatelli had organised the safari, but Rodrigo was manipulating the strings. He and the others were all simply puppets.

After they had crossed the river, they got back in the truck and drove for another two hours till they reached the salt water lake of Sao Martino do Bilene. They unloaded the blankets, as they would be sleeping out at night: the girls under the only hut near the beach, the men on the sand near the water. From here on nothing would be left to chance, and anything was possible.

It was no accident they were in this amphitheatrical setting. The light of the sun altered the colours of the set and later, as night fell, the moon shed its beams, slowly moving them from one corner of the stage to the other.

It was no accident that thousands of fireflies danced an enchanted ballet, urged on by that instinct that rules both fireflies and human beings.

It was no accident that thousands, millions of frogs around the lake had organised the greatest chorus that had ever been sung, from evening till daybreak, with unparalleled continuity, with the same repeated cries, as incessant as the tom-tom which drives men into the world of intoxication and mystery.

It was no accident that when they went to swim in the incredibly clear water, millions of micro-organisms played the game of nature with them at every turn, glowing in the water around them like spotlights lighting the protagonists, as if the stage had become an aquarium.

It was no accident that they were in a part of Africa where the ceremonial drama is an indivisible part of life, where the symbolism of the myth mixes the fantastic with the real in an abstract whole, which only the cosmic force of intuition can comprehend.

When later, around the campfire they had lit on the beach, Alexis decided to divulge these thoughts of his to the party in the hope it would change the course of stop the development of the drama he felt would follow, Rodrigo cut him short by changing the subject.

It was the prologue, the introduction to the last performance. The recitation of the myth when the audience is not obliged to separate truth from fantasy.

"The various levels of existence are united by the 'life force" Rodrigo began. "At the summit, the Supreme Being, at the base the infernal powers. On right and left, the super-physical beings, idols, spirits and the souls of ancestors. In the middle, human beings. At one with the plants, minerals and animals in his own magical world, in the heart of the universe, with the universe as his soul.

"Eternal, like the universe. Because although he is due to live in the heart of the universe only for a fraction of time, he will be on its circumference before, after, and forever. In the few years we live as flesh and bone, as we do now, we must close the circle of life. We set off from human non-existence, to be completed as a 'concept', only to return to the world of the spirits where, as people, we will be, once more, non-existent.

"In order to be complete as human beings, we have to suckle at the breast of our mother, men and women alike, without distinction, to mature separately; half as men, half as women, like the fruit on the trees. Seeking love, true love. Love without end; and when we find it to depart for the hyper-natural, where the senses endure for centuries, where it makes no difference to anyone if you are man or a woman. Because man has inside him the seed of woman and woman the seed of man and death is not a denial of life but a petition to immortality.

"Because only the continual quest for love drives from within us all negativity toward whatever is around us, on land, on sea or in the sky. And you know neither hate nor aversion.

"We are here, now, at this moment, all of us, in the middle of a ceremony, in the middle of a drama, like the day some of us were at the initiation ceremony of the young men of Namaacha, as part of a new initiation in the endeavour of mankind to find completion.

"In today's performance we are staging my own initiation. It is a performance which began when we first met which is why it does not begin like other performances at the beginning – nor will it end today; it will be continued tomorrow and maybe beyond tomorrow ... I really don't know.

"And I, as protagonist and director, have called you here, to be both actors and spectators of my own festival which is also your festival, because all people evolve together, hand in hand, and one blends into the other.

"Whether you understood or net, we have been living and are still living through a Wagnerian festival in the great theatre of the world.

"In the gallery, the first dress-circle, and in the pit are our consciousness, the stars, the trees, the birds and the spirits. On stage, the illusions of our existence; we, the human pawns, acting in the play, are directed by the spectators, our very own selves. Every so often we rebel and leave to play our own game. The words are incomprehensible to the spectator, our actions absurd and the prompter, who is concealed in each of us, comes to make a correction, to bring us back to the cosmic scenario, to the dialogue that doesn't require words, through sacrifice and punishment.

"Every work of art is a confession, Goethe once said. Here, before us, with African nature as our stage, here, where myths are born, without bound or barrier, I make my confession.

"With you Teresa, I lived the first and second acts of the *Flying Dutchman*. You are Senta, the woman who would break the curse, the woman who sent me wandering until at last I found my roots in this place, and you managed it. Because for the first time I felt as though I belonged somewhere, for the first time my panic over life had left me.

"Alexis replaced me in the third act and, sailing with Senta in the stormy seas of the Indian Ocean, changed the fate of the Flying Dutchman, before he rejected life. You, Kiarka, are Venus, the goddess of flesh, who introduced Tannhauser to carnal pleasure, but also gave him the strength to repudiate it for the more complete love of Elizabeth, for your love, Yvonne. The two of you, along with Viriatou, who is none other than Wolfram who loves you, taught me the meaning of forgiveness, just like Tannhauser when he made his pilgrimage to the Pope.

"But then a solution, a sacrifice was needed in order to avoid the death that would bring salvation to Tannhauser in his desire to remain a poet and a child. Again Alexis shouldered the burden of the last scene. He sacrificed three cows for me which, as you know, are sacred animals, taking sin upon himself Through the sacrifice, the Wagnerian drama changed course once more to save me. I am now free to go further and be the leading man in the great initiation of life.

"As of now, two Wagnerian operas are unfolding at the same time, but have not yet reached their conclusion. In one, Tristan plays the leading role, in the other, it is Parsifal. Isolde is between us and does not know that tonight she will love me. For it is ordained by fate, which does nothing more than take an old character and restore it generation after generation."

All eyes turned toward Maga. She was the only one of the single girls in the group he hadn't mentioned, as Samia was sitting some distance away, behind the party, near the forest.

"There is nothing difficult to fathom here. I travelled in the same boat with Maga, when she came to Mozambique to marry the Governor's son, just as Tristan travelled to Cornwall with Isolde who was to marry King Marke. Isolde hates Tristan, who killed her fiancé Morland. Maga hates me, Rodrigo, because she can never forget that I struck her best friend during a game, when we were children."

No one spoke, no one laughed, either at the words or the serious expression on Rodrigo's face. They all listened as if under a spell. It might have been the magic of the African night, but they listened to what Rodrigo was telling them as if it was the most natural thing in the world. Not even Maga reacted to his words. He went on.

"When she drinks the love potion that will be given her by Brenghene, the hate that she feels for me will disappear without her even knowing it and she will love me."

Only then did Frederico, the courteous Portuguese, get up to speak, angry for the first time, "But Isolde chose the death potion! What kind of game are you trying to play, Rodrigo?"

Rodrigo kept cool, as if he hadn't heard.

"Frederico, you are Kurneval, my faithful friend, the steadfast person who exists in every Wagnerian opera, the person who tries to help, to reconcile; and don't forget that the faithful Brenghene substituted a love potion for the death potion."

Rodrigo then took a bottle of dark liquid from a sack he had next to him. He held it out toward the fire with both hands. "Samia, come here," he called out.

Samia approached as everybody's eyes turned toward her. She kneeled in front of Rodrigo and awaited his orders.

"Take this bottle and give it to Maga. It was given to me by my friend the witch doctor of Beira."

Samia, whose every movement was a call to love, got up, went over to Maga and gave her the phial. Only then did Maga start to laugh, and it was hysterical laughter which echoed and mixed with the croaking of the frogs over the lake. When she stopped laughing she shouted: "I'll drink the love potion, just to show you, you conceited Lothario, that if there is one person on this earth who doesn't love you, it is me!" And she gulped down the entire bottle.

"Don't drink it Maga," Frederico shouted but it was too late.

It was clear to everyone that Maga was in love with Rodrigo. Despite her words, it was the first time that she had had fire in her eyes. In order to relieve the tension of the moment, Teresa said, "Aren't you going to tell us what parts Karl, Donatelli, Dalia and, of course, Alexis are going to play?"

"Shouldn't we wait for the results of the potion first?" Karl said teasingly.

"The potion will have its way, whatever happens. Fate doesn't change and nothing can be forced," Rodrigo answered.

He turned toward Donatelli. "Our story isn't over yet. You, Donatelli, are the magician Klingsor in 'Parsifal'. You lead astray the knights who protect the Holy Grail with the blood of Christ, the blood of Nature, which is continually renewed, and wound the helpless animals with the spear that wounded Christ."

Donattelli was sitting next to Alexis. He whispered to him: "I told you the very first time we met that his mind runs away with itself"

Rodrigo went on: "You, Dalia, are Kundry. The woman who laughed before Christ, on the way to the cross. As a beautiful woman created with all of nature's good things, you should be in her service, but you are a devil-woman in the service of Klingsor. You will repent when I have learned what forgiveness is, what compassion is."

"Now I know you are mad," Dalia shouted at him.

"Karl, my good friend, the smiling one, is also a figure like Frederico. He is Gurnemanz, the wise knight who gets his wisdom from the ancient myths of his homeland and who knows why I, Parsifal, came to the Palace of the Grail. Because as I told you, today and tomorrow the drama is being acted out on two sets. Today, in the palace of the Knights of the Grail, where we are at this very moment, with the gifts of nature all around us, and tomorrow, at the royal hunt of Tristan and Isolde. It's just that the characters in *Parsifal* and *Tristan and Isolde* do not have the same weight in both sets. The protagonists in one will be the supporting actors in the other, since our theatre, the magic theatre of the imagination, has no hierarchy. And then there is Alexis, who has no set part. But from the first moment I met him that night on the beach I felt that he was a kindred spirit, a man who understood me, the *deus ex machina* who finds, through his own imagination, the solution to my salvation, to the completion of my initiation."

"What about Samia?" Alexis asked.

Rodrigo paused briefly and then said: "Samia can play every part. Just a while ago, as Brenghene, she gave the potion to Maga. But Samia is also an innocent observer, who has within her all the sensitivity of the universe, who communicates through the eyes of the soul, without the distortion of speech. The instinct of nature in human form, containing all the important concepts of wisdom, love, forgiveness and compassion. Samia was born with these, she doesn't have to pass tests. She is without egotism, narcissism or ambition – even though she is the most beautiful of us all and the best."

"Ohhhh!" All the girls in the group cried in one voice.

"She is the 'presence' which is needed for the drama to be acted out. The continuity on the screen of the soul. Good night!" And he put the emphasis on the 'Good', then left. He went to find a spot on the beach to lie down without waiting for the applause, which didn't come.

"He outdid himself tonight," Kiarka said, after a brief moment of general embarrassment.

"For the first time he gave me the impression that he really does experience everything he says," Teresa added.

"I'll get my revenge for the crazy things he said about me," Dalia said in anger.

"That was the only time he may have been right," Donatelli said sarcastically, addressing himself to his wife, but Dalia's angry glance froze him on the spot.

Viriatou tried to take Rodrigo's side. "But can't you see that it's all a game? Why are you all taking him so seriously?" he cried.

"Even if he was serious, what harm has he done to us when you come down to it?" Karl added.

"He frightened me and I was lucky that our affair ended when it did," Yvonne said.

The only one who didn't say a word, but stared at the fire as if hypnotised, was Maga. It was as if she wasn't hearing what was going on around her.

Samia, as soon as Rodrigo left, got up and went over to lie down at the edge of the beach outside the hut, away from the white women.

Alexis remained silent and thoughtful. He got up. He said goodnight to everyone with a nod and then to Teresa separately, touching her on the shoulder; he took his blanket and went to lie beside an overturned boat next to the water.

One by one the others got up, the five women heading for the hut and the four men each choosing a place on the sand.

The fire had nearly gone out. The frog chorus went on. The moon and the stars, nearer than ever before and more intense as the night advanced, lit the dome of the stage.

Alexis, wrapped up in his blanket and lying on his side, couldn't sleep. With one hand he played with the sand trying to sift his thoughts through the grains which glistened in the moonlight, as he let them trickle slowly through his palms, trying to see into the future, to guess the outcome of Rodrigo's great game.

And then a female figure with black hair cascading over her shoulders came out of the hut and walked across the sand in the direction Rodrigo had taken. At first Alexis thought it was Samia, but when he looked closer he saw that the dark body, which appeared black in the moonlight, was not Samia's. It was not difficult to recognise Maga then. The love potion had worked. She had become Isolde. Even Alexis, who was closest to Rodrigo's imagination and soul, felt his mouth hanging open. What more is in store for us! he wondered.

He was trying to go to sleep when he thought he heard steps behind him on the sand and suddenly a female voice called out, not very loud, but near: "Alexis, look out! There's a snake behind you!"

He jumped up and just caught sight of a thick snake, about two metres long, moving off across the sand and slipping into the bushes. Dalia was standing in front of him with the moon lighting her face. She was wearing a long, transparent green dress which left no doubt as to the perfect lines of her body.

"I came to make love with you," she said straight-forwardly.

"Did you send the snake as a symbol?" Alexis replied, not to show his surprise.

"I saved your life. If I hadn't called out, you would have been bitten. And there is no antidote for a mamba bite!"

"And now you want your reward, or is it your revenge, as you warned earlier?"

"I wanted to make love to Rodrigo's soul brother," she said ironically.

"Why do you hate him so much?"

"Because he told me that making love with me was the best ever and then suddenly he rejected me with the excuse that the spirits advised him otherwise."

"That's what he says to all his women, but it's also the way it is, because each time he feels love more deeply. But I'm getting tired of being second in line! Always being wanted as a replacement for Rodrigo!"

"Don't you like me?"

"Listen Dalia, we've hardly exchanged a word except when we were introduced in Rodrigo's office and this morning as we crossed on the ferry. I won't hide it from you that under other conditions I would be very flattered. Even now I have to hold myself back to keep from lying down on the sand with you."

"So?"

She came within breathing distance of him.

"So? No! I don't like being used especially when it's to take revenge on someone else."

"Do you think that if I didn't like you too, I would have used this method of getting revenge?"

She put her hands on his shoulders. She had offered him an excuse which, however, reminded him of a phrase French women used to say to their ephemeral American lovers after France was liberated in the second world war; "I love you too, Johnny!"

But should he miss the chance for a magical night with such a woman who had given rise to so many fantasies? When she placed her lips on his, he at first gave in completely but when he realised that it was Kundry kissing him, he pushed her away in alarm and rejected the woman he hadn't chosen himself. He was a mature man and he mustn't betray Parsifal. He never thought of Donatelli for a moment.

He wanted to explain to Dalia, but she was already far away. She had left, deeply insulted and doubly dissatisfied. Dissatisfied in love, but even more so because she hadn't gained revenge. However, as Alexis watched her moving away from the stage on a lonely walk down the beach, he could distinguish the sounds of her weeping amid the voices of the frogs. Had Kundry repented? Had she again become faithful to the Knights of the Grail?

It was more psychological than physical factors that made Alexis sleep deeply and when the first rays of the sun awoke him he wasn't sure if Dalia had been a vision, a dream or real. He dived into the lake to recover his senses. As he was ducking his head in and out of the water, he again saw the silhouette of Dalia walking on the shore, but, this time lit by the first rays of the sun. The harsh countenance of the preceding night had disappeared and a glorious, laughing figure had been reborn with the sun, ready for the life this day would bring, and she looked like she was the day. He looked around for Karl, Viriatou and Frederico but didn't see him.

"If I was going to paint Night and Day," Alexis thought, "I would draw Dalia. Dalia yesterday, Dalia today. Is it tears that change the day into night and laughter, night into day?"

When Dalia drew even with Alexis she stopped. She made a friendly sign to him, looking around her. No-one had awoken yet. She took off her dress and, naked in the sun she entered the lake, as she would have entered the large stage at La Scala in Milan. The water was shallow and covered her only up to the waist. Alexis watched her, dazzled by her appearance. She walked over to him, splashing the water playfully with her hands.

"I came to ask your forgiveness. You were right. Sometimes love is an escape. Last night, Maga left the hut and went to find Rodrigo. My whole body rebelled. The man who leaves the whore – don't be startled by the word – for the virgin. However, a man, to become a man, must experience the whore. Immature, still uninitiated, he must make love without love, take without giving.

"The whore is the fire that slowly sets a man, cauterises all his imperfections and awakens him to the magical world of carnal pleasure. Because the whore consciously loves her body, her sex, and indicates this love to the man, who gradually loses his fear of woman and breaks loose of the maternal embrace.

"Then he seeks the virgin, the untouched, the unsullied, who will awake in him the feminine element, so he can find a balance with his tempestuous masculinity and become a human being aware of real love and beyond love, true pleasure. That void, which is like death at the moment of orgasm, when neither the man fears the woman nor the woman the man. Rodrigo did nothing more than live the cycle of love on a stage open to spectators! He said so!"

She splashed her body and face with salt water and the drops glistened on her like gold in the early sunlight. As she was at that moment, half in and half out of the water, she seemed to be an extension of the sea and the sun, a mermaid born of the sea and the sun.

"Why did you come to me naked? The provocation before the penance?"

"My penance is that I didn't succeed in making love with you last night. But as I was lying on the sand, Karl heard my sobs and came up to me. 'Wake up, Kundry, wake up!" he said.

'Stop crying and imitate the frogs and the animals in the forest' and he left with a smile as if he had come to tell me a joke. His words were so strange, they disconcerted me and I was startled. I stopped crying and began to croak like a frog: croak, croak, croak, croak, croak, croak till I broke out in nervous laughter and suddenly felt relieved."

Dalia approached him as she had done the previous evening, moved against him and kissed him just as she had a few hours before.

The taste of the salt on her sensual lips, her throbbing body and her pliant breasts, did not leave Alexis any room for choice and he was ready to make love on the illuminated stage of nature, with the curtain wide open, without taking into account that from one moment to the next Rodrigo or Donatelli or the entire group might appear. But this time, Dalia pulled away from him.

"Last night I wanted you out of revenge. Perhaps revenge was just a pretext to make love to you. But now, its too late. My tears on the beach cleansed my impure desires. But I want you to remember my kiss, as I will remember this moment of love with nature, which is perhaps the greatest pleasure. My final coquetry; on the stage of a theatre that has become a temple, the fate of man who hopes for happiness and who cannot find an answer without the help of a priest, an artist, a saviour."

"The mission of Parsifal who baptised Kundry in the name of God, has been completed," Alexis answered her simply; "and as you see I am part of the game – 'once more'" he added to himself.

Dalia swam out of the water, bent down and picked up her dress from the sand and put it on just as Rodrigo and Maga, hand in hand, returned from their hiding place.

As soon as Rodrigo saw that there were at least two spectators, one on the beach, one still in the water, he stopped and recited:

"The day, the day
the longed-for day
to my worst enemy, hatred and fire.
As you hold the torch
I will seize the light of day, to save those in love
from the harsh torture of the light.
Oh night, blessed night
holy, noble
night love
when you enfold us
when we are blessed
how will we awaken without being sad?

He kissed Maga who went to join the other women in the hut and then moved off, certain of the impact of his provocation on Alexis,

Dalia and on the women of the group who, he knew, must have heard his powerful voice through the woven branches of the hut's walls. Samia, under a blanket next to the hut, seemed or pretended to be, fast asleep. So were the men on the beach.

Dalia turned and looked at Alexis, who was still in the water.

"Change of scene. *Tristan and Isolde* Act Two, Part Three!" he called from afar, just loud enough that only she could hear.

Tristan and Isolde!, Parsifal! Two dramas being played at the same time, Rodrigo and Alexis, two lives that intersect. And the great game goes on Alexis said to himself, as he came out of the sea where the others were now coming down to splash water in their eyes, still heavy with sleep, in the high spirits of the morning coolness.

A swim in the sea and a snack on the beach was the last intermission before the finale. When they got back in the truck for the crocodile hunt on the Limpopo, the feeling that the curtain was about to rise for the last time was pervasive. Wasn't Rodrigo's recitatio from the royal hunt in *Tristan and Isolde?*

The girls knew that Maga and Dalia had been missing from the hut the whole night and it didn't take much imagination to realise that Maga had spent the night with Rodrigo. If they had the slightest doubt, Maga's radiant face erased it from their minds. They did have their doubts about Dalia. She could have gone to her husband but the different expression on her face made them think twice.

Only Teresa asked Alexis, as if by chance: "Did you see Dalia on the beach last night?'

"I did see a silhouette on the beach but ... I don't know if it was her." And they left it at that.

Around nine in the morning they parked close to the Limpopo. They left the truck in a clearing, among tall trees, and went along a path through the dense jungle that Donatelli knew. The path wasn't wide enough for two and they were strung out in a line, Donatelli holding his gun in front and all the rest behind, man and woman alternating, with Alexis next to last and Samia last.

When they reached the river, Donatelli motioned for them to sit down, some on a rock, others on the ground, while he went ahead with his gun to the riverbank. At this point the Limpopo was wide and the water slow-moving. The current was less powerful than at the ferry-crossing.

Seeing Klingsor with his spear lying in ambush for the crocodiles, Alexis didn't know if it was the royal hunt in *Tristan and Isolde* or *Kingdom of the Grail*, once more.

But from then on, everything unfolded with lightning-like rapidity.

An enormous crocodile, about two metres long, swam near the bank and was closing in on them. Donatelli took aim with his gun and waited. The crocodile, like a disdainful knight, drew closer and closer and when it was level with Donatelli and he was ready to pull the trigger, Rodrigo leapt up and was beside him in one jump; he made the sign of the Cross, which is the sign of life, to remove the magic of Klingsor from the face of the earth and grabbed at the gun from his hands. Donatelli was startled and resisted. The gun went off. Rodrigo staggered and slid into the muddy waters of the Limpopo right in front of the crocodile, who opened his jaws wide ready to devour him. But Klingsor's magic had been nullified. Donatelli, who was holding the gun in his hands, aimed at the open jaws of the crocodile at close range and fired twice, filling the water with blood and staining Rodrigo's white shirt, already wet in the mud.

The white women jumped up, the men in the group ran to pull Rodrigo out of the water, but he stopped them with a gesture. Samia, the only one who didn't seem terrified, got up calmly, took two or three steps to the bank and dived into the water on top of Rodrigo who was practically embracing the dead crocodile.

Rodrigo started to climb out of the water but Samia held him in her embrace. He was dripping wet and covered with blood from the crocodile, as he knelt in the water, with Samia supporting him, full of mud in his hair and on his face; he signalled for the others to be quiet and began to recite again:

"*She who can*
close my wound forever
is coming to heal.
Disperse people
as I run to her,
Isolde, Isolde!"

He turned to look at Samia. "You are the true Isolde. The Isolde who will sing as I close my eyes:

> "Noble, tender
> look at his smile
> look at his eyes – half-open –
> look at him
> can't you see him?
> More brilliant, more luminous
> born in the stars
> there on high.
> Don't you see him?
> How his heart
> proudly swells!
> Look at him, friends,
> you feel, but you don't see him.
> Can it be only I
> who hears this enchanting, glorious sound?"

"Well I'll be damned!" Frederico exclaimed, "he's using Isolde's words to talk about himself."

"The greatest egotist I've ever known," Viriatou added ingenuously – and said to Rodrigo almost in a mutter, "Madman, who are you addressing? May God protect you!"

Rodrigo wasn't able to continue the monologue. At that moment another crocodile approached. Alexis who was watching this tragicomic scene in horror, reached the river in two steps and quickly, almost violently, pulled Rodrigo from the water, shouting: "Enough of this stupidity, get out!"

Then with a second quick movement he pulled out Samia while Donatelli fired again and killed the second crocodile.

Rodrigo reacted, looking at the sky. "*The deus ex machina* alters fate again and brings Tristan and Isolde to life."

Alexis, angry now, told him: "If Donatelli hadn't been here to kill the crocodile, Isolde herself would have recited the final words and not you on her behalf!'

Rodrigo didn't even seem to listen. He turned again to the others. "Samia! The true Isolde! Ready to die for Tristan. You see, I made a mistake when I thought that Isolde had to be white. She was black! It couldn't be otherwise. Shaped from the dew on the leaves, from the caress of the breeze, from the rays of the sun and the moon, from the damp floor of the forest. Ready for the great sacrifice, the great love of mankind, which touched God."

Samia was standing next to him like a queen, with her head high, looking around without fear. Samia, playing only for a moment the part of Brenghene at the evening performance, had come on stage and had stolen the leading role.

Maga wanted to cry, but the tragi-comic tension of the scene seemed to deprive her of all reaction – as if it were the antidote for the love potion, a shock, that made her forget more quickly than anyone would have imagined.

The others in the group, caught between compassion and laughter, watched in a daze.

Only Alexis was seething with anger. Rodrigo had overdone it. He had been willing to risk his own life to get to the finale of the two Wagnerian dramas, *Parsifal* and *Tristan and Isolde*. He turned and spoke to Teresa who had understood him. "I'm certain that he deliberately used me once more. He was sure I would save her – didn't you hear? 'The deus ex machina!' But Donatelli, Klingsor himself, altered the finale of *Parsifal* killing two Knights of the Grail!"

"I was afraid Donatelli would find it convenient to leave Rodrigo to the crocodiles," Teresa replied.

"It was the actual repentance of Klingsor." Alexis was thinking of Kundry's morning repentance.

"What about the finale with Isolde? How could he know that Samia would jump in the water?"

"Consciously he didn't know it of course. He may have thought that Maga would become a victim. But in his unconscious, he knew, perhaps, that Samia would have the final word. But hadn't he already given Samia the great part in the evening by keeping her out of all the other roles, using her only to give the love potion to Maga? A master move. Maga begins the story, Samia finishes it. In his imagination he had no trouble in changing parts and actors on the spur of the moment, but they unfolded in line with events. Just as he used me for a stand-in. And maybe he found it convenient. In reality, Samia was perhaps the only woman who really attracted him. The woman who didn't cause him problems, who let his personality roam freely, without boundaries. Samia is the woman who nourishes, who protects, who gives rebirth through her silence, leaving the active forces to the man, to the Conqueror!

"At the beach in Lourenco Marques, a few days ago, I watched a small boy who was building castles in the sand and a little girl, she couldn't have been more than two, who, already conscious of her role as a woman, was quietly and without complaint carrying water for him, leaving the creation to the man, who was very proud, like Justinian in front of Agia Sophia. And if his eyes could have expressed his pride and his egotism he would have shouted: 'Solomon, I have defeated you!"

Oddly, Justinian's phrase kept coming back to him; he had quoted it to Rodrigo that first morning in Lourenco Marques, but every time he said it, it made him feel uncomfortable. Was it the guilt arising from provocation? As when sometimes, in a conversation, he would use the phrase: 'spitting image'.

"So you too believe that the character of the human race is male?" Teresa said to him. "You're nothing more than a misogynist, like all men, in terms of your incompetence. If you were sure about yourselves, if you weren't afraid of women, you wouldn't think that women are only passive."

"It's not only men's fault. When a woman loves herself, respects her existence and learns to say no, only then will she take fate into her own hands and find, even in lovemaking, her true role, which always begins with self-love. Tristan and Isolde is a sad tale of two people who never matured, who never believed that true love existed on this earth. Sacrifice, any sacrifice, is also a deplorable hypocrisy. The worst form of escape because we are unable to face ourselves. Remember how Rodrigo's eyes gleamed in his mud-spattered face in his vain endeavour to garner applause, even with a sacrifice. He upset us all, both he and Samia missed by a hair becoming crocodile food, but it doesn't matter to him. He played his part, and now he thinks he's won eternal forgiveness, that he's become a fulfilled human being, that he's become, a man."

He raised his voice: "Poor Tristan! What a parody! You made a complete cycle, I don't know how many women you've gone through, to return to the primitive woman, to the woman who functions by her instinct, to the woman without speech, but with the wisdom of creation, like 'mother'."

"It's the first time I've ever seen you so angry! But you and Rodrigo sail in tandem!"

"It's my rebellion, my outburst. I grew up, he didn't. For Rodrigo I am the *deus ex machina*. He himself didn't want to play his role to the very end. As for myself, I am the kind of person who does not accept destiny, who strives as hard as possible to carve out his own fate!'

Turning to the others, as if he had now taken things into his own hands he said with the momentum he'd acquired: "Ladies and gentlemen, the performance is over, it is time to go."

No-one objected, and they slowly went back to the truck, silent, without speaking, but also relieved that the royal hunt had ended, that the Palace of the Grail was far away.

Until then, Rodrigo had usually been the connecting link of the group but in the weeks that followed he rarely made an appearance and Alexis and the others didn't seek him out as before. Perhaps they had become wary of his own overbearing presence. Now they entered a period where they all tried to distance themselves from the events on the excursion. No-one talked about it. It was as though they had made a silent pact to erase the arresting images of the adventure from their memory and perhaps they were afraid to resuscitate, even for a while, the inexplicable forces that had moved them around.

There were a number of developments in the group. Karl had been sent to the north for a while where the company he worked for was involved in various projects. Donatelli and Dalia no longer appeared. Kiarka had returned to Johannesburg. Viriatou, Frederico, Yvonne, Maga, Teresa and Alexis met in the morning or the evenings at the sea or the Polana coffee-house, but seldom went out at night in a group.

Nearly every evening Teresa and Alexis took a long walk on the beach before they went to sleep either at Alexis' pension or Teresa's house, when her parents were away.

The reticent Viriatou, who had always had a tender spot for Yvonne had now declared himself. In a place like Lourenco Marques, where one needed to share the warmth of another, it was natural that the logic of preservation should prevail.

Maga, the Isolde for one night, whose role was taken away from her at dawn, was not inconsolable as one would have thought. Maga, that dark beauty, who was perhaps wiser than she appeared, had awoken in Frederico a feeling of protectiveness the day Rodrigo abandoned her. They saw each other quite often, but no-one knew what her feelings really were. Her fiancé was still away on exercises.

Alexis had seldom been alone with Maga. One morning however it was just the two of them in the coffee-house, as they waited for the others. Alexis tried to get her to open up. "Maga, we've been in the group for some time now, and it's strange but you and I have never spoken longer than the time it took us to dance a samba and then only to talk about whether we preferred the samba to the tango or how beautifully Rodrigo danced, so, of all the women in the group, you are to me the most enigmatic."

Maga looked at him with faintly sad eyes and said: "I spoke to you, but you didn't hear me."

Alexis didn't immediately understand what she meant and didn't answer.

"I always had the feeling that I was communicating with you. Don't be upset. I felt a kind of certainty in your presence. That I had a friend I could count on. I'm shy when it comes to words and I'm romantic too."

Alexis nerved himself and said: "Is it true that you're not in love with either your fiancé or Rodrigo?"

"I thought I was in love with Rodrigo, like all the girls, but perhaps my instincts pushed me into a fling with him, to clear up my feelings about my fiancé."

"Frederico is in love with you – you do realise that?"

"He's nice, very nice, tender and considerate but it's a little early yet. Everything is so confusing."

"Maga, I'm restless when it comes to love, like Rodrigo. Frederico is a good friend. Remember what he said to Rodrigo? 'Stable people make good companions.' Remember how our good friend reacted when Rodrigo said that Brenghene would give you the love potion? And how he tried to stop you from taking it?"

Maga didn't reply, but when Frederico arrived she kissed him on the cheek more warmly than ever before.

One morning, Fernando knocked on his door and along with the morning tea brought Alexis a letter. He was still in bed with Teresa next to him. He had no secrets from Fernando any longer. He opened the letter. It was from the Greek Consul in Lourenco Marques, notifying him that all Greeks abroad had to return to Greece as soon as possible, to report to the army.

Alexis' feelings were mixed. He knew that the Civil War was raging, but he almost felt relief. He asked himself why. He was getting along well, he had a woman next to him who suited him – why did he always feel that things were temporary? Did he really want to stay in Africa? As much as Africa enchanted him, he missed Europe. Had he perhaps been spoiled by 'culture'? Did he live in primitive Africa with that zest for the new, that nonetheless recognises that sooner or later the exploration always comes to an end? Was this simple piece of paper his own 'deus ex machina' which solved all his problems because there was nothing else he could accomplish? The letter was written in English. It appeared that the Consul didn't speak Greek. He showed it to Teresa.

Teresa had been under no illusion that they would spend their lives together but her eyes welled up. Still, she was a strong woman and Alexis knew she wouldn't make a scene. Perhaps he would suffer more, but he knew that distance would quickly cure him and that Teresa would remain a part of his soul for the rest of his life, like a beautiful dream, as with the other women he had known. They never disappeared. Each one took her place in his soul and they all lived together in harmony.

"We lived a dream, without dreaming ..." Teresa was already speaking in the past tense and it helped him make the decision that would once more change the entire course of his life. 'Mother Greece' had taken him by the hand. At that moment it suited him well, to think that he would once again be a soldier in the service of his country.

He left Teresa still in his room and went straight to the agency. He didn't have enough money to return by air and he liked the idea of going by boat.

The ships that the agency handled sailed usually out of Lourenco Marques along the coast, loading oranges in three or four South African ports, then into the Atlantic, unloading their cargo in a harbour in a Western European country. He would ask some captain to take him along, maybe even as a crewman, if they were looking for one, since he had been at sea. He told his idea to his boss who was sitting behind his desk in the lotus position, as usual. "My joy at being rid of you is so great that I will help you get on the next boat! It's arriving tomorrow and leaving in three days," he replied.

"Well, one of the reasons that I prefer to go and fight in the mountains of my homeland is so I won't have to look at your repulsive, ironic smile, thank the Lord, and listen to your cheap philosophy."

It was their only way of communicating, and perhaps the only way of having any contact, at all, which is why, maybe, neither of them ever had any problems with the other. They had found their 'modus vivendi' in offensiveness.

"I'll go to the captain of the ship in the harbour presently and ask him to sign you on as a cadet officer. I wouldn't trust you for anything higher."

Alexis knew the boat. It was an English ship, owned by the Union Castle Line, the *Roslin Castle*. She would be loading seven thousand tons of oranges for London and Rotterdam. It would take them about twenty days to reach London because the *Roslin Castle* would stop in South Africa: Durban, East London, Port Elizabeth and Capetown, then on to London, stopping only at Las Palmas in the Canary Islands for bunkering. Once in London, Alexis would think about getting to Greece.

Three days. Only three more days left in Lourenco Marques. Three days in Africa. Three days with Teresa. From that point on the countdown began. He had closed one more cycle in his life. The burst of joy you feel when you make a big decision, began to slowly dissipate and contrary processes came into play. He had had a wonderful time in this oasis. Despite all the adventures, despite all the absurd situations – perhaps, because of them. It was natural he felt sad. Moreover, he had come to Africa with the intention of spending a number of years there and overnight he had made an about face that would change his life, without much thought, by instinct alone, just like the natives.

He nursed these thoughts as his steps took him unconsciously to Rodrigo's house. He was going to tell him that he was leaving. It was not only a friendly act, it was an obligation. Yes, he felt it was an obligation.

As on the first time he visited Rodrigo, Samia opened the door. She was wearing the same red dress and her humility hadn't changed. Isolde had become Samia again, Rodrigo's slender shadow. She led him into the empty living-room and gave him something to drink until her master arrived. For the first time Alexis heard her voice. "Mr Alexis, have you come to say that you are leaving?"

He looked at her in surprise. "How did you know?"

"I saw it in your eyes."

Woman, the sorceress, who reads the soul. Perhaps Rodrigo was right. Not Teresa, not Kiarka, not Yvonne, not Maga! Rodrigo had chosen Samia.

"I want to thank you. You saved my life and Rodrigo's too," she added humbly.

"I didn't save your life, Samia. Donatelli saved you. But you, Isolde, were saved by Rodrigo. He was pulling the strings. I and the others were just puppets."

"Thank you, you saved our lives," Samia repeated, ignoring Alexis' words.

As soon as Rodrigo entered, Samia withdrew discreetly. She knew they wanted to be alone.

"Rodrigo, I came to tell you that I'm leaving. I've been called up by the Army."

There wasn't a lot of explaining needed with Rodrigo. Why? When? How? These were questions for ordinary people. Furthermore, Alexis had never known for sure whether Rodrigo had been influenced by their friendship as much as he had. One thing was certain, Rodrigo was the more egotistical of the two. He looked at Alexis calmly and Alexis thought, or wanted to think, that the faint surprise in his eyes was sadness. They stood opposite each other.

"We went through a lot together," Rodrigo told him.

"We lived parallel lives," Alexis replied.

"Parallel lives that met in infinity and now each of us will go his own way."

"We lived beyond life in the magical world of dreams."

"We also lived, beyond dreams, 'the life'."

"The women you loved, also loved me."

"The women we loved, we loved in our imaginations, not in our hearts."

"I broke the bonds of nature, you didn't."

"I was driven by magical powers, the spirits around me."

"You directed the Wagnerian myths, surrounded by zombies."

"If I hadn't had this creative imagination in me, then I would have followed my heart. I would have become a saint, like Wagner."

"For you I replaced the idols of Africa with the Greek gods who were born in the light of dawn."

"You made the sacrifices so that love could dawn."

"The greatest sacrifice is to reject women when you have nothing to give."

"You didn't believe in the apotheosis of love through death, in salvation."

"Not even you sought death, you sought innocence. And you found it in Samia."

"In the dawn of love! In Amaranthea!"

They embraced, shook each other's hands firmly and parted without another word. Rodrigo stayed in the living-room. Samia stood at the door. As Alexis left, she looked him in the eyes and then bent her head, while from inside the finale of *Tristan and Isolde* could be heard. The most magical music ever written. A cry, an outburst, an apotheosis of the senses.

Alexis and Teresa took their last walk on the Mirrador.

"I went to say goodbye to Tristan this morning," Alexis said.

"Why not Parsifal, Tannhauser or the Flying Dutchman?"

"Because he never managed to get a woman the way the Flying Dutchman or Tannhauser or Parsifal did. Nor did he go on to fulfil the myth because he always longed, after the sacrifice, to return to the world of the living, by himself, free. But as Tristan, at the final moment of the sacrifice, he did replace the woman with a doll, Samia. And it was not by chance that he played Parsifal and Tristan at the same time. The two heroes supplement each other. Parsifal eradicates the Kingdom of Magic so that Tristan can transform illusion into Nirvana, which, for him, is nothing more than the refuge of his childhood, refuge from the age-old fear of growing up. He is living a Nirvana at this moment. As I was leaving the house, the record-player was playing Isolde's last scene."

It was dusk. The monkeys were jumping from branch to branch among the upright and proud trees on the Mirrador. For a long time they watched the monkey mother on one branch holding a baby monkey in her embrace and stroking its head.

"You see, Teresa, even the monkeys who live freely among the branches have need of the same love, the same protection from the fear of emancipation."

They walked slowly to the end of the beach and lay down again on the wet sand. Night had fallen. Alexis rested his head on Teresa's belly which formed a hollow between the bone of her sternum and above the two hooks of her hips. His head felt comfortable, protected. One of his hands moved slowly up to her breasts and the other to her lower belly. After he had stroked her two breasts for a while they made love for the last time. They wouldn't be going to his room that night.

"I don't want to say goodbye to you in bed, I want to say goodbye to you in nature," Teresa told him, "and then let's go and dance all night and in the morning I'll take you to the boat."

In the early morning hours, they sat by themselves at a table in the Costa del Sol, after dancing all night, and Costa came to sit with them.

"I'm jealous you're going home ..." Costa said to Alexis.

"At this moment, Costa, my heart is split between two continents. As though I'm at the equator and I'm being pulled by the North Pole on one side and the South Pole on the other."

Don't forget to call my brother in Aghios Nikolaos, in Lassithi, and tell him that nostalgia is a great torment. Bon voyage and may the Saints protect you …"

It was already dawn when Alexis and Teresa started back to the Pensao Polana to collect his things. The boat would be leaving sometime in the morning as soon as loading finished.

"When I think of how far I've come, when I think of where the world ends for me, my mind will return to this corner, here at Costa's beach, as the final beacon on earth."

He expected that the parting with Fernando would be upsetting. He would be losing his master, his protector, the person he worshipped. Oddly enough, Fernando, like Samia had the same remote expression in his large eyes, as if they had known deep down, that parting was a ritual of life, like birth, love and death.

This outwardly emotionless last meeting gave Alexis the courage for the final farewell with Teresa, who was waiting for him at the entrance. He gave Fernando all the escudos he had left and kissed him on both cheeks. Fernando made his final bow: "Goodbye, my Lord, Great Master!"

He took his bags down to the street.

Madame Mendoza was standing in front of the cab with Teresa and for the first time there was a trace of humanity in her face, as she said goodbye.

At the ship's gangway stood Frederico, Viriatou, Maga, Yvonne and Karl, who had returned from the north. He knew that Rodrigo wouldn't be coming. They had said goodbye. Nor did he want to see him again.

Viriatou was holding a large package. He gave it to Alexis, telling him that it was a gift from the group. Alexis opened the cardboard box and began to read the titles: *Flying Dutchman*. There was no need to go on. The four works of Wagner that he had acted out with them, were inside the box. As well as a record of African music and a book of African poetry.

He felt like an explorer who had completed his mission. He looked around to see if perhaps Dalia or Donatelli would appear. He had not seen them since the safari. Didn't they know he was leaving? Impossible. Nothing stayed a secret in Lourenco Marques. However, neither Klingsor nor Kundry had come to see him off.

"No matter how many years go by, you will remain the best friends I've ever had even if we never see each other again," he told the group.

He kissed them one by one, beginning with Maga. "Isolde, erase Rodrigo from your mind. Frederico is your friend for life."

Alexis embraced Frederico. He'd always liked him, perhaps even more than the others.

Maga whispered in his ear: "Last night I broke off with my fiancé. Frederico doesn't know yet." Her smile showed that she had been liberated.

He turned to Yvonne. "Elizabeth, you have found your way. The magic has been dispelled. You helped too with your ... sacrifice." The smile was intended for Viriatou. He kissed both of them warmly on the cheeks.

"Karl, the blond Viking, who knows about the sea and storms, you take care of my Teresa!"

Karl squeezed his hand in assent.

Finally, he turned to Teresa: "Senta, it's time for you to become Teresa again."

He didn't kiss her. Nor did Teresa kiss him.

He climbed the gangway. A sailor took his luggage. At the top of the gangway his boss, the Indian, gave his last instructions to the captain, bored as usual. Alexis knew the captain from his last call to Lourenco Marques.

"Another lazy bum leaving Mozambique," Adi Munjab said to the captain.

"If I told you I'd miss you, it would be a lie!" Alexis replied and for the first time they shook hands before the 'boss' went down the gangway, being careful not to trip and fall.

Alexis went up to the bridge and stood waving at his friends on the wharf.

In a while, the cables were loosened and with eyes full of tears they said 'saudade' as the boat turned its prow toward the South.

They took on oranges in Durban, they took on oranges in East London, they took on oranges in Port Elizabeth, they took on oranges in Capetown, against the imposing background of Table Mountain, which divided the earth from the sky, like the edge of a knife.

After Capetown, they headed for the Atlantic rounding the Cape of Good Hope, the southernmost part on the earth that he would see on this remarkable trip.

Dawn broke at the the Cape. Alexis had awoken early. He sat in the stem and read the last words of Alan Patons book: *Cry the Beloved Country*.

"For it is the dawn that has come, as it has come for a thousand centuries, never failing. But when that dawn will come, of our emancipation, from the fear of bondage and the bondage of fear, why, that is a secret."

He closed the book and glued his eyes to the Cape of Hope, of Good Hope.

The weather was good and the days went by peacefully. Every so often Alexis assisted at the watch on the bridge and the rest of the time talked to the English officers and sailors on the ship or read the collection of poems his friends had given him.

For all of them it was a game to call every boat they passed on the radio, to learn its name, nationality and destination.

For all of them it was a game, when the flying fish landed on the deck and they went to collect them and throw them back in the sea or when they gazed for hours at the sails of the Portuguese men-of-war as the English call these fast swimming fish who travel like escort ships in a convoy right and left of the boats.

For all of them it was a game when they woke in the morning to see if the bird who had roosted on the peak of the mast before they pulled away from shore was still with them. They put out food for it on the bridge every day, and it would come down, eat it and go back to its perch.

And they waited anxiously to see what kind of soup the cook made in the evening so they could criticise it, the captain shouting that there was too little salt or too much, but never the right dose ... that too was a way of passing the time.

There was one passenger on board who was going to England. He was a retired English Captain returning to his homeland. What little they saw of him was mainly during the morning hours when he was sober. From midday on he locked himself in his cabin with two bottles of whisky and did not reappear till the following morning to gather round him all the members of the crew who were not on duty and tell them some jokes and some great truths about life before disappearing into his cabin again.

"Tom," he was saying that morning, "bought a new boomerang, and spent the rest of his life trying to get rid of the old one."

They all laughed at the idea of Tom trying to throw the boomerang away and how it was ever faithful, and always came back. Alexis laughed too but his thoughts were with Rodrigo.

"What is life but a boomerang? You try to get away from yourself? You make a circle, and always return to the same spot. To non-existence, before birth, to the mother's womb, the womb of the universe ..."

As they approached the equator the weather became hotter and it was difficult to sleep at night. It was almost impossible to sit in the sun or in the cabin. On the bridge and in the officer's mess sweat ran like a river despite the fans that were whirring in every corner.

Eight days after leaving Capetown they crossed the Equator. Everyone who has ever crossed the equator on a boat, knows about the tradition that when you cross the imaginary line that cuts the orange of the earth in two, there is always a costume party with a baptism in a pool. Since the *Roslin Castle* didn't have a pool, a hose did the job. Officers and seamen put on make-up and when the captain blew the whistle as they passed the line of the Equator they turned on the ship's hose and began to spray each other. They felt such pleasure in the sea water smacking into their sweaty bodies that they began to shout as wild as children.

As they leapt around like Africans on the canvas hatch covers over the holds full of oranges, Alexis' thoughts turned again to Rodrigo and the African festival at Namaacha. That was the initiation, he said to himself. Now, the catharsis. Isn't this the innocence that Rodrigo was looking for? For Alexis the crossing of the Equator, the Baptism, was the final deliverance from being bound to his alter ego, Rodrigo. But would it be?

They only stayed in Las Palmas for two or three hours to take on fuel. On the wharf were dozens of dolls in colourful Spanish dresses, about one metre high, standing on their legs ready to be sold like slaves. "Blondes, brunettes, redheads, serious, laughing, romantic, lively, for all tastes. Only one hundred pesetas for any one you choose!", the seller called out.

Alexis went down to the wharf and examined them one by one. Later he walked around to loosen up a bit after the long trip, and on his return, bought the doll in the red dress he had had his eye on from the beginning, to give to his little sister. The blondest, the most romantic, the most ethereal one. Even though 'she' wasn't black, when she blinked her eyelashes her eyes reminded him of Samia. He paid the one hundred pesetas and took her by the hand to walk the few steps up the ship's gangway.

And as he was climbing the gangway, he remembered a poem by the African poet, Ralemenanhaca:

"No hand, none
will ever be able
to undo the bond
or sever the eternity of magic."

He amended the lines:

"Of all the hands that may hold me,
none will ever be able to take from me
the magic of imagination."

He took the doll to his room, put her on the upper berth, laid her on the pillow and as she closed her eyes she said, "Mama!"

Alexis jumped back. But then he smiled and, without undressing, also lay down on the bottom bed, lifted his right hand and hooked his fingers through the holes of the wire mesh under the upper berth. Thus, hooked as he was, he turned his head toward the bulkhead of the cabin and, closing his eyes, saw the image of the young Hamlet, on a deserted beach, his first night in Lourenco Marques, reciting: "Freedom ... is born from the withdrawal of the soul ... which remains suspended in the stupor of withdrawal."

"But dream is also born in withdrawal," Alexis added.

He fell asleep with a feeling of sweet remembrance.

PART THREE

THE NAME OF WOMAN

Alexis has just been discharged from the Army. One of the milestones in a man's life. For three years, everything in his life had been cut and dry. He had learned how to take orders and give orders – but there had always been someone above him who was in charge. Now he was starting from scratch. New questions, new quests. He got his discharge papers and bade farewell to his fellow officers.

"I'll drop by to say hello, now and then."

"Everybody says that but we never see them again!"

He would be no exception.

He went home, took off his uniform, folded and hung it carefully in the closet. Without it he felt naked – to the bone. He was standing in front of the mirror naked, still holding his hat in his right hand. He put it on and saluted his naked self for the last time. He set the cap on the closet shelf, with the royal insignia facing outward, and looked in the mirror again. "So now what? Who are you?" For a moment he felt a sense of panic. So many problems were solved by wearing a uniform! He tried to convince himself that the clothes don't make the man, but still …

The end of January. He was pale and thin, which didn't do much for the dynamic image he would have liked to convey. He tried to give himself a dressing down: "You fool, be grateful that you belong to yourself again. What do you mean 'who are you?' You are what you are, no matter what clothes you wear. You are the same person you were when you were released from prison during the Occupation, the same as when you were leaving Alexandria, the same as when you were called back into the Army, from Africa. Each experience should have made you stronger. It should have! But I feel like the youth whose mother said to him: "My child, if you're ever in a bad mood, lift your head high and shout out: 'I'm in a bad mood!'" The mirror, returned a smile.

He didn't go out that evening. Instead he looked through his old photographs from Egypt. In one he was sitting on a camel near the pyramids and Ellen was holding the reins, in another he was rowing on the Nile. As he looked through them he came upon a faded photograph taken on the bridge of a freighter on which he had embarked years before. He stared at it for a long time. He took it out of the pile, set it on his dresser and put the others back in the drawer. One day he would arrange them in an album. It was the fate of photographs to be stuffed in drawers, just like memories. You took them out only when they were useful to you.

As he fell asleep he wondered why he had selected that one photograph in particular. One often does things seemingly for no apparent reason, but there is always some sense to it.

Next morning, he got up without too much thought and took the train to Piraeus. He went straight to the offices of the company that owned the freighter in the photograph. His unconscious mind had been at work in the nightly cogitations of his soul.

He was received warmly at the offices, congratulated on his discharge by all those present and then asked, "What are you going to do now?"

"That's what I'd like to know too. Don't you have a boat for me just until I can get straightened out? But not for too long, one or two trips, till I get used to being a civilian again."

"Anything for Alexis! He held the fate of Greece in his hands for so many years! We owe him our very existence. We'll man a ship for him immediately ... is there any place in particular you'd like to go?"

"Cut the comedy. If you have a job, give it to me – if not I'll look somewhere else."

"They're right when they say soldiers don't have any sense of humour." Then somewhat sarcastically: "We have something that ... we think you will really like, it suits your style. A three week trip to places you've never been to. There's also a little adventure in it."

"I don't want adventure. I've had enough. I want to get used to being a civilian – you hear me, a civilian! I only need the job for a transitional period, till I join University."

"What would you say to going to Russia?"

Alexis' eyes lit up.

"You see? And you said you didn't feel like adventure. People don't change, my friend."

Odd, he had thought the same thing in front of the mirror the previous evening.

"Where in Russia, if it's not confidential?" he asked with the suspiciousness of the soldier, who is still way deep inside himself.

"We have a new passenger ship, the *Semiramis*. In a few days she's leaving for Odessa to pick up 300 Spanish prisoners of war from the Compania Azure, the Blue Berets, who fought with Hitler against the Russians. They're letting them go after eleven years of captivity."

"I've never even heard of the Compania Azure – but if they fought on Hitler's side, it serves them right!"

"That's not our problem. The ship has been chartered by the French Red Cross who carried out the negotiations for their release. If you want to go along as a third officer, you'll be doing us a favour, because we've been looking for one. Hopefully you haven't forgotten all about seamanship from your trips on the freighter. Later, you can go to University and become a bookworm. You'll pick up the POWs in Odessa and take them to Barcelona. If you're not ... held up in Russia, you should be back in about twenty days or so."

"You talk as if I've already accepted."

"We know you. You wouldn't let such an opportunity slip by."

Very few people had sailed to Russia since the war. The great bear still hadn't opened the doors. Communism! He was as frightened by the word as children are by the bogeyman. And now, he was being given the chance to see the homeland of this terrifying new religion.

Over the years, his mind had become more open. He was aware that there were other worlds, other religions, and he couldn't see why his world had to be the right one, the only one, at all costs. Up till then he had done his duty and he saw duty as whatever his parents, his school and his church asked him to do, along with the moral code that he had made up for himself down through the years. But he didn't reject anything out of hand and he had learned to accept any creed even if he didn't agree with it, or understand it.

When he made the decision to sail with the *Semiramis* he felt relieved. Now he had a purpose. Till that moment he had never had any long-range goals in his life. "Play it by ear", he'd said. Whatever God sent. See and do. He wanted to let his instincts work and come up with results, served on a tray. Consciously, he was leaving decisions to his unconscious! In order to make a decision," he'd always say "you have to have the information that you don't have or that you don't know you have. But your unconscious has it. So let it handle things. One less problem."

After he left the shipping office, he walked around the wharves for a while looking at the few boats in the harbour and thinking how odd it was that he should have taken the picture on the freighter out of the drawer the day before. It couldn't have been by chance. He had had several such experiences in his life and they had both given him heart and frightened him. Did he have powers he wasn't aware of? One Sunday morning, a while back, he had gone to the flea market with his girlfriend. They had stopped at a cart full of hundreds of photographs and old postcards, some written or stamped with postmarks, others blank, perhaps out of the sale of items from a house, full of memories, ending up as junk. He was seized by melancholy as he looked at all those old photographs – ladies in long dresses drinking tea in a drawing room and smiling at the lens, families arranged in classic poses, with the moustachioed grandfather in the middle, men and women on the beach in old-fashioned one-piece swimming suits. Entire generations who had been photographed, had written, mailed, read ...

He imagined an old woman in an attic, her only company the photos of her life which, when she died, would lose their meaning. He stretched out his hand to pick up a photograph lying face down with nothing written on the back. He turned it over, looked at it and said to his girlfriend: "Look at this, there are even pictures of kids in Carnival costumes here."

It was a picture of a girl during some Costume Ball in the past.

"That's me!", the girl gasped in surprise. "I was fifteen years old. But it's impossible! How can that photograph be here? Out of all these thousands how could you just happen to pick up one of me?"

"But are you sure it's you?"

"Don't you think I know myself? Don't you recognise me?"

"Yes, I do, but it seems so unbelievable. What's this photo doing on a push-cart in the flea market?"

"That's what I wonder. Maybe from my old nanny from when I was a child. How should I know?"

"What if I told you that just a moment ago I got this image in my mind of an old woman in an attic, whose friends sold off everything, even her pictures – would you believe me?"

"I might believe you but it would frighten me."

"Nothing happens by chance," he told himself again.

Telepathy? Prophecy? Vision? He had no explanation but he would never believe it was coincidence.

Certain now that he had a sixth sense, that he was a veritable Moses, that he … received 'commandments', his mind returned to the trip to Russia. Two photographs in the period of a few days had revealed unknown forces to him – he didn't know if they were his own or coming from beyond. But what difference did it make? "If I have to go to Russia then there must be some reason for it. But what could be the reason? Should I think about it or wait for a sign?" The sign wasn't slow in arriving.

After the war no-one had truly got to know or to describe Russia. Would they let him move around freely? Of course not, indeed they might not even let him off the ship at all. But he would be travelling for days with three hundred prisoners who had lived in Russia for eleven years. What a source of information!

Maybe this was the reason for his trip. To bring back first-hand accounts from Russia. He thought it over. OK, in any case, when the prisoners-of-war arrived in Spain they would give interviews to journalists from all over the world who he imagined would have gathered there to meet them. Who cared? He would get the information first hand. The next morning he presented himself at the offices of *Ta Viima*. He explained what he had in mind and the editor seemed to be excited at having an 'on-the-spot' reporter.

March 17, 1953. He sailed out of Piraeus on the *Semiramis* with a double mission: as an officer on the bridge of the ship, he would help sail the ship through the Dardanelles and the Black Sea to Odessa, and as a reporter – he preferred that word to journalist – he would be going to conquer Russia, something that neither Napoleon nor Hitler had been able to do!

Alexis had known the commander of the *Semiramis*, Captain Gerasimos, since he was a child. The first mate, Captain Yiannis, he met for the first time. The same applied for the doctor, Costas. Alexis was a few years older, but they hit it off right away. Costas was a radiologist. He himself said that he didn't have a clue about medicine ("I'm just a photographer") and he went on sea voyages every so often for a change of air. He could only make two diagnoses: to send them to bed with Dramamine at the first roll of the boat and to say to the women: "You need fresh air, come up on deck at midnight for a consultation!" He was married to a central American girl who spoke only English and Spanish. He knew only Greek and French and neither of them made any attempt to learn the other's language. "It's better this way," he'd say, "we never quarrel." He was always laughing – one of those fortunate people who never take anything seriously.

Besides the crew, two representatives of the French Red Cross were also on board: a man of around fifty, and a nurse of around thirty-five who had no distinguishing characteristics except for her heavy eyeliner, rouged cheeks and her strong French perfume. They would be receiving the prisoners-of-war on behalf of the Spanish government, as Spain did not have diplomatic relations with Russia.

On the very first night they ran into heavy seas. It was Alexis' watch and they were sailing among the islands. The captain didn't sleep a wink and stood next to him on the bridge. "They don't have too much confidence in me," Alexis thought, "and they're not wrong either!" He got the lighthouses confused a couple of times and was forced to look at the map again and again – without of course offering any explanation.

They would have reached the Dardanelles by afternoon if things had gone well. But with the storm they made very little headway and it grew dark again. The sea calmed as they entered the straits and the further they went the calmer it got. The mate, a tall, gaunt fellow with an ascerbic wit, was now on duty on the bridge and Alexis kept him company more to listen to his stories than anything else.

Approaching Canakkale, they saw two ships moored in the sea lane and it seemed to Alexis that they could gain time if the *Semiramis* went between them.

"Why are you going around them, Captain Yiannis?" he asked.

"We wouldn't fit," was his curt reply.

As he looked at the dark night and saw only the mooring lights of the ships without being able to make out their silhouettes clearly, he asked again: "How can you tell that we wouldn't fit?"

"If your shoes hurt you, can't you tell?" snapped the Captain.

Alexis went to the corner of the bridge, sorry he had opened his mouth.

"Anyway, when you're at sea you should always keep in mind the old proverb: 'He who takes care of his clothes, will always have something to wear'" the mate shouted at him.

"You have a distinctly sartorial sense of humour, Captain Yiannis. First you talk about shoes and now it's clothes," he ventured, trying to put things back on an even keel.

After that, a tangle of images began to flow into his mind: Canakkale, nearby Troy, the Trojan Horse, the Dardanelles, the Naval Battle of the Elli in the war against the Turks 1912–13, the Battleship *Averof* and the remains of the Patriarch Gregory V which had been placed somewhere along the coast, or so he had been taught in school.

He had gone to Turkey, to Constantinople, for the first time when he was four years old, before he started to read history, and when he saw with innocent eyes. Since then, he had learned about the 1922 Smyrna Disaster, and the slaughter, fire and rape in the fall of Constantinople. The minarets, the fezzes, the domes of Topkapi had a bloody history and they aroused bitter feelings in him.

"Why can't we separate images and emotions? Why can't eyes and thought decipher things without the interference of the unconscious? And why all these thoughts right now?", he asked himself. Perhaps it was the peacefulness of the sea, perhaps the twinkling lights of Canakkale and the stars, perhaps the motionless outlines of the mountain peaks and the soft colours of the night that gave rise to such peace that it was impossible for anyone to think like a Greek or like a Turk. Greek or Turk – involuntarily he had again made the separation. The lights of a coastal town at night, and their reflections as you approached them by boat, had always been an enticing image for Alexis, as if the earth were sending vibrations out to the sea, and he was the receiver. He pulled himself up short. "My mind is really churning tonight," he thought, "one would suppose that I was being employed to do some work around here."

He looked right and left with a serious expression to see what was going on and realised that the Skipper had also come up to the bridge and had brought the engines first to 'slow', then to 'stop', while he waited for the Turkish authorities to give them the green light to pass through the Dardanelles. But his thoughts were soon derailed again as the lights of the caiques carrying the Turkish police and customs appeared in the distance.

The Turks are coming! He ran to the gangway to look at them from up close. He was expecting to see faces with huge, curved moustaches, flashing eyes and angry voices. Instead, when their caique pulled alongside, he saw two laughing Turks with small moustaches, in well-pressed uniforms; they seemed affable and courteous, signed the ship's papers, thanked the Purser for the traditional gift of two packs of cigarettes and left nodding away like old friends.

"See how right I was," he thought. "Neither people, nor domes should be given historical connotations." From the domes of Topkapi his mind flipped to the domes of the Kremlin. "I am sure that the Russians will be less 'Red' than they appear to be." For him, Red was something negative. He had even connected the colour itself with an ideology and had excluded it from any place in his surroundings. He liked blue – the colour of his flag, the sea and the sky. Then came green – vegetation, the meadows and forests, and that brought an end to his chromatic ranking. "But then the day departs in a red sunset," he said contradicting himself, as he often did, trying to be objective and counterbalance his impulsiveness.

He was again on the bridge. From twelve on, it was his watch and the ship had set off slowly to traverse the Dardanelles. This required particular care, with so many ships coming downstream assisted by the powerful current from the Propontis towards the Aegean. You had to navigate and at the same time keep an eye peeled for other ships. Green with green, red with red, he knew the theory, his mind had settled on the domes of Topkapi and the Kremlin, trying to isolate them from all other meanings and to see them only as beautiful forms. But why domes? Why not minarets or braziers or samovars? Could it be because his mother had nursed him for eighteen months?

He laughed at himself and the skipper, who hadn't left the bridge during the crossing of the Straits, asked: "Why are you laughing Mister Uniform ...?"

"Why Uniform?"

"Ten days ago you were still a second lieutenant in the army, now you're a third mate – there isn't a uniform you haven't worn! If you had stayed at the Cadet School you would still be a second officer in the Royal Navy!"

"Yes, and I was still thinking about ..." and he finished to himself, '... my mother.'

"What did you say you were thinking about?"

"Nothing, Captain. Sometimes I dream and once in a while I talk to myself."

Discreet Captain Gerasimos, born and bred on the sea, called forth respect and confidence. Knowledgeable and composed, he knew what to say and what not to say without beating around the bush. "Dream as much as you like, Captain Alexis ... just as long as you watch the boats going south," was all he said in that deep voice of his.

A phrase which had become a classic on the boat and which the lowest ship's boy knew how to imitate was the way Captain Gerasimos used the dialect from the island of Cephalonia where he was born, when there was a sea mist. "Ehei athoura, ore" and the 'thour' didn't come just from his throat but from his whole being.

It was a strange sensation to sense the sea, it's reactions and the phenomena around, as if they were part of your body and soul. To feel the waves, the winds, the clouds in your very marrow, and Alexis knew he had that feeling.

When he was small and heard the waves breaking on the beach below the open window of his room, at night before going to sleep, he was able to visualise them: one long, one short, one long, one quieter, another with a little foam, another one churned up with bubbles. It was as if he was sitting on a rock watching them as they were flirting with the shore.

He looked at Captain Gerasimos who appeared to be at one with nature, in complete harmony with it – all you had to do was see his calm expression when there was a heavy sea. As vast as the sky, a part of the cosmos – why not?

That night Alexis' watch ended at four in the morning and he went to bed. When he awoke again they had entered the waters of the Propontis. "The pincers have closed," he thought. "Turkey ahead of us, Turkey behind us." Fortunately, the smiles of the Turks in Canakkale had given him hope that the pincers would open again on their return. "Imagine now going beyond the Bosphorus. Another set of pincers. Iron curtain pincers this time! Rumanian, Bulgarian and … the U.S.S.R.! God protect us. Straight into the mouths of the wolves!"

The Dardanelles were behind them. In the afternoon it would be Constantinople and the Bosphorus. Sometimes the days seem endless when you're sailing on the open sea but Alexis always found something to stir his interest – a lighthouse, the chance boat passing, a bird that would perch on the mast. He would make a symbolic projection for everything. Now, the crew stood waiting to see that legendary, that renowned city, Constantinople. His unconscious refused to call it Istanbul, which was also derivative of the Greek 'eis tin poli' – 'to the city'. Early in the afternoon, the doctor and the two French had joined the captain and the officers on the bridge.

The doctor, more down to earth than the others, was trying to ingratiate himself with the French nurse who till then had kept him at a distance. The rest of the crew, although she was the only woman on board, were repulsed by her overpowering perfume, and decided she was not worth the effort.

"France has such beautiful pussy …," the foul-mouthed doctor whispered to Alexis, "why did they have to send us this one? But never mind – beggars can't be choosers."

"You never know, she may have other qualities ... if she's wearing that cheap perfume it is certainly not to inspire the fish!" Alexis replied.

When the skyline of Constantinople first began to appear, silence fell on the bridge. As they drew nearer and the calm hills, the domes and the minarets of the mosques, the Galata bridge, the Golden Horn and the Princess islands took shape, Alexis felt tears come to his eyes.

"Some day, some time, it will be ours again! Under King Constantine, as prophecy goes, we'll take back Constantinople and Aghia Sophia." Words he had learned like the alphabet. How could they not have become part of him? Never for one moment had the idea entered his head that Constantinople might never be Greek again ... one day ... somehow ... "during the reign of the six-fingered king." They say that the present Crown Prince Constantine has six fingers ... could it be?"

A thoughtful silence ruled the bridge. Only the doctor seemed on edge. A combination of his celibate days on the boat and his doubtful chances of laying the French woman. Alexis heard him say to her, "Non, pas Istanbul, Constantinople" as he pointed out the city, taking her arm at every opportunity. "Oui, oui," the French woman told him trying to cool his ardour. Actually in a white nurse's uniform with that blue beret she's not all that bad looking. The doctor may be right Alexis thought.

The *Semiramis* moved slowly, in order to enter the Bosphorus just at the moment of the evening when the minarets of Aghia Sophia speared the sinking, dark red sun. But the colours were blurred by the tears in his eyes as he watched in awe the church of Aghia Sophia, the symbol of Orthodoxy, built by the Emperor Constantine and then rebuilt by the Emperor Justinian.

"Now here's a red that you do appreciate," Alexis said to himself in another moment of self-criticism.

The last rays of the sun lit the banks of the Bosphorus in silence and their eyes and souls tenderly caressed the outlines of the palaces while only the slow throb of the *Semiramis'* engines kept beat with the whispers of History.

"A little to the right ..., straight ahead ..., steady as she goes." Even the Captain had subdued his voice so as not to disturb the imposing peace of this moment as they passed through the straits between two continents.

Leaning toward the prow of the ship, Alexis reached out his right hand as if trying to touch Asia. Ahead lay Asia Minor, the Caucasus, Siberia, Persia, India and China! He then stretched out his left hand toward Europe and in his imagination he was touching two worlds. He closed his eyes for a moment and saw Chinese dragons on one side and soldiers of the English Royal Guard in their bearskins on the other, sacred elephants of India to the right, prostitutes of the Place Pigalle to the left, Persian mosaics from Isphahan and last, the bullfighters of Cordoba.

On the portside, after they had passed the Palace of Dolma Bakce with its beautiful gardens and other grand buildings remaining from the times of Byzantium, just as the Bosphorus began to widen at Karabournou, Therapeia came into view, the famous old Greek summer resort with restaurants along the Bosphorus, serving a fine fish, the Kalka, explained the well-travelled Captain Yiannis. And the doctor didn't miss the opportunity to tell the French nurse that 'therapeia' is the word for cure in Greek.

After Therapeia came Kavakia, at the exit from the Bosphorus, and then: the Black Sea! The name itself filled one with awe. Kara Deniz in Turkish! Alexis had never doubted that the Black Sea really was black and he waited for the waters at the exit from the Straits to darken.

It was not yet dark when they passed the lighthouse at Kavakia and the Captain ordered full steam ahead. A cold north-easterly wind brought Alexis back to reality. The numerous whitecaps on the waves, turned the sea grey, as the sun set, while a few clouds covered the *Semiramis* as it sailed north.

"So the Black Sea is grey. One more compromise!" He was disappointed. To carry a picture around in your mind for years and in a few minutes to have it change its most basic feature, the colour! "Always compromises! I'm compromised! Although I can't bear compromises ... the greys, the pinks, the beige. Is, maybe, compromise the middle way of wisdom! Ah, it's about time you stopped this silly chromatic philosophy and thought about your work. What are you talking about? Wisdom? Pink? Bah!" he said shrugging his shoulders and scorning colour. "Shut up! Where are we, helmsman?"

"Right on course, twenty one degrees."

"Did you know the Black Sea wasn't black?"

"Are you pulling my leg, Captain Alexis?"

"Can't I joke?"

"Not when it's as cold as this, Captain Alexis. Save it till we get back to the Mediterranean!"

He didn't carry it any further. He had learned in the Army that you could joke with those of lower rank only up to a point – beyond that they began to get lippy. A couple of slaps on the back so they felt the warmth of your presence, a few personal questions to show your concern, but always keeping your distance so they would respect you. As long as you were good at your job, and were fair of course!

Right now, here on the bridge, where he wasn't sure how much they thought of his naval expertise, he should be even more watchful of his attitude, to cover up a lack of confidence.

But at noon the following day, something happened to alter his relationship with the crew. They were travelling through the heart of the Black Sea under an overcast sky. To get a fix on their position at midday Alexis took the sextant and pointed it at the overcast sky, even though he needed the sun for a fix. He would play it for all it was worth. This was like Russian roulette. He concentrated like a hypnotist until, like a vision, the sun appeared in his mind at a point in the sky. He took the angle, then went to the Chart Room, made his calculations and put the point on the chart under the pitying look of the Captain who was saying to himself: "The poor fellow, he even turns science into fantasy!"

"What did you find, Captain Alexis?"

"Our fix, Captain Gerasimos."

"Do you have your own special radar to locate the sun, Captain Alexis?"

"I seemed to see it for a minute but ... I may have miscalculated," he said to justify himself.

Captain Gerasimos looked at the point on the chart and with the intuition of the good sailor who knows more or less where his ship is at any moment, calculated speed, wind and drift and shook his head in amazement.

"Let's tune in on the radio direction finder," suggested Captain Gerasimos.

The radio direction finder fix was precisely the same as the one Alexis had made.

The story made the rounds of the boat and from that moment on the crew looked at him in a different light. "He saw the sun through the clouds!" Fortunately, for the rest of the trip, the sun was shining at midday so he wasn't forced to repeat the experiment.

At their table that evening the doctor made a few more passes at the Frenchwoman but she didn't bite. The doctor turned to Alexis. "Let's play a little poker since we're not going to be screwing tonight either!"

"I don't know how to play poker."

"You don't know five-card-draw, seven card stud, deuces wild, Spit-in-the-Ocean. Nothing?"

"I never had the patience for cards. Except for Old Maid and Hearts which I used to play with my grandmother."

"Sit down and I'll teach you. I just hope you won't read my cards like you read the sun behind the clouds!"

Alexis tried to concentrate on the doctor's cards, since he was beginning to believe in his extra-sensory perception, but he drew a blank.

They were to arrive in Odessa the next afternoon. It was foggy and the Captain stayed on the bridge. It was getting steadily colder. Every so often Alexis pulled the cord on the ship's horn and the thundering echo cut through the fog on all sides, giving an other-worldly tone to the setting.

Then, around one-thirty there was a sudden dull thud as if the vessel had run into something. Alexis turned uneasily to the Captain, wondering if they'd hit a reef, without stopping to think that there was no reef in the area.

The Captain, undisturbed, acted as if he had felt nothing. He was aware of Alexis' uneasiness and with his usual slight smile said:

"It looks as though this is the first time you've come across ice, except for the ice-cubes in your ice-box!"

Alexis looked out the side of the boat and, despite the fog, could make out hundreds of small chunks of ice which grew more numerous as they approached the coast; the boat slowed down so they wouldn't hit the pieces of ice so hard.

Because of the fog, the Russian coast wasn't discernible for a while. It must have been three-thirty when, ever so faintly, the land began to appear and soon after, there was the harbour of Odessa, bang on the prow. They were all on the bridge again as the boat stopped so the pilot boat could draw alongside the *Semiramis*. On the mast of the pilot boat was a large red flag with a hammer and sickle which made Alexis shiver, remembering the walls splashed with them during the civil war, in Kaisariani, a stronghold of the leftist guerrillas.

The pilot climbed up the rope ladder and was soon greeting the Captain on the bridge. The first Russian Alexis had ever met seemed quite a likeable old fellow. 'It's like coming into contact with your childhood fears, with the bogey man and the Vampire!' Once more he thought – why do we look at people in terms of banners and systems? 'I like you, old pilot. I may not like the ideology of your country, but I'm sure that every morning you tenderly embrace your wife and children as well as your grandchildren ... if you have any, that is.'

The Captain offered the Pilot coffee and cigarettes. The pilot wouldn't take them.

Every pilot in the world drinks the coffee and puts the packs of cigarettes in his pocket. Why didn't he? Alexis wondered.

The *Semiramis* slowly entered the harbour of Odessa while a sailor raised the Russian flag on the forward mast. Just like the *Potemkin* first raising the flag in the 1905 Revolution as it entered the harbour of Odessa. 'I hope we don't end up the way those first revolutionaries did, in prison!' Alexis said to himself.

In the freezing cold and as the first buildings appeared around the harbour of Odessa, Alexis felt a pang of disappointment. He has thought he would see domes like those of the Kremlin or the palaces of Tsarist Russia. Instead, he saw warehouses in the red brick harbour and cranes, like gigantic hooks ready to tear you to pieces. But it made the mystery grow even greater. Boundless Russia was now hidden even further back.

Which Russia? His mind went back to the *Potemkin*.

"Oh, Mr Potemkin! By what miracle did you manage to upset the mind which the whole world considered to be one of the best in Europe?" The words of Catherine the Great to her lover. "How many secrets are hidden away in History that no-one will ever learn?" He'd always wanted to solve mysteries, to shed light on puzzles, and felt a tightness in his head when he didn't have the answers.

Which Russia? Chekov's Russia?:

– *"An oppression. A weight from which you must get free at all costs.*

– *"A night of terror ... an impenetrable fog ... the wind that blew in a rage through the folds of my cloak."*

– *"Nature resembles an endless property forgotten by God and people."*

And Mikhail Gorky on Chekov: "One has the feeling that he is living in a sad, autumn day ... everything has a peculiar loneliness, motionless, without force. The people colourless ... you burst from boredom and indolence. Small people who think without being aware of it – one is sorry for them. A deepening nostalgia in the face and the heart."

"Oh Chekov, Chekov, Chekov!

– *"In this grey mass of mankind they call out to them: 'How badly you live, brethren.'"* Alexis imagined these brethren in endless, motionless isolation, trying to seize hold of something, anything. But what? God perhaps?

– *"God gives us passing memories ... we'll see about the eternal ones."*

– *"For the love of God! Let us warm ourselves."*

– *"Tell me, in the name of God!"*

– *"Goddamn it, this stove won't light."*

– *"God gave him a large forehead because he was wise."*

– *"He only showed his red nose to God!"*

– *"Siberia is like Russia. It has the same God and the same Tsar. The Tsar comes down heavily and God comes down heavily."*

Which Russia, Tolstoy's Russia?:

– "*The intelligentsia plays at religion. It will take tens of thousands of years for mankind to know the taste of the 'true God'. But there must be no haste! Tens of thousands of years!*"

Infinity, even in time.

– "*In the infinity of time, in the infinity of the universe, a cell is born, it multiplies for a moment and dies. I am not that cell. Why? Leven asks Anna Karenina.*"

– "*One must not live for himself but for God, the musician answers.*" Fatalism?

– "*Think, it is for the salvation of his soul. Oh, what terrible duties a Christian has!' Anna Michailovna sighed.*"

– "*Behind the puppets which you must move, I see something metaphysical, something startling. The shadow of the infinite is always present. A mute question-mark from the ungraspable. A long drawn-out sigh for fate in the void.*" Melchoir de Vigne said in Resurrection.

Which Russia? Michael Lermontov's Russia?:

– "*The road is desolate and the fog is before me. It turns and turns and takes me far away. The night is silent and every sound on earth has been stilled. Nature rests on God. Each star is speaking to another.*"

Listen to Trofimov:

– "*The world advances and perfects its powers. Whatever cannot be grasped today, will one day be understood. But one must work with all one's powers to find the truth. The intelligentsia that I've met are not capable of work. You think you belong to the intelligentsia but you speak to the servants in the singular and you use the musicians like animals. The workers eat in despair and sleep without pillows, thirty, forty, in one damp room, with bedbugs for company. It is a filthy morality. Asia is mud and barbarity. And the others ... philosophise. I don't think I like serious countenances and I dread serious conversations. It's better if we don't speak. Has anything changed? Has the Tsar left? Has God left?*"

"Has anything changed? Have the Tsars left? Has the true God been found?"

Alexis would have liked to know more about philosophy and history. To feel in the very depths of his soul the total realisation of History. There was so little he still remembered from his school days. But why should he have memories especially from Russian literature? He had tried to cast out those heavy, those immovable words from his mind, but they had dug their claws in all the more.

At that moment, wherever his thoughts turned, they induced in him an unbearable weight. Was he prone to melancholy and depression? An endless deep winter when the boots stick in the mud and the nose freezes without hope. He envisaged the frozen soldiers of Napoleon and Hitler, on the endless steppes, motionless along with time. And it was as if he himself had become a frozen statue without hope.

He looked at the pilot. He had a smile on his lips as the *Semiramis* weighed anchor and pulled into the harbour of Odessa. The smile of repletion. The ship had entered the safety of the harbour. A ray of sun in the mist. To Alexis, looking for a breakthrough, that faint smile opened the window of hope.

Slowly the visitors on the bridge filed down to the salon to wait for the Russian authorities who were already on the pier. Only Alexis stayed on the bridge, lost on the steppes of History.

Before he left, the pilot approached the captain and asked him for the cigarettes he had earlier refused.

"He probably didn't want to accept them in front of the others," Captain Gerasimos explained.

A woman in a blue uniform with stripes on her shoulders who turned out to be the port doctor, was the first to board the ship. The hat on her head, cocked slightly to the left of course – framed a beautiful round, rosy face with blue eyes. An old-fashioned blonde braid completed the image of strict decorum.

She was followed by another woman, also in uniform, but without any stripes: a brunette this time, with short, tousled hair and a less polished type of beauty than the doctor's.

Both of them were of medium height, their uniforms clean but rumpled, as if they'd been pressed with an iron that wasn't hot enough, wearing thick cotton stockings, which did not permit a western eye to run over their shapely legs.

Besides the two women, two soldiers in smart-looking great coats – they must have been of high rank, no-one on board could make out their insignia – and two others in grey uniforms, probably policemen or customs officials, had gathered in the salon. And there was a strange person with hollow cheeks and a funny looking moustache, in a black overcoat with a turned-up collar, and a black hat which he didn't take off even as he sat down in a corner of the room, obviously to keep an eye on everything.

"A caricature of a commissar," Captain Yiannis whispered to Alexis, "and be careful what you say, because he will understand Greek, for sure."

The harbour authorities, the captain, the purser and the ship's doctor, sat around the table in the lounge, while the military and the representatives of the French Red Cross sat at another, to discuss details for the handing over of the prisoners.

Alexis joined the captain and also sat with the port authorities, while Costas, the doctor, was all smiles for the Russian doctor, who remained serious and aloof. They spoke broken English. The steward approached and asked the ladies if they'd like coffee or tea.

"No, it is not necessary!" both of them answered just as the pilot had done, and so did all the Russians.

'A strange kind of pride,' Alexis thought. 'Is it that they don't want to show that they have any use for our western products?'

He was waiting impatiently to find out how long they would be staying in Odessa, when the prisoners would be arriving and whether the crew would be allowed in town. The brunette, who was the secretary of "Inflot", the State Shipping Agency, told them that only the captain and the representatives of the French Red Cross would be allowed on shore by the authorities and that the rest of the crew would have to remain on board. The prisoners would be arriving at any moment.

It was a great disappointment. "Sailing all the way to Russia, through three seas and two straits, and then not being allowed to set foot on dry land! What could the Russians be afraid of? A counter-revolution by five idiots from the *Semiramis*? Whatever the reason might be, two armed soldiers patrolled outside the ship and a third stood guard near the gangway.

When the formalities were completed all the Russians except the two women and the commissar went ashore with the captain and the two Frenchmen. It was now dark and the Russian women onboard sat across from each other and the commissar, still in his look-out corner, like a suspicious tiger.

Alexis, the doctor and the chief steward, Fylachtos, who had all accompanied the captain to the gangway, returned to the salon and stood in front of the bar.

"Watch and see what I'm going to do to the commissar," Fylachtos said with a wily look. He approached the man and without warning spoke to him in Greek.

"Can we offer you anything?"

"No, it is not necessary!" the commissar answered in faultless Greek.

When he realised his blunder, he got up and left the ship in a huff, since his mission no longer had any meaning. As soon as the commissar was out of sight, the two women appeared to relax. They called to the steward and asked him if perhaps they could now have the tea he had offered them below. They changed place and went to sit at the table where Alexis had placed English and French magazines – *Paris Match*, *Life*, *Time* and *Marie-Claire*.

Alexis and the doctor watched the women leafing through the magazines and casting a glance at the door every so often to see if the commissar was coming back. They paused for quite some time over the cover of *Life* magazine which showed Marilyn Monroe in a long sumptuous skirt. They shook their heads over the Christian Dior, Marcel Rochas, or Desse models with their provocative poses, the striking ads for Elizabeth Arden and Helena Rubenstein beauty products, the affected jewellery of Cartier ... an enchanting, unapproachable world. For a moment Alexis felt sorry that he had been responsible for this temptation. It was like watching two small children who had their noses glued to the frozen window of a Christmas display, tears running down their cheeks.

"Let's go talk to them," he said to the doctor.

"Of the two, I rather fancy my colleague and comrade-in-arms," the doctor answered, not waiting to be asked a second time.

They sat down, Alexis next to the secretary from the Agency, the doctor next to the doctor.

Alexis tried to start a conversation, hoping to get their minds off fashion, cosmetics and jewellery, but the less sensitive and more blunder-prone doctor, seeing that they were looking at an ad for nylon stockings which showed a male hand stroking two lovely legs, could not let the chance go by. "I have two pairs nylons in my cabin – I give you them," he said in the broken English that he used with his South American wife, and which he suddenly blurted out now.

The women's eyes glistened but they didn't say yes or no.

"Where did you get the nylons?" Alexis asked him in Greek, so the others couldn't understand.

"I was told you could buy anything you wanted in Russia with nylons." And turning to the girls: "Would you like to come to my cabin to try them?"

This time Alexis intervened decisively.

"Let him go and get them; in any case there are only two pairs – you don't have any choice."

"Are you trying to ruin everything for me?"

"You can buy Leica cameras with nylon stockings, if you want, but not women, doctor!" Alexis retorted angrily.

"Why not? Don't you think they'd like a little adventure with a descendant of Hippocrates?"

"Not for two pairs of stockings. Besides, need I remind you, that in order to calm your ardour they might send you to Siberia?"

At the mention of Siberia, the doctor gave up and went to fetch the stockings.

Alexis took the opportunity to lighten the atmosphere sensing the women seemed perplexed about what was happening.

"The doctor likes his little jokes, but he's a good fellow and generous."

"How is it that he has ladies stockings in Odessa?"

"Ah! Yes, he explained that to me. He got them for his sister on a previous trip to Europe ... France I think it was, and he didn't have time to give them to her."

Too bad if the stockings turned out to be Greek! He would have put his foot in it, so to speak ... The doctor returned at that moment, and before Alexis could tell him about his lie, both of the women protested as one.

"But is not right you should give us your sister's stockings!"

"My what ..."

"Doctor, shut up. You do have a sister!"

He didn't understand, but Alexis's tone had been so gruff that the doctor didn't say a word. He gave each of the girls a pair of stockings. Alexis now had control of the situation and fortunately the stockings turned out to be made in France.

"Look, you'll make him unhappy if you don't take them. We're on our way to Spain and the Doctor will get some new ones there for his sister. Right, Costas?"

"If you say so!" Costas was puzzled, but then began to laugh again in his explosive way.

The women thanked him with a little smile and hid the stockings inside their jackets.

"What are your names?" the doctor asked.

"I am Olga," the secretary said.

"I am Natasha," the doctor said.

"Natasha ... Olga ..." the doctor repeated trying to sound like Charles Boyer. "Aren't you going to put the stockings on?" he urged.

"Not now!" Olga replied with a polite smile.

"Don't you have nylon stockings in Russia?" the doctor insisted.

They didn't answer the question directly, but the ice had been broken a little, and the smarter Natasha, who was catching on, said, "You think we are jealous because you saw us looking at the magazines? No, we are not jealous, we do not suffer the pangs of looking in the mirror. Well, maybe just a little bit – we are women after all, are we not? But the true values lie elsewhere," she quickly added, to keep up the doctrinaire pretext.

"Be that as it may, they pocketed the stockings fast enough!" the doctor remarked in Greek.

"You're right!" Alexis interrupted. "Fashion in the West may have imagination but it's oppressive. A woman goes out to buy a watch band and ends up with a whole wardrobe to match the colour of the band. How much freer a person would be if he didn't pay attention to fashion and what his male or female friend will say if he isn't dependent on the tyranny of fashion. One day skirts go up ten centimetres, the next they go down thirty centimetres. Green is the colour to wear this year, red the year after. Wide skirts with pleats in Spring, a suit with a cord on the collar and puffed sleeves in the fall. Hemstitch in the summer, pleats in the winter."

He knew he wasn't convincing anyone, but at least he had exhausted all avenues to make them feel at ease.

"What do you mean?" the doctor protested, not understanding Alexis' signals, "Fashion is the expression of the human imagination! If you stop the human imagination what's left? Open *Marie-Claire* to the page for Guerlain's perfume – I was looking at it yesterday. Give it to me and I'll find it for you." Then suddenly turning to Natasha, "Why, smell Natasha – as a matter of fact the smell of her perfume makes my head swim."

"We do wear perfume," Natasha answered calmly, ignoring the doctor's clumsy manoeuvres. "All women, from ancient times, wear perfume."

"There, at least, you haven't broken with tradition ... the women who want to provoke!"

"It is not provocation, it is the joy of a beautiful aroma."

"How many different kinds of perfume do you have in Russia?" The doctor was on the attack again.

"Everywhere in Russia they make perfume – a different kind in every place."

"Let's say here in Odessa, how many choices do you have?"

"Three or four, I do not know – what difference does it make?"

"You mean to tell me that most women here smell alike? That you can walk down the street and not be able to tell one from the other by the aroma of the perfume? Not to be able to say, she smells like 'Moscow Nights' or she wears 'The Mystery of the Volga?'"

The ladies laughed.

"How do you know there is a perfume called 'Moscow Nights'?", Olga asked.

"Is there? I didn't know, I made it up. But the 'Mystery of the Volga' – that doesn't exist, does it?"

"No, but there is 'Woman's Secret'."

"Are you trying to tell me that woman has changed in Russia, when she still has her secrets? When she's not an open book to the eyes of the Party? When she can dream on the sly?"

"Why should we not dream?"

"Because dreams take you far away, away from the road they have paved for you, and no-one can control them: certainly not the parties, or even ideologies," Alexis ventured to say.

"We can have dreams but there is also the reality and they do not always work hand in hand," Olga replied.

"But if you can't move in the direction of dreams, what sense does life have?" the doctor suddenly added, showing another side to himself, unknown to Alexis.

Neither Olga nor Natasha spoke. The doctor went on: "... Why, are there only three or four kinds of women? Doesn't each one have her own character, her own sparkle, her own smile, her own colour? Have you ever found two women to be alike? Even the natural aroma of the skin – is it ever the same? Then why do they have to wear the same perfume or the same clothes? Here is the ad I was telling you about. Listen to this: only about the perfumes of Guerlain – fourteen different brands! Listen: 'Night Flight', inspired by the Saint-Exupery novel. 'The Music of Love', 'Mitsuko', 'The Secret' – which shows that women have their secrets irrespective of geography – 'Nature's Canto' and one that you will like, 'Red Dress'. Listen to the descriptions: 'Mitsuko'. Powerful, tender, sinful. A fragrance coaxed from oranges, wood and oak root. 'Night Flight'. Exotic, provocative, dangerous. A perfume concocted of herbs, wood and delicate iris petals. 'The Secret'. Discreet, aristocratic ... (you might not like that), fresh, forceful. A perfume blended from lavender, the bark of the fir tree, mint, pergamon and basil. 'The Forest of Love': Warm, oriental and sinful again – and don't try to tell me that all these tend toward sin ... 'A powerful scent of herbs, vanilla and essence of sheep's wool', which I don't think I would find so appealing, etc., etc., 'for all tastes, for all dreams!' For all nights," the doctor added slyly. "Do you want to hear the magazine's comments?" Another perfume, Zicky. 'Full of athletic vigour. Fresh and robust for the woman of action. It is also worn by men.' About Parure: 'a distinctive presence, harmony and elegance for day and night.' "About Charmade: 'arouses the teasing curiosity of youth. Vibrant. A journey into the unknown, into adventure, the novel!' 'Unknown', 'new adventure' – words that have been wiped from the communist lexicon. All that for a few drops of perfume behind the ear – isn't it incredible? And look at the bottles! What shapes! It's pure sculpture. The famous 'consumption', isn't it the popularisation of art in all forms of daily life? Doesn't that say anything to you?"

"Certainly it does. Words that are meaningless," Olga replied. "For us, art is what gives to people the basic means, art springs out of real values."

"And isn't it a basic requirement that for a perfume to reach the nose of a woman it must have been thought of and produced by the cultivator of the flower, the person who conceived the idea of the scent, all those who helped to process it – the one who designed the bottle, others who designed and manufactured the boxes to pack it in, others who dreamed up the ad, others who wrote the descriptions I just read to you, still others who decorated the window displays, not to speak of the merchants who sell them?"

"No, they should all be working in factories, or on farms to feed the millions of starving people in the world," Natasha interjected obstinately.

"Why should the western world – because that's what we're talking about – be responsible for everyone who is needy," the Doctor replied impertinently.

"Because it has exploited poor countries for so many years."

"We're sliding into a deep political analysis of history again. I was talking about a woman's dreams – can't they be the same in Moscow and Paris?" the doctor was now trying to wriggle his way free.

The conversation was beginning to take a dangerous turn toward politics and Alexis tried to steer it in a new direction. "Who knows, perhaps Natasha and Olga are happier not having to worry about what their girlfriends will say."

"They may not, but every woman suffers in front of the mirror!" the pragmatic doctor replied, "and just let them try and say they don't!"

"Why? Don't most exotic birds spend their whole life in the same feathers without ever looking in a mirror?" Alexis paid an oblique compliment.

"Yes, but they ruffle them up when they meet the males and besides, they have nature as a decorative background!", the doctor insisted.

"Why, does a person not have nature as a background as well?" Olga asked.

"Where does creation start and where does it end? No painting, no architecture, no music – except for standardised dwellings, furniture and utensils so we can preserve the other values you girls are talking about, but which ones?" Costas wouldn't leave it alone and it was too late to stop the conversation now despite Alexis' attempts to counter his arguments.

Natasha found the solution.

"There are some human values beyond art and science. Simple love, simple existence, simple speech without embroidery, without multi-coloured chandeliers, without complex processes of the mind. But do not be afraid, it is utopia. We will continue to cut the flowers in the fields to decorate our homes and we will frame the moon, and we shall store the sun in our prison to have it in reserve for the dark, and we will put aside the shadow of the mountain so we can dig labyrinths for our towers on mother earth. And where does it all lead us? Nowhere, or rather, always back to the same point. And we will sit cross-legged in our silk stockings, knowing that the eyes of men go straight to the heart ..."

"Not just the heart!" the doctor added, changing the tenor of the conversation once more. The mere mention of crossed legs had aroused him again. "How well you said that Natasha! Of course, you are a scientist like I am and I know that medicine has made great strides in Russia. What's the name of that fantastic drug you have for ulcers in Russia? Would you like to come and see my dispensary on the lower deck?"

"Here we go again!" Alexis groaned.

He was curious, however, to see if the woman doctor would agree to go, and perhaps leave him alone with Olga who wasn't talking much, but had a gentle presence and with whom he felt a silent contact had been made. The commissar, who returned at that moment – most probably under new instructions – took care of that problem, for the women got up immediately, thanked them and left the ship.

The elusive tender gleam in Olga's eyes had rent Alexis' heart. Would she come back? They hadn't spoken.

The doctor, of course, had a well-armoured heart. But Alexis was so angered by the unexpected appearance of the commissar forcing the girls to leave, that he spoke almost savagely to him in Greek without thinking too much about the consequences: "Where were you born?"

There was no way to avoid it and he answered: "In Greece ... in Florina."

"You couldn't have been one of the children taken East by the communists – you aren't young enough."

"Don't ask any more questions – I won't answer them."

They were standing in the salon near the window facing the wharf. Alexis looked out the window at the dock-workers who were unloading a freighter and humping the sacks on their backs to the warehouse about one hundred metres away. Among the men there was a short old woman who was bent under an enormous sack. From the white tracks the workers left behind they had to be carrying flour. "So, even old women," (he didn't want to say slaves), "carry large bags of flour?"

"Haven't you ever seen old women in the villages in Greece carrying firewood on their backs?" the commissar retorted.

Alexis shut up and went out on deck to see Olga and Natasha who were departing into the Russian night. He thought of running after them but the guard at the door didn't look very accommodating. He whispered to himself: "Olga ... what a sweet, tender face. Iron bars are erected between people for a thousand reasons but being fenced off for politics is just simply stupid! Olga! You belong to another world that won't let me touch you and speak to you, except with my heart. We met for a few moments and I know that both of us felt a warmth in our souls. And neither you nor I are free enough to ignore the commissars and ideologues. And we're afraid. I don't know if my world is any freer; perhaps not. But my fear is greater. Olga, even though they won't allow us to set foot on this great Russian earth, the trip was worth it for the look you gave me as you left. I will carry it away with me. And this cold night you warmed the 'folds of my cloak'."

He went back to the salon and sat down in an armchair next to the doctor. Both of them fell asleep and they didn't wake until the Captain returned with the French representatives, past midnight.

"Welcome back, Captain! How did they treat you?", the doctor asked.

"They fed us caviar and vodka," the Captain replied laconically.

The French nurse appeared to be in good spirits and the doctor tried to exploit the opportunity. He began to sing to her the only Russian song he half knew. "Oci Ciornia ..."

"You have a beautiful voice, doctor," she said.

"She's nibbling, she's nibbling," the doctor murmured happily to himself. He got up from his armchair and did his best to imitate a Cossack dance. Michelle watched him under the startled look of the commissar who didn't know whether or not he was mocking Russian songs and dances.

After that things followed their natural course and Michelle, dancing along, followed the doctor into his cabin to complete the night.

"Let's hope that satisfies the doctor for a while," the Captain commented wryly, "it was getting to the point where even we were all in danger from his attentions."

At that moment Alexis felt very alone. The doctor at least had someone to share his loneliness. He again looked at the window of the salon, frosted over with the cold and closed his eyes. The buildings in the harbour and the roofs beyond disappeared. He saw a boundless snow-covered plain with three dead trees along one edge and a sleigh being pulled by two black horses, fading, fading, into the night. A woman wrapped in a thick, black cape, with a fur hat, was holding the reins and whipping the horses to make them go faster. Every so often she would cast a glance over her shoulder and Alexis recognised the disturbed, tear-stained eyes of Olga. At the end of the plain, rose up a marble tower, but it seemed like a miniature tower, hardly taller than a human being. At the doors of the tower, Olga pulled on the reins, ordering the horses to stop in an otherworldly voice that echoed in Alexis' ears, alighted, and with a last look behind her, opened the door and entered a round, empty space with the walls and the ceiling made up of mirrors. On the floor was a deep red carpet with an enormous hammer and sickle embroidered in the centre which was reflected on all the surrounding walls. A bright sun, imprisoned in a cage hanging from the ceiling, lit the room and countless fragrances spilled from every corner. Olga closed the door, threw the cape and the fur hat on the floor, and stood naked in the middle of the room, holding a pair of silk stockings in her hands.

Alexis abruptly opened his eyes and stared at the frosted-over window. Then closed them once more. The naked Olga was now also reflected in the mirrors which left no part of her body hidden. She had a pure white skin covering her soft curves, and her flesh was tender and innocent.

Then, she suddenly lost her frightened look as she gazed in one of the mirrors, became arrogant and haughty and leaned over to put on one of her silk stockings. As she straightened up, caressing her well-shaped legs, their length multiplied endlessly in the many mirrors, she shuddered all over as she saw, reflected in the mirrors the black silhouette of the commissar, who appeared from nowhere without warning. She remained frozen in place for a minute, closing her eyes to the cruel moment of lost joy she sought in isolation, but there was no escape. When she re-opened her eyes, the commissar stood in front of her, grim and implacable. He pulled the second stocking from her hand. Olga began to cry. The commissar bent over to remove the stocking she was wearing, but as he knelt in front of her naked body, he rested his head on her thighs.

Olga gazed at the silk stockings in the commissar's hand in surrender, and stood motionless, while the commissar began to kiss her, then laid her down on the red carpet and, without taking his clothes off, ravaged her like a brutish beast.

At that moment, Alexis was certain he could hear her voice, calling out his name: "Alexeii!" Ignoring the guard, he jumped off the deck of the ship onto a white horse on the dock and began to race away like a demon, over the dark snowed-in steppes.

When he got to about one mile from the tower, lit up by the reflection of the stars on the white snow, he whipped the horse which started galloping even faster, but the distance did not seem to lessen. They always seemed to be in the same spot. Then, the horse stopped, reared up on its hind legs and threw him on his back in the snow.

As Alexis stood with his eyes closed, in front of the frosted window, he began to sway as if some force was pulling him backwards. The chief steward who had been watching him for quite some time, thought he was going to faint and hurried over to catch him before he fell.

Alexis opened his eyes and couldn't understand what George Fylachtos of the *Semiramis* was doing on the frozen steppes. "The horse threw me, thanks for coming to pick me up. By the way, I just realised that your surname means 'saviour' in Greek."

"You need a doctor, you're delirious and you almost keeled over. Sit down in the armchair and I'll go and get the doctor."

"No, don't", Alexis exclaimed. He could imagine the doctor just reaching climax in his erotic clinch with the French nurse.

"I'll bring you a little water."

"Don't you have vodka? I'm cold."

A part of him was still in the snow.

"Vodka? The supplier didn't bring us any, but I'll give you some retsina with pleasure."

"Then give me some brandy, retsina only warms the mind."

"Why don't you get a little sleep – you've been up for two nights."

"First of all because I'm on duty. We're waiting for the prisoners and we don't know when they're coming. Then, I can't sleep, I feel super alert, everything seems like a fairy tale to me."

"You always look at everything like a fairy tale!"

"Could be, Fylachtos – but does it matter?"

"If I hadn't been here to catch you, you would have cracked your skull! That's why it matters!"

As Alexis sat in the armchair, brandy in hand, he looked toward the corridor that led to the deck and was still trying to separate truth from dream when he saw Olga's silhouette at the end of the corridor.

"I must have slipped away again," he thought, "but no, it can't be – I'm not all that crazy. It's her! She came back!" He leapt out of the chair and rushed toward the girl who was slowly coming toward the salon. He stood in front of her and blocked her way.

"Olga! I dreamed about you! I was riding a white horse and I was chasing you over the Russians steppes. But the horse threw me off into the frozen night."

Olga looked at him in astonishment.

"I know you don't understand, but that's how it is. My own truth is different than yours. But who can say which is best?"

"Excuse me, but what are you talking about? My English is not so good and I do not understand. Do not speak so fast."

She was cool, perhaps frightened, but she did not try to leave.

Alexis opened the door of a cabin and took her by the hand.

"Come, let's sit in here. The black commissar is back in the lounge."

"I cannot. I come to inform you that in one hour the train with the prisoners will arrive."

"It's a good thing you told me. I'm the one in charge. Do you have time to talk to me at least?"

"But …"

She didn't want to show him that she was afraid, so she followed Alexis into the cabin.

Alexis locked the door, Olga sat in the only chair in the cabin to avoid sitting on the bed.

Alexis related his dream to her, but he didn't get the tender look she had given him when she left before. She was now in control and wasn't going to give way to any emotion, she was sure of herself, like a great aristocrat. And she spoke to him severely: "My father was in the Tsar's Court, he was killed in the Revolution. My mother, the Countess Marlova, lives by herself in a room in Leningrad. I have my own life to live. I am not unhappy, I am not sorry about anything and I do not want anyone to feel sorry for me."

Her sharp words reverberated in the small cabin; a lesson to a spoiled child of western, capitalist society.

"Olga, I would like you to stay on the ship, to stowaway, to go with us." He said it as if in a delirium, without believing it. "I've never seen a woman like you. Proud, aristocratic, with a childlike romantic innocence but also power; I can't understand how you can keep it in check behind your tender beauty."

He tried to hold her hand, to approach her, but Olga sealed his mouth with two fingers of her hand as she pulled away. "To each his own world. I thank you for your beautiful words."

Was she a little shaken?

"Please, you will peek into the hall to make sure no-one is there," she said to him.

Alexis opened the door and gestured to her. Olga went out and entered the salon by herself, to wait for the train with the prisoners.

Alexis remained in the cabin, troubled and discontented and decided to try and refresh himself with a little sleep. "To hell with the watch! I'll wake up with all the fuss when the prisoners arrive."

At that moment he believed that he was in love with Olga and he was annoyed by her cold and, to him, inexplicable stance.

The trucks carrying the Spaniards arrived at the docks next to the boat. The prisoners got out, escorted by Russian soldiers and began to climb up the gangway of the *Semiramis* demoralised and silent, without fuss, without waiting for anyone's orders, as if they'd rehearsed it and each one knew his part.

The sailor on duty woke Alexis. He ran to the gangway, where he should have been in the first place, rather than in bed, and decided not to go to the lounge to see if Olga was still onboard. He knew there were no more words to be said, but the idea tormented him. He very much wished to meet her once more, even if it were the last time.

He tried to focus on the prisoners. He looked at the faces of the Spaniards as they came up. They boarded the ship silently and with their eyes humbly lowered, like children in an orphanage going for a Sunday afternoon walk. Loaded down with eleven years of captivity, they had learned to accept their fate and it seemed as though their approaching freedom hadn't had any particular effect on them. Perhaps they didn't really believe that the ship would be taking them to freedom.

The sailor on the gangway greeted them one by one with the one Russian word he had learned: "Pajaloushta, pajaloushta."

"What are you saying to them, Dimos?" Alexis asked.

"I'm saying 'welcome' to them in Russian."

"But they're Spaniards. They've been prisoners in Russia for eleven years. That's a fine way to receive them!"

"I don't know any Spanish, Captain Alexis. Anyway, after so many years here they must have picked up a little Russian."

Dimos' 'pajaloushta' must not have been all that comforting to the Spaniards who were guided into their cabins by the Frenchmen from the Red Cross and Michele, who had surfaced after her night of love with the doctor.

The doctor, of course, had shown no sign of life and was probably sleeping off his erotic binge. Meanwhile, the Captain, the officers and all the rest of the crew had collected at the embarkation point as the last of the prisoners climbed on board and the chief Russian officer asked the French representatives from the Red Cross to sign the delivery papers, just as he would have signed a bill of lading from a cargo of wheat.

No Spaniard was in sight. They had all been escorted to their cabins and none of them came out to go around the ship. From then on everything happened very quickly. The Russian escorts and other authorities left the ship first, followed by the commissar. Olga was the last to disembark as soon as the pilot arrived. She paused by the gangway in front of Alexis, looked at him and said with a smile full of melancholy: "Irazoshlis oni kak v more korabli ... and they passed like two ships on the sea."

She went down the gangway without turning to look at Alexis' tear-filled eyes.

"Like two ships, each going its own way", Alexis corrected and got back into the rhythm of the job and the new emotions and his tears dried quickly. But not forever ...

He led the pilot to the bridge, the gangway was hauled up, the ropes loosened, and the tug boat that was on stand-by picked up one of the ropes and began to pull the *Semiramis* out of the harbour.

Alexis looked around. Near total silence had spread through and around the ship that morning. He looked at his watch. It was eight o'clock. The soldiers who had come to hand over the prisoners were still on the dock, looking after the ship, with who knows what thoughts going through their minds. The dock workers hauled their loads, as always, without looking right or left. On the boat, the Spaniards were still in their cabins and on the bridge the Captain, the mate, Alexis, the two French representatives and the helmsman watched the manoeuvres silently. Only the pilot's commands disturbed the morning peace.

Alexis eyes caught in the morning mist a motionless silhouette, leaning on the wall of a far-off warehouse, smoking a cigarette, but he couldn't swear it was Olga.

The Spaniards, as soon as they heard the ship's engines working, began to furtively peek out the port holes to make sure the ship really was setting off. When they saw the open sea and the pilot getting into the tug-boat and disappearing into the fog which hid the Russian mainland, they plucked up courage to come out on deck, one by one, still silent, serious and stunned.

The following minutes were like a pause in time, where mind and soul stop and everything stays suspended, before the swing that would bring you from the lowest depths of despair to the highest peak of elation.

Then, as if an invisible conductor had raised his baton, came the outburst and tears of joy, more powerful than those of laughter. Explosive weeping. The unique spectacle of three hundred young men all sobbing in one another's arms. The lament of a chorus in an ancient tragedy, but a lament of joy.

Alexis and all the crew on the bridge watched in awe. Suddenly the Spaniards, as if directed by a secret, inner voice, all flung their Russian caps, symbols of their captivity, up into the air and overboard.

The foam of the propellers swept them up and hurled them further out, drowning the memories of the three hundred soldiers, as the caps swirled and were lost in the wake of the *Semiramis*. 'In a desperate dance of symbolic revenge,' Alexis thought.

At that moment, the doctor peeked out with bloodshot eyes, glancing right and left in amazement as he headed for the bridge. Sleep had spared him all the morning's emotions and, barely half awake, he was trying to piece together the events from the time he had retired to his cabin with

Michelle. He remembered the boat as being tied up in the harbour of Odessa whereas now she was sailing in the open sea with a host of weeping passengers. It was for him difficult to connect the scenes in his mind.

Alexis greeted him on the bridge. "From the look of you, doctor, I'd say you weren't even aware that we'd started on our way back."

"That pussy wore me out!", was the doctor's only excuse. "But why are they all sobbing? And I see that your eyes are wet too."

"I suppose that's the way it is when you have lost all hope and you're afraid the whole thing is just a dream. Perhaps it's the fear that you will lose what you have gained, you just can't believe that you have won. Perhaps it is utter abasement before fate. Afraid in case 'fate' might change its mind. Sorry if I am a little melodramatic about it. It's only natural that I would be moved too, like everybody else on board, by six hundred eyes shedding hot tears into the freezing Black Sea."

But back inside, he knew that his own tears weren't only for the sobbing men, but also for another image left behind, and becoming ever more blurred as the distance grew.

"My my, such lyricism so early in the morning – and rather cheap too, if you'll pardon me!"

"Are you getting aggressive in order to try and justify being asleep and not taking part, or is it simply that you're being cynical?"

"Does your question contain a touch of jealousy?"

"I hadn't thought about it, but it's not impossible. You mean because I slept alone?"

"No, what I mean is …"

"The doctor has gone from being a radiologist to a psychologist. It doesn't suit you."

But he began to look at him differently. It was the second time the doctor had surprised him.

"Let's go on to the bridge, because I'm beginning to get chilled," the doctor said.

"Maybe you have a hunch that Michelle might be there?"

"Who's playing the psychologist now?"

They opened the door to the bridge and the doctor went in first.

"Bonjour every one!" he called out in a loud, jolly voice and exchanged a guilty look with Michelle.

"Sleep well?" the Captain asked dead-pan.

"Some celebrate with vodka and caviar and others ... hit the hay. I received a full report, Captain, the minute I woke up, from the chief gossip on the ship!"

"I see you had a rewarding French lesson last night" Alexis pulled him up short.

The doctor ignored him and went on with a professional bearing this time.

"The chief steward told me about you too, Mr Alexis. What happened? He said you were about to faint and wouldn't let him call me. Not that I would have come. Hah, hah, hah!"

Is it wrong I didn't want to interrupt your ardent embraces?

"Come on, tell me what happened."

"Let's go and sit in the salon and I'll tell you."

The ship was at full steam now, having passed through the ice-field, and the party on the bridge began to leave, the Frenchman first.

He called out, "So long Captain, we're going to see the Spaniards – in any case, the donkey knows the way home, it doesn't need our help!"

Captain Yiannis had the last word, saying between his teeth: "Trafalgar ..." and turning to them: "The gentleman was treating us to a little Gallic wit!"

Michelle followed, brushing by the doctor and giving his hand a quick squeeze so that no-one would see what everyone saw!

The doctor waited a while for her to get ahead, to avoid extending the uneasiness in front of others after a first guilty night and then left the bridge, Alexis following him.

The Spaniards on deck wiped away their last tears as they faced towards the open sea, then looked at each other and put arms around one another's shoulders, as if each needed to have proof of his presence, to really believe in the truth of the moment.

Alexis detected a fleeting emotion even in the eyes of the doctor. They went down to the salon and sat in a quiet corner.

"You won't believe me, but when you left with your woman last night I had a dream standing by that frosted window – but no, it wasn't a dream, it was too real, it was like a vision. I don't know what it was."

Alexis related his dream to the doctor. "... and as I was falling from the white horse onto the frozen snow of the Russian Steppes, Fylachtos caught me while I was still in a stupor, and made me sit down on the couch!"

"So? What could be more natural for a dreamy type like you? Dreams are very important in the starting point of all psychoanalysis."

"I told you, you are full of surprises. You might not know a lot about medicine, being ... only a 'photographer', but as an analyst, you're something of a Freud."

"If you're a good radiologist, you can even photograph the soul. Your dream doesn't need all that much analysis. In your eyes Olga thirsts for luxury and ran off to the tower to hide her desire. The only eyes that admired her in the mirror were her own. Remember Natasha's words: 'the pangs of looking in the mirror?' I don't think the red carpet with the hammer and sickle needs any explaining. But her sense of guilt is more powerful than her desire to escape. The commissar catches up to her and then you identify yourself with him. Fatalistically, she puts up no resistance as she has no other choice. Afterwards, comes your own guilt! You mount the horse and ride and ride – but always stay in the same spot. First, because you're afraid to meet your true self, the rapist that is you, not the commissar, and, anyway, remember the words of Natasha again which still ring in my head like a bell – not that I understood all that well what she was saying at the time: 'And we will store the sun in our prison to have it in reserve for the dark, and we will put aside the shadow of the mountain so we can dig labyrinths for our towers on mother earth – all of which will lead nowhere, and will always bring us back to the same point'. Here is your tower, here the sun in a cage, here is your horse that keeps galloping, while glued to the same spot. I don't think I need to analyse further your dream about the thousands of fragrances and I've had enough of you and your fantasies."

"I'm the dreamer but you have the imagination, doctor. What's worse, all you say seems to make sense. Then Olga returned and I saw her and spoke to her and asked her to sail with us."

"You did what? You mean the reverie goes on?"

"No, this was in real life. She returned before the prisoners arrived and left before we sailed."

"Did you tell her about your dream?"

"Yes. More or less. I was upset, but she didn't show any reaction at all. In fact she was cold, almost hard."

"What did you expect? The girl has to protect herself from young men like you, who don't have their feet on the ground. She walks on solid ground, while you're walking in the clouds!"

"Her mother was a countess and her father in the service of the Tsar. Do you think that might be one of the reasons that in my dream I saw her in a tower?"

"You didn't know that when you were dreaming and they say that dreams are never prophetic. However, a ... sensitive person can charge the batteries of the unconscious with information from the past and process it, as a computer may predict what is to come. But as the Greek folk-saying goes, any prophet after Christ is a jackass!"

"What about my fainting?"

"You were so intensely involved with the dream that you would have collapsed anyway ... after two days without any sleep! You still look pale and tired."

"I can still imagine Olga in front of me. Back on the bridge, I saw her flying in the clouds, swimming on the waves, standing on the prow of the ship."

"It would be best if you went and laid down for a while till it's time for your watch."

Which is what he did.

It took two days and two nights to reach Constantinople, where they would stop long enough for a committee of Spanish officials to embark. They had been unable to go to Russia as the two countries did not have diplomatic relations.

The weather was better than on the trip out – not as cold, fewer clouds and a light northerly that only raised small, choppy waves.

The Spaniards began to move about on the ship and to get used to the idea of freedom.

"It's like a resurrection," Captain Palladio, the superior officer among the prisoners (a tall, gaunt figure, long-faced in the style of a picture by El Greco), said to Alexis as they ate together at the same table on that first evening, with Monsieur Dupont, Michelle and the other Spanish officers. The doctor ate by himself in a corner but in the end couldn't bear his isolation and came to join the group.

"It's strange that after the first emotion, you feel that all the years of captivity have never existed, as if you'd made a jump in time, like you'd been asleep and woken up eleven years later. Now my mind is back in Spain and I think that I will find everything the way it was. I know it won't be like that, but that's how I feel," Palladio said.

And of course there was an immediate barrage of questions by the others around the table.

"What can I tell you and where can I begin. All those years we thought about how we would describe our experiences when we returned to our homes and now all we want to do is forget. And everything is so perplexing! I will tell you one thing: the best school for a young communist is a trip to Russia," Captain Palladio rambled.

"Were you in concentration camps all those years?" Dupont asked and Lieutenant Castillo this time answered: "Yes, but we were not only in concentration camps, we also worked on the Kolholz, the collective farms, and in factories."

"The transit camps, Parasilka, they call them, where they have the facilities both for prisoners of war and ordinary prisoners: they usually put you up in grand old hotels. They exist in every town in Russia," another Spanish officer, Rammel added.

"The prisoners are a huge mass of people who are constantly being moved, according to need, from compulsory labour, to concentration camps, to prisons. Twenty-five million souls from many races, covering the gamut from German prisoners-of-war to Georgians, Jews, Armenians, dissidents and Russians sentenced by criminal law. And this number is the present estimate, after the amnesty Malenkov granted," Castillio explained.

Alexis looked at him sceptically, because the number sounded rather inflated.

"Didn't you ever try to escape?" he asked.

"Are you serious?" Palladio answered. "Many have tried but few have succeeded. In the vastness of Russia which way would you go and what would you do when you got anywhere? There are organisations that give you forged papers and if you have learned a little Russian, you might be able to reach the border areas – though who knows who might betray you for a crust of bread – but these zones are the most treacherous, their inhabitants being the people most faithful to the regime. Entire groups are relocated in order to make the twenty to twenty-five kilometres deep border areas secure."

Then it was Claudio Rammel's turn to tell his story: "I worked for a long time, at the beginning of my captivity, in Caraga. A coal mine in Siberia. The phrase alone gives you the picture. All day, bent over, pick-axe in hand, hauling coal on your back through tunnels hardly one metre high. Now they tell us they have brought in electric drills. What can I say? They may have, I wouldn't know."

"I also worked in a coal mine, in Cresnapo," Castillio picked up. "It's a small town, quiet and depressing, amid endless steppes. You seldom see a soul in the streets and the display windows of the few shops that you can count on one finger are as empty as the shops themselves. But when a committee of Scandinavian coal miners came for a visit one time, the streets were decorated, the windows filled with goodies and new mining equipment was deployed. They even took us captives for a tour of the town that day, as though we were going to a festival!"

Rammel leaned down and took a loaf of bread from a bag. "This hard black bread is what we ate. The farmers who cultivate the wheat in the grain-producing areas eat the same thing. Try it!" he told Dupont.

"No, thank you," the Frenchman replied, thinking of freshly-baked baguettes in the French bakeries.

"Where does the good wheat go?" the Frenchman asked.

"It all goes to the State, which distributes it as it sees fit or exports it."

"But I thought the Russians imported wheat because they didn't have enough," Alexis said, thinking that something wasn't quite right about this story.

"We have no way of knowing what kind of game they are playing. We were only captives. I know only one thing, this is the bread we ate throughout all those years."

'Was his answer an evasion?' Alexis questioned.

Captain Palladio was the most taciturn, as if he wanted to avoid the questions that would inevitably lead to *the* question: "Why did you fight with Hitler's forces?" So he tried to change the subject.

"To be able to eat real food at a table laid with a white tablecloth, porcelain plates and proper knives and forks – what a feast! Thank you all!"

"We've only cooked plain food for you. Rice with meat in tomato sauce so that the change in diet from captivity won't be too sudden; anyway the ship's cook doesn't know how to cook paella," Michelle added eagerly.

"We have a soldier who was a good cook in Spain, if you let him cook and give him rice, chicken, shrimp and saffron, he'll make you the best paella you've ever eaten! I'm sure he hasn't forgotten the recipes. The expectation of making a paella again one day kept him alive."

They raised their glasses of red wine. The question was finally brought up by ... who else ... the woman: "Tell us, why did you volunteer to fight with the Germans against the Russians? I hope you don't consider the question indiscreet."

Dupont, Alexis and the doctor cast approving glances at Michelle for the courage they hadn't had themselves.

"I've been expecting that question, since all of you on this ship, whether French or Greek, fought and defeated the Germans and ... as things turned out ... were allied to the Russians during the war. But let me tell you one thing and let there be no doubt in your minds. Russia is preparing for another war. This time against the West. From the day the Second World War ended, it began to prepare for the next one. Soviet communism *must* conquer if it is to survive. Tsarist Imperialism under the guise of the communist ideology. We were the soldiers of General Franco who volunteered to fight against communism for our children to live in a free world. That is why we also fought during the Civil War in Spain. Not for profit, but for freedom. You Greeks and French ought to understand that better than anyone else."

"But the Spanish Democratic Army wasn't communist! At that time free men stood at the side of the Democrats, Malraux, Picasso,

Hemingway and so many others. It was Franco who was strangling freedom!"

This was the doctor, speaking with passion, and his flushed cheeks had become even darker.

"This man is a constant revelation on this trip," Alexis said to himself, once more.

"You are talking about freedom and you fought with Hitler?" the doctor pressed on.

"Don't be deceived!" Captain Palladio said, calmly but clearly upset.

Alexis thought that perhaps it wasn't the right moment, on the first day of their liberation to attack them in such a way, but it was too late to stop this discussion now.

"We'll talk about it again in a few years. If you had lived for eleven years as a captive in Stalin's Russia, you would see that we made the right choice. We don't regret it. Being there confirmed our fears."

So they hadn't repented! And now they were all eating at the same table – winners and losers. What was odd, was that despite their ideological stand, they all felt some compassion for people who had lived as prisoners-of-war for eleven years, no matter who they were.

Alexis remained silent for a moment and then asked a simple, very naive question: "But are the Russian people unhappy? Despairing? Don't they laugh, have fun, sing?"

There was a touch of anguish in his voice that only the doctor was able to catch. He whispered: "Olga?"

"Yes, Olga, I want to know!"

"How can you sing, when you can't speak or move about like your mind tells you to?" the doctor interrupted anticipating the Spaniard's answer.

"You talk as though you're translating from ancient Greek, dottore!" Alexis said with a smile and added, with a touch of hope in his voice: "but the canary sings, even when it is caged!"

"And who knows if his canto isn't a sad one?" the doctor answered and turned toward Michelle for approval of his momentous utterance!

Michelle, who had been trying to keep up appearances, this time met his eyes with a look of admiration.

"Not only a good lover, but a psychologist and now, a poet as well!" Alexis said sarcastically to the doctor and went on seriously: "During the occupation of Greece by the enemy, we were in a cage too and we fought and we had only very little food to survive on and no heat but our songs were not sorrowful."

He stopped with that to let his mind calm down for a while, to withdraw from the discussion into his own world, on the ever receding Russian steppes.

Michelle had lost her caution of the first days of the trip – you'd think the doctor had deflowered both her and her controlled behaviour. She lifted her third glass of wine and drank to the freedom of the Spaniards, "and to you Doctor," then turned to Captain Castillio. "Tell me about the women in Russia."

"I will tell you two stories that say a lot. One winter, on a deserted street in Charkov a well-dressed woman was out walking at night. She was wearing fur and silk stockings, an example of the Party's favour. On a street corner Ukrainian autonomists of the 'Black Cat' organisation, which often staged robberies in residential areas and which that night were in high spirits, waited in ambush. At the same time a simple woman was passing by wearing thick, woollen stockings, a pinned up apron, long skirt and the classic quilted coat. The 'Black Cat' jumped on both of them and in a flash they had undressed them and exchanged their outfits. The one, stripped of her finery, quickly ran away. The other stayed long enough to say to them: 'I thank you for the fancy clothes, but I was much warmer in my own!'"

Alexis suddenly awoke from his torpor.

"You see," he told the doctor, "silk stuff doesn't keep you warm!" He realised he had left a piece of his heart in Russia.

"What about the other story?" Michelle prompted.

"I was working in a factory in Charkov. Working next to me was a woman who was expecting a child. She was in the final days of her pregnancy and the doctor at the factory wouldn't give her leave to go home. Even when labour started she was forced to continue working. She gave birth right there, on a made-up table in the factory. Fortunately, without complications."

"And ... by the way ... didn't you have 'relationes amorosos' with Russian girls all that time?" the doctor jumped at the occasion to talk about his favourite subject.

Juan Iglesias, a tall, dark Spaniard, perhaps the Casanova of the group, who approached the table at that moment, undertook to answer without sitting down. "Of course we did. Women in Russia don't find love as we know it in the West, at least not today. The present-day Russian men & women are violent. They, got a little tenderness from us. When conditions of survival are harsh, emotions are set aside."

"There's the answer!" Alexis thought immediately. "That's why Olga was restrained" – and satisfied his egotism yet again.

"In women we found a little kindness, even if we only could meet secretly," Juan Iglesias went on.

A new shock for Alexis who was trying to get his emotions in order, but wasn't being helped by the controversy under discussion.

"Was your captivity harsh?" Michelle asked.

Franco Diaz, who had also joined the party, attempted to explain. "There were so many thousands of us captives. We, the 286 on board are the only survivors. Some died, some vanished into Siberia. In one concentration camp, the guards gave one of ours a heart of a colleague who had died the previous day, to eat, without him realising it of course. I can still hear their laughter. As soon as they told him. Perhaps that was the most terrible story I carry with me from those eleven years in Russia. Otherwise, they fed us simply, but well enough and every so often there was a package from the Red Cross. The thing that destroys you is not having any contact with the outside world. None! Even now we don't know if our parents are still alive, or our wives or our children. We are looking forward, but with anguish, to getting to Istanbul for the Spaniards you told us, Mr Dupont, will be coming on board, with news of our families. It won't be easy."

The first to leave the group was the doctor. His intentions were obvious for he winked at Michelle as he bade goodnight to the group.

The *Semiramis* was a slow boat but with the weather to the stern the return trip was faster. They could have reached Istanbul earlier but they would have arrived during the night and the Captain preferred to cut speed and be at the mouth of the Bosphorus at dawn to anchor opposite Aghia Sophia in daylight.

It was around nine in the morning when the rattle of chains announced the casting of the anchor. The sacred ceremony of the bell was conducted on the prow with the bosun as the high priest; he struck it so the sound would carry all the way to God, the Captain, and it was followed by the clatter of the loosening of the chains till the ship had been made secure.

There was enough time for the Greek crew to gather on deck to gaze with reverence at Aghia Sophia once more, before two boats approached, one carrying the authorities and the shipping agent and the other the Spanish committee. All the Spanish captives were on deck, but made no attempt to greet the representatives of their country or show any particular emotion at reaching the first city of their new-found freedom. They were waiting with bated breath for the news that was being brought them.

Alexis wanted to tell them about Constantinople, about Aghia Sophia, about Byzantium, but remained silent, respecting their anguished state. He limited himself to leaning on the bridge and watching the two launches which had drawn up to the gangway. Their passengers came up one by one. He made out a woman among them … Olga?

He rubbed his eyes and then peeked again at the tall, twenty-year old girl who climbed the steps with regal bearing. She wore a nurse's uniform like an imperial cloak, and her semi-circular starched cap like a valuable tiara.

Alexis glanced around. If the fire in the three hundred pairs of eyes of the Spanish prisoners and the Greek crew which focused on her legs as she ascended step by step had been real, they would have put her to the stake like the Maid of Orleans. "A holocaust in Constantinople", he thought to himself and closed his eyes, as usual, when he was … off track!

No, it wasn't Olga. He tried to reconstruct this new figure in his mind for she had now disappeared from his sight. Was she the most beautiful woman he had ever seen in his life? From afar he had made out large eyes like a gazelle, long, carefully curled eyelashes, the delicate hued skin. Each of her features had its own personality. The fresh lipstick on her sensuous lips, the hollow cheeks, the ancient Greek profile! But why did he feel resistance? Normally, he would have gone down to the salon to receive the committee with the other ship's officers and to translate for the Captain who spoke only Greek.

But he hadn't budged from the bridge. "If they need me, they'll call for me," he told himself. And so they did. It wasn't long before a sailor showed up with the Captain's orders. With a heavy heart he went down to the salon to meet the new group of people who had joined the Captain, the Doctor, Monsieur Dupont, Michelle and Captain Palladio.

As he approached, the doctor said in Greek: "Hey, get an eyeful of this dish!"

After Alexis shook hands with the Greek Shipping Agent, and Turkish authorities, Captain Palladio introduced the members of the committee to him one by one, leaving till last Senorita Estrella Gomez Sebastian, the princess of his new fairy tale.

Alexis didn't know why but he had planned on snubbing her, to keep her at a distance, to feign indifference and with an expressionless look to try to avoid her eyes which fixed themselves on him with no hesitation. But when she shook his hand, an electrical current scuttled all his plans. His "How do you do?" in English seemed to hang there and his glance was uncertain. A confused picture, like a double-exposure on a slide, with two figures, one over the other, slid before him. One made him feel a tug at his heart whereas the other triggered a negative emotion, mixed with admiration.

But the figure of Olga was now on a second plane. He shook his head a little to drive the transparencies from his mind and to translate for the Captain the polite formalities.

"Captain, we wish to thank you and your crew for bringing these brave men of the Companie Azul back to their homeland. The name of your ship will go down in history of Spain, in the unending battle of men for the realisation of their ideals, just like the *Santa Maria* of Christopher Columbus, which will be bedecked with flags to welcome you into the harbour of Barcelona!"

"Captain!" Alexis began to translate with a slight smile, word by word and the only thing he added on his own was "no more, no less than" when he mentioned *Santa Maria*.

Captain Gerasimos was unused to ceremonies and speeches, but with the certainty of the experienced sailor who never drowns in shallow water, he replied simply: "Ladies and gentlemen, to be able to help people is always satisfying. It is God's work. During the war you save a shipwrecked person no matter which side he belongs to!"

He put things in their proper perspective and then added in a wily tone: "I regret though that we didn't return with the spoils of Columbus!"

Alexis hoped that the Spanish would consider the words of the Captain to be an example of modesty and not irony and he stressed them accordingly. They shook hands.

Dimitris Zervoudakis, the Greek agent, born and bred in Constantinople, with the traditional courtesy of the Constantinopolitans, and the open-handed eastern custom of making presents, handed to all, Chatzibekir Turkish delights, one of the most famous treats of Istanbul, before he bade them goodbye and left the ship with the Turkish authorities.

The *Semiramis* was ready to cast off again.

To leave the salon, the Captain and the other officers had to squeeze their way through the Spanish ex-captives who had lined up in the corridor waiting to be called by the committee.

Up with the anchor, three hoots of the horn, a wave from afar to the agent and the Turks who were leaving in their boat, one last glance at Aghia Sophia and full steam ahead for Barcelona.

But the speeches, it appeared, hadn't ended. The voice of the principal Spanish official boomed out from the loudspeaker.

"Heroes! General Franco sent me to welcome you and bring you back into the embrace of the homeland. There are men who fight with courage because they are asked to do so by their homeland and become heroes. But what does one call those who voluntarily give themselves to the greatest ideal, the ideal of freedom? They are called free people – a word greater than hero!"

Alexis, who was listening carefully, would have been moved by the words if they hadn't been uttered by a representative of a Dictator. "How people play with words!" he thought while the loudspeaker went on: "Let us observe a moment of silence for all those who were lost in the endless nights of Siberia."

Once more the engines of the *Semiramis* kept the rhythm during the sixty seconds of silence. When they had passed, Alexis, hurried to the bridge in exasperation and pulled on the cord of the ship's horn which let out an incredible sound, reaching well beyond the minarets of Constantinople out to the plains of Eastern Thrace, a moment which the silence of the three hundred Spaniards and the crew made even more impressive.

The second officer, who was on duty from four to eight, was a little under the weather and asked Alexis and Captain Gerasimos, if they could, to take half of his watch.

It was around five in the afternoon and Alexis was on the bridge. They were still sailing in the Propondis before entering the Dardanelles. He was bored and the few boats they had passed weren't enough to entertain him.

He had been on duty since noon. No matter how far your mind travelled, five hours standing was too much. He looked at the foam rising from the bow as it split the sea. It was always his final ploy when he had exhausted all his thoughts and dreams. The endless motion of the foaming waters held his eyes and relaxed him, until he heard the helmsman whispering:

"Captain Alexis we have visitors!"

Alexis looked to the left since the wind was blowing from the Starboard side and anyone coming up to the bridge used the protected side.

The helmsman corrected him: "On the Starboard side, Captain Alexis, not the Port side."

He turned his head the other way and there was Estrella standing behind the half-window of the closed door, her hair loose and streaming in the wind.

His first thought: "God, not yet another vision!" Since that night in Odessa he hadn't trusted his eyes. Particularly when he was in front of a window! If the helmsman hadn't announced visitors, he might have hastily averted his eyes to avoid another dream episode.

His second thought was: "An advertisement of L'Oreal for auburn hair!" as he saw the figure of Estrella framed by the window and the aggressiveness he had felt when he had first seen her came to the fore again.

Estrella looked at him with a faint imploring smile on her lips and in her eyes a look that said: "Open up!"

'What a curious combination. Arrogance and humility,' Alexis thought. And although he had not intended to respond, he opened the door and gestured her in. "When there's this much wind you should come up to the bridge on the other side if … if you don't want to ruin your hairdo," he instructed her first severely, then changing half-way into irony. And then kicked himself. Damn it! He usually had more self-control and had never liked to offend people.

"I'm sorry, I didn't know, it's the first time I've been on board ship," Estrella replied politely.

Alexis relented a little: "You seem a little sad. Am I being tactless?"

"The last Spanish prisoner has just passed before the Committee. If you had been present you would have been sad too. One discovered he had lost his parents, another his brother and sisters, the wife of another had remarried and made a new home, thinking her husband was dead. To live in hope for eleven years, and then, just when the solution seems at hand, to see it slip away!"

"It sounds tragic. But don't forget they were all volunteers. They took fate in their own hands. They played and lost."

"How can you be so cynical about these heroic men?"

"I'm not being cynical, quite the contrary, but you see I am a pragmatist and besides, forgive me but … they are not heroes. They are adventurers, in the good sense – don't get me wrong. Soldiers of fortune." He heard his voice but he couldn't recognise himself. For any other woman, for any other person, he would have found words of comfort.

"Doesn't eleven years of captivity count?"

Alexis heard a flash of anger in her voice. "They had no other choice."

"You don't seem like a cruel person and I don't understand you."

"I am not, but don't forget, we were the soldiers fighting on the other side."

"I do understand and I've heard that you went through a lot in Greece with the war and Hitler – that Monster! He even had France duped!" Estrella said innocently.

"Shall we change the subject?"

"You started it." She had regained her composure and wanted to have the last word. "What are you doing up here?"

"Guiding the ship." And he added modestly: "Supposedly!"

"But isn't the gentleman at the wheel guiding it?"

"He is looking at some numbers on that machine that is called a compass so that we will stay on the right course. Let's say he's the reason, the consciousness if you like, of the ship, who always brings it back on the right course if it veers off course in its imagination."

"And what do you do then? Does the ship have imagination?"

It was partly a personal question and Alexis warmed to the subject.

"Does a ship have imagination? And how! Isn't she a she? They say fantasies are useful. I make sure that we don't collide with other ships using their own reason and imagination – I try to reach a compromise between their fantasies and those of my own ship. Only when you wed reason and imagination can you sail smoothly. A journey of endless compromise."

Estrella couldn't really tell if he was speaking seriously or being ironical, but she seemed to enjoy it.

"And who are you? Why did they bring you all the way from Spain with the Committee?"

"Well, I am also a volunteer. A nurse, as you can see. I am here to give the prisoners the comfort of a female presence."

"A volunteer nurse? You mean you're from one of those aristocratic families of Spain who use philanthropy to assuage their guilt."

His aggressiveness had come to the fore again.

"What is it you have against the world, against people? What's so bad about the desire to help others? Why should I feel guilty? Because my family is one of the Grands d'Espagne? I'm proud of it and I don't owe anybody anything!"

Alexis knew very well why he was reacting the way he was, but he didn't want to admit it to himself. She was so beautiful when she expressed herself with her whole body and with theatrical gestures! "What do I have against the world, against people? Do you want to hear my confession? I've never confessed before in my life, not even to a priest. Do you want me to confess to a nurse for the first time, when I've only known her for a few moments?"

"Why not? If you can speak to me in this imprudent, this impertinent manner, you can also confess or be psychoanalysed if you want to be more modern. I am a Catholic. Once a year I kneel before the confessional."

"And where will my confessional be?"

"You know the boat, you choose the place."

"In your cabin."

"I knew you'd say that. But all right, I'm not afraid of you. You need someone to teach you a lesson!"

'Why did she say that?' He thought to himself. 'What right had she to invade my soul? Did I offer it to her unknowingly?'

"After the evening meal then."

"After the evening meal."

Estrella opened the door on the port side of the bridge by herself and glancing back said: "As you can see, I'm going out the proper side so I won't ruin my hairdo. My cabin is number 4."

Alexis was left perplexed, as he closed behind her the door she had left open.

"I don't know about you, Captain Alexis, but I think these Spanish ladies are hot stuff!" the helmsman blurted out in his Corfiot accent, a silent witness to the conversation, despite the fact that both of them had ignored him. "I don't know if you're aware of it," he went on, "but if I hadn't changed course twice we would have had two victims by now: a Turkish caique and a Russian trawler! You may be a good sailor Captain Alexis, but you don't make the best skipper. That Senorita turned your head. If we left things up to you, you would tie a cable from the bow to the nearest cloud and let it take you wherever it chose!"

"Look who's talking! Our Corfiot troubadour who would be far better off serenading in the Spianada in Corfu, rather than fooling around with the sea and ships." Alexis said mocking his accent, as Captain Gerasimos came in to replace him.

Alexis went straight to see the doctor in his office. It turned out the doctor was reading English ballads in French translation. He started to talk to him but the doctor cut him off. He turned a few pages of the book and began to recite, translating into Greek:

"St. George then looking round about,
The fiery dragon soon espied,
And like a knight of courage stout,
Against him did most fiercely ride;
And with such blows he did him greet,
He fell beneath his horse's feet.
For with his lance that was so strong,
As he came gaping in his face,
In at his mouth he thrust along;
For he could pierce no other place:
And thus within the lady's view
this mighty dragon straight he slew.

"Doesn't that story remind you of something? The horse, the Dragon ... Alexeeei!" his voice echoed in the small cabin.

"You're impossible. Where did you get those English ballads?"

"Believe it or not, from one of the prisoners. A book from 1880 that was given him by a Russian girl from her family library."

"Listen Doctor, Estrella, the dish as you call her, was on the bridge and when I spoke to her each one of my words had a tinge of irony, criticism or pure malice. Since you have become my psychiatrist – tell me why?"

The doctor appeared to be thinking deeply.

"That she was on the bridge, I am already cognisant of. Nothing secret can prevail upon this ship. The problem, my child, is very simple. If you'll permit me, I'll go on reading the ballad:

When as that valiant champion there
Had slain the dragon in the field,
To court he brought the lady fair,
Which to their hearts much joy did yield.
He in the court of Egypt stayed

Till he most falsely was betrayed.

"Doctor you're rambling. Stop trying to be another Delphic oracle!"

"How should I speak? Like a gypsy: 'There is one who has betrayed you but another who must pay' or even "Love was born in icy Russia and replanted in fiery Spain!"

"Are you trying to say that I see Olga in Estrella?"

"Yes and no. You want Estrella to be a continuation of Olga, but you revenge yourself on her for what she has that Olga doesn't and since Olga kept her distance and this one makes advances you lash out at her. It's easy to hurt the one who loves you. The others don't wait around for you to attack them."

"Hey, what do you mean she loves me!"

"In a manner of speaking. She's purring. I saw the way she looked at you when she was introduced to you. Besides, why else would she come up to the bridge? Was it to find out which way the wind was blowing?"

"Do you know what she said to me? That I needed someone to give me my comeuppance. Can you imagine that? And that I should go to her for confession."

"Well, that girl is smart and sensitive as well. And knowing you, you agreed, which also means you accepted her coming down hard on you. The child runs to its mother's arms, the nurse, the good, the pure, the protectress. But, just like with our mother, we try to pull away."

"It seems to me that both of you are round the bend. Confessing, oracles, gypsies, psychoanalysis – the two or you have got me surrounded."

"The Furies, my son, the Furies!"

"Come on, let's go for dinner. We'll eat in the crew's mess. I don't want to meet Estrella during the meal. I'm hungry after six hours on the bridge and I want to see food, to touch it with my hands, to put it in my mouth, to do something completely instinctual, something basic because we've overdone the 'spirito and anima' as our Corfiot friend the helmsman would say. But tell me, in your interpretation of my dream the Dragon is the Commissar, fine, I understand that, but the courtiers who betray St. George, who are they?"

"Who do you think is holding Olga captive? It's so simple! Where's your imagination?"

"It's my fault for taking you seriously."

"Your case is a classic example of what psychiatrists call 'fusion'. I'm just telling you if by chance you need to use the word during the course of your confession!"

Alexis remembered the blending of the two images that he had experienced when he first saw Estrella climbing the gangway. Like a double exposure, he thought or better yet, like two transparencies, one over the other! Could the doctor be right?

The desire to eat with his hands that Alexis had expressed was not just a figure of speech. The agent in Constantinople had brought them red mullet from the Bosphorus and the cook fried it for the crew. Alexis devoured the fish from head to tail, leaving only the bones. During the meal he didn't speak, only mused over whether he would go to his appointment with Estrella or not. He had almost decided not to go but his encounter with this woman had shaken him. Finally, at nine precisely, when he figured that she would have finished her meal too, he knocked on the door of her cabin. It was convenient because No. 4 was on the boat deck with the door facing the deck so no-one could see him entering.

Estrella opened the door. He had imagined her waiting for him in some gossamer nightdress, at the most, a silk robe. Instead, she was still wearing her well-tailored uniform, without a wrinkle, as if it had just come from the cleaners. On the bridge she had been wearing her blue cape and one could only have an inkling of the perfect proportions of her body. "I wasn't certain that you would come especially after what I said to you about ... teaching you a lesson. I'm sorry, perhaps I was a bit extreme."

"I wasn't even sure that I was going to come myself. Not because of what you said to me but because it seemed like you were trying to enter my soul uninvited."

"And wasn't your rudeness a kind of invasion?"

"But I ... I've known you for a long time!"

"What are you talking about?"

"It's a strange story. The doctor explained everything to me; he's a radiologist but also plays the part of a psychologist."

"So you confessed to him before you came to me?"

"Thank God, because otherwise I wouldn't have known what to say and I would have stayed mute or reacted in the same manner as before."

"Whereas?"

"Whereas now, I know why I acted like that."

"And why is that?"

They were still standing in the open door. She finally decided to let him in: "Come and sit on the couch and tell me." Her voice was courteous and tender but firm. She was in complete control of herself.

"You see, it was this girl in Russia – I met her less than two days ago and she already seems like dream."

"What was her name? Did you fall in love with her?" she asked calmly without a trace of uneasiness in her voice – she seemed so sure of herself!

"Olga. Did I love her? I only knew her for a few hours. But perhaps I empathised with her. Like me, she was from an old family – part of the Tsar's court – and now she is a minor employee, in Russia's Shipping Agency, without family, without town, without silk stockings."

Estrella tugged her skirt down to cover her legs and her expensive stockings. This modest action showed him that she cared about his feelings – and he appreciated it. "You see how easy it is to confess?"

"Without a doubt, it's easier to confess to a pretty little face like yours than to the stern beard of some austere Byzantine figure called Seraphim or to the doctor for that matter!"

They took each other's hands as they both laughed. Alexis thought that from there on developments would follow their natural course, and that the next step would be to kiss her, so he duly tried, but Estrella politely pulled away. "Look. You may have misunderstood me when I came to the bridge and when I let you come to my cabin. But now it is I who must confess something to you: I do want your company. To travel on a boat for the first time on such romantic seas is like a dream to me. But I don't want to build up your hopes. I'm engaged to a Spaniard and I love him and then – be prepared – I'm a virgin."

"You mean you want to *play* with me?" Alexis was aggressive again.

"Don't start the same thing all over again. I am being frank with you. Don't forget I'm a Catholic and even though I don't believe much in formalities, certain things are deeply ingrained in me, whether I like them or not. I'm not a prude, I'm not afraid of a man. Besides, as a nurse I have met a lot of men, some of them stark naked, as you might imagine, but I want to arrive at the threshold of the church not only in a bridal gown but with my virginity intact," she said with a smile.

"If I've learned anything, it's to respect people even when I don't understand them. Don't worry, I won't rape you!"

"Kiss me!"

"You see how you're playing with me?"

"Kiss me! You won't take my virginity with a kiss!"

Alexis was completely at a loss and, almost hesitantly, leaned toward her, but before he was able to press his lips to hers, Estrella embraced him tightly and kissed him on the mouth passionately. Now and then she pulled back to say: "You can squeeze me too!"

Now and then she stroked his hair and whispered: "Mi vida, mi vida ... my life!"

Alexis thought: "I'm holding a very beautiful woman the like of which I've never seen before and perhaps will never see again in my entire life – but I don't feel any passion. I wish she'd let go of me."

Estrella felt Alexis wasn't involved, and a moment later pulled away. "You're thinking about Olga! I know it!"

"But shouldn't you be thinking about your fiancé?"

"Maybe. But that's my business," she said, irritated.

"If I say that you're a spoiled girl from 'high society' will you get angry again?"

"You don't look as though you were born in a stable either!"

"Why, what's wrong with a stable? Christ was born in a stable."

"You know very well what I mean!" She was angry again. "Maybe it's my fault. Maybe we said too much tonight and maybe we did more than we should have. Good night! I'm not throwing you out. Just leave."

But at that point Alexis became furious. If he hadn't been afraid of the whole boat hearing him he would have shouted even louder. "You ought to be locked up. If anybody needs a psychiatrist it's you. Behind your angelic figure – and you do have an angelic figure – lies the Devil. Of course, I'm leaving and don't speak to me again till we reach Barcelona!"

"Go and gaze at the vision of Olga over the waves!" were Estrella's last words.

Alexis went out on deck and stood at the rail so the cold air would hit him and bring him to himself. He wasn't a little child. He'd seen all kinds of women but this one was something else. He couldn't place her in any category nor identify her with any other type. Was she jealous of Olga? Was it her Spanish temperament that made her fickle? He ran off to find – who else? – the doctor. He had to give him a full report and by talking to try and put a little order in his rattled mind. He found him in the salon talking to Michelle and two Spaniards.

As soon as the doctor saw him he asked: "You got through rather quickly. Are you a Speedy Gonzalez? Or did things fall apart?"

"I don't want to interrupt you, but I have to talk to someone or I'll go mad."

"Come on, let's go and sit over there," and turning to Michelle and the Spaniards he asked them to excuse him for a few minutes. "On second thought let's have Michelle come with us. We're a small, close-knit family by now and perhaps Michelle, as a woman, can shed a little light on things. In any case, women have a more down-to-earth mind than we do and usually see things more clearly. If you don't have any objection of course."

"The way things have been going, why not, I'd be curious to hear her explanation even though I'm very doubtful about the mind of woman, tonight at least! But I need to drink something to sharpen my mind and remember Estrella's every word, her every gesture, and maybe come to some conclusion."

Alexis, who had taken the initiative, ordered Grasshoppers for the three of them without asking what they wanted. It was what they usually drank on the ship after the evening meal.

"It's just the thing when your mind is in a dither," he told them – and went on: "Any person, more or less, can draw up an image in his mind about someone he meets, man or woman, either through perception or knowledge, sketching their character either by a logical process or instinctively, by receiving the beams his soul transmits. But this Pucinella has completely jammed my receivers." The words came out more like a condemnation rather than a question that required interpretation.

"Maintenant, doucement, one thing at a time," Michelle interrupted with French logic. "Let's state the problem: Posons le problème."

Alexis remembered his French lessons: statement of problem – analysis – conclusion. "Why not? So listen. A woman shows you that she likes you, she invites you to her cabin, she announces to you that she is a virgin, she kisses you passionately and them throws you out. What conclusions do you draw?"

But the doctor knew better. "Wait a minute, wait a minute. You're telling it too telegraphically and obviously leaving out small details which may be essential."

"All right! I talked to her about Olga and when she was kissing me she said I had Olga on my mind and threw me out."

"Haven't you heard of a word that is very common in daily life called 'jealousy'?", the doctor asked.

Michelle, who was listening, didn't know enough of the story yet to take a line.

"What should she be jealous of? She called me to hear my confession, that's what she said – and, instead, she confesses that she's a virgin!"

"What did you tell her about Olga? There's your problem."

"My problem? My problem you say? My problem is that she was the one who almost forced a kiss on me and then was annoyed because she thought my mind was on Olga?"

Michelle came straight to the point: "Was your mind on Olga or not?"

"It may have been. But since I had spoken to her about Olga she shouldn't have kissed me. I would have understood if she hadn't wanted to screw – chère Michelle, to call a spade a spade – but since she insisted on kissing me she shouldn't have cared about the presence – presence in a manner of speaking – of Olga! 'I'm a virgin, I'm not a prude, I have principles, kiss me! That's more or less what she was saying. Now try to make something out of that one! Bullshit!"

Michelle found the solution to the problem while the doctor watched her in admiration. "Precisely. Bullshit. You seem to have known women in your life but it appears you haven't learned anything about them, yet."

"That's why they're always a surprise," the doctor interjected with his shaking laugh which Alexis hadn't heard in some time.

Michelle went on: "You think everything is black or white, that there are no other shades in the soul and consequently in the way we express ourselves. On the other hand Estrella wants you – after all, all women were virgins until a few seconds before they were deflowered, and on the other she has her taboos and uses Olga as the most convenient excuse, something to hold on to, to help resist temptation at the moment when she is ready to abandon herself. And it is you who gave her that excuse. So don't complain. Right, doctor?"

"The best psychiatrist couldn't have made a better analysis."

But Alexis kept on: "And on top of everything else she's engaged to be married!"

"So? That is something that you men shouldn't concern yourself with," and she looked coyly at the doctor.

Alexis hadn't been absolutely convinced by Michelle's words but they had been reasonable enough and besides he wanted to give Estrella the benefit of the doubt. At any rate, he went to sleep no longer feeling that he had been insulted by the woman who had thrown him out of her cabin.

It was the third night since they'd left Odessa but Olga was still a real presence in Alexis's mind. "Tomorrow you'll see," he told himself, "things will be clearer." From former experiences he had learned that 'great loves' lasted for three days from the last time the face was seen, like a mild fever. Three days go quickly. The French phrase: "Loin des yeux, loin du coeur', 'out of sight, out of mind (and heart!)' had become a living experience for him and the idea that his feelings weren't deep didn't bother him. Perhaps it even suited him. On his night watch, the image of Olga had already grown faint and if there was a way to meet Estrella again he really wanted to. Besides, she had aroused his curiosity and he needed to figure a way to approach her without deflating his ego.

He didn't have to take any initiative, Estrella took the initiative once more by knocking on the door of his cabin the following morning. He was still half-asleep when he heard her voice: "It's me." He reacted with mixed emotions because he was tired and would have preferred if she had come by a bit later. For a moment he even thought of not opening the door. Now that her return had been assured he could afford the luxury of acting a little macho, to preserve his dignity in her eyes, despite the fact that he considered his withdrawal from her cabin the night before had been performed with great dignity. He had left shouting and calling her mad!

"Open up, I'm cold."

Her voice was working on him like the teasing voice of a little child. "She's changed roles," Alexis thought and got up from his bed to open the door. "Excuse my pyjamas – but when I'm sleeping I don't get dressed to receive ... uninvited visitors!"

"Do you want to punish me? Should I come in or leave?"

She had him cornered again. How did she always manage to get the upper hand? Now he had to ask her in, but was in need of an excuse. "I don't want to be responsible for you catching a cold, if for no other reason than that our doctor is a radiologist and I doubt if he would be able to treat you. Besides, he's a great womaniser and you'd be in danger!"

"You can say what you want, it doesn't put me off. I come humbly to ask your forgiveness. I'm impossible, I know. May I sit down? On the bed or the chair?"

"Wherever you like and excuse the mess."

"Shall I make up your bed?"

"Have you decided that I'm not going to sleep any more? Or does the unmade bed prejudice you and frighten you?"

"Neither the one nor the other. It is simply a question of aesthetics or perhaps professional training. The first thing you learn as a nurse is to make up beds. It also has a symbolic meaning. A mother making her child's bed."

"Ah! Now I know why you told me I should get my comeuppance yesterday! Your professional training! That's why you're wearing a uniform too, you want to be my nanny. And since I won't let you, you want to spank me."

"You're a real joke and you don't know what you're talking about. I'm wearing my uniform because I'm not allowed to do otherwise. Do you forget that I'm here on a mission?"

"Ah, yes, I'm sorry. How could I forget! In any case, you are executing your mission wonderfully!"

"This is our third meeting and it's not going any better than the first or the second, I can see that!"

"If you want to be a mother lie down and I'll arrange for you to have a child, so you can offer the fruit of your love to your fiancé – it won't be his, but what's the difference? You will be a fulfilled woman while now you are still in the 'process of development.'"

"If I'm in the process of development, you're completely underdeveloped. And no matter how much you hate me you have no right to speak to me like this, when I came to humbly ask your forgiveness. But how am I supposed to follow your absurd thinking? It would be better if I left again, it was a bad idea to come in the first place."

He started to say, "If you think that I hate you, I really don't. To hate, you have to have an interest in some!" But his good upbringing wouldn't allow him to hurt her any more. "I have never hated anyone," he told her instead. "Make up the bed so the environment will have the aesthetic balance you're looking for and sit down on the chair. I'm going to lie down."

"You say you've never hated – but have you ever loved?"

He had a hard time answering. Had he ever loved? He tried to avoid the question by saying: "Didn't you tell me my mind was on Olga? So ..."

"So what? I'm talking about real love, great love, love that leads you down a road of no return."

"And what about you?"

"I'm searching like one possessed. For me this trip is an escape on a great quest, for the great adventure, to a different world, free, without clouds."

And just as on the previous evening, she grabbed his head and began to kiss him and to stroke his chest. She unbuttoned his pyjamas in a frenzy and mixing words with kisses continued: "Without clouds, far from prejudice, far from the fear of punishment, far from the fear of being swallowed up by the bourgeois images of Hell." And she talked and talked maybe so she wouldn't think about what she was doing and with her eyes closed so she wouldn't see, as her hand now crept inside his pyjamas, while her other hand led Alexis to caress her under her white and unsullied snow-white skirt, like a bridal gown!

Alexis followed everything passively. When all was said and done, why should he feel any remorse? – though the idea of her fiancé down there on the Iberian Peninsula did bother him. And now Estrella was sobbing as she talked. "I'm afraid. Can't you understand? I'm afraid that I'm not living. What do you make of a life, if it's not to live through dreams and emotions? I had the chance to leave Spain, to travel the open sea under the open sky, so I used all my influence to accompany the Committee on this expedition. It wasn't difficult. They chose me more for my appearance than for my professional abilities."

Alexis began to loosen up and to participate more actively in the early morning love feast, to kiss her on the throat, on the breast, to stroke her silken skin above her stockings and finally around her moist velvet cave, so Estrella again would cry out: "Mid vida, mi vida ... my life!" How strange! She didn't seem to question where this ceremony would end up. He let himself go and enjoyed the moment with this volcano and suddenly her look changed. She moved her face away from his and looked him in the eyes triumphantly, as if she were holding the banner of victory, as if she had conquered him utterly.

For Alexis, lovemaking was a ceremonial process which was why he always began it humbly, tenderly. He expected the same of the woman. He didn't like to be conquered and to have her crow in triumph at the end of it all. Automatically, as these things happen, without anyone knowing the how or the why, the image of Olga, the inflexible priestess, passed through his mind – and the weapon Estrella was holding became an innocent little mouse.

She lowered her eyes and pulled away her hand. "Of all the insults you have thrown at me, this is the worst! Don't you desire me at all?" She got up, straightened her clothes and left in humiliation and tears.

"This is a sick situation!" the doctor told him when they met later in the evening. "And I don't know what to say to you anymore. Leave it alone! Estrella wants to build up a great love affair between Constantinople and Barcelona. Chance brought her to you – I don't want to insult you, but whomever else she would have found young and somewhat ... presentable, would have served as well. There's the Greek expression you must be familiar with: 'she's got an itch that needs scratching' and all the rest is bullshit. But you're not completely on the side-lines! Look at how Olga came back at the critical moment to turn you off!"

"Lately, you've been the confessor, the psychiatrist, the poet and the good friend – and now you're being the cynical quack on Hippocrates Street!"

"Why Hippocrates Street?"

"Asclepius Street if you prefer! Because you are only following the path of your predecessors."

"You're the one that didn't get what you wanted! And you're taking it out on me. Life makes you cynical by itself. Either you survive or you fade into the background. Choose! Unless you want to be straddling the fence your whole life."

"And how am I supposed to avoid Estrella from here on? We still have three days left. The *Semiramis* is not an ocean liner. I can't isolate myself in my cabin or on the bridge. Do you think she intended to sleep with me today?"

"Do you want me to ask her? You're the one taking all the risks. I certainly wouldn't have such reservations!"

"As if we didn't have enough sex maniacs around already!"

Suddenly he felt very alone, abandoned, shrunken. Even the doctor didn't take him seriously any more. And he was furious with himself. To lose his desire for the most beautiful woman he had ever seen, and from such close contact. "Christ! I never suffered that kind of catastrophe at Gabriela's whorehouse and then I lose my hard-on with the Venus de Milo!" he shouted.

"I'd lose mine too with the Venus de Milo," the doctor said, "too cold, pale and too ... white!"

"Cold? Maybe the one in the Louvre but not this one I can assure you. If we had made love you would have seen the *Semiramis* bucking around like it was in a force ten gale even if it was dead calm (he paused). But white she is ... her pure white skin, her white stockings, that she never takes off and ... you know what she told me? That a nurse arouses maternal feelings in a sick person."

"Aha! Why didn't you say so? That's why you couldn't ... And don't call me cynical again. No-one sleeps with his mother. Hah, hah, hah!"

"Hah, hah, hah. A little while ago you told me my problem was Olga."

"So what? You've become involved with two women here, Olga and Estrella, so why not have another one in the game? Anyway, the mother always pops in somewhere."

"Dottore, it seems to me you have become completely confused and from here on in I'm going to follow my own instincts. So, I'm not going to drive her away. I've had it! I'll find her, I'll grab her, I'll lay the bitch and I'll give her the back of my hand and we'll see who's looking for Mommy or Daddy!"

"Now we suddenly have a Marquis de Sade."

"Oh why don't you go and ..." Alexis said and left.

He had to come up with a plan. 'Let today go by,' he told himself. 'In any case, she won't get over the passion so quickly, it will last. Don't try anything tonight, sleep a little and tomorrow, with a fresh mind, during the midday watch, make a decision. Nothing gets done with a tired mind.' Suddenly he felt better. Now he was on the attack. That night he slept peacefully and, oddly, didn't dream the way he usually did.

The next day, without trying to avoid Estrella, he still only once caught a glimpse of her, from the bridge, speaking with the Spaniards in the stern. After the uproar during the preceding days the Spaniards now roamed around the ship day and night like ghosts, waiting to really become human being again when they would set foot on

Spanish soil. Alexis hardly spoke to them anymore. He had been photographed with them once so he would have a souvenir. He would have liked Estrella to have been in the picture. To show his friends what kind of woman he had conquered on his voyage. Conquered? "What a fool!" But it was time to put together a plan. He watched the waves from the bridge, as one followed the other ceaselessly; the waves he had gazed at thousands of times, always ready to swallow him up or lullaby him, depending on his mood of the moment.

They had crossed the entire Aegean, having passed the Cyclades, coasted the Peloponnese, and cleared Kavomalia and Kythira, and were now travelling in the Ionian Sea heading toward the straits of Messina. He was sorry he didn't have someone to share the sights of the islands with, the coasts, the ever-changing hues of the sea, and the sky as they sailed first south and then west. If Olga were here I'd tell her about Iphigenia, Achilles, Troy, Odysseus, the Trojan Horse, about Mycenae, Agamemnon, the beautiful Helen of Troy. 'I should have abducted Olga, as Paris did Helen! Instead, I met a Clytemnestra, as beautiful as Helen, and I had better take care that she doesn't leap out of some corner with a bull-fighting sword!'

He would have spoken to Olga about the Cyclades islands, their chapels, their small narrow streets, and whitewashed houses made to man's measure, about the processions on Good Friday, and the Resurrection Ceremony in front of the Churches at midnight before Easter Day. In another month it would be Easter! He could have told her about the Byzantine splendours of Mistras, Sparta, Thermopylae, Olympia and the Olympic runner Spyros Louis ... the first ever to win the modern marathon race at the Olympic games.

Jumbled thoughts on history and time and the complaint that he didn't have anyone to share them with. 'Not even Estrella!' Things didn't seem to work according to his fantasies. 'Now what? The places coming up? The Straits of Messina ... Scylla and Charybdis! That's where I'll corner her. I've got it! I've have to concoct something. That should be a cinch for the descendant of the wily Odysseus! He was from Ithaca, I'm from Cephalonia. Two islands hardly more than a stone's throw from each other. Odysseus, Ithaca offered you that wonderful ... Odyssey! Without the blood of

Cephalonia running in my veins I wouldn't be on this sea venture, in your wake.' He recited into the wind:
> ... *hope your road is a long one,*
> *full of adventure, full of discovery ...*
> *Laistrygonians, Cyclops,*
> *wild Poseidon – you won't encounter them*
> *unless you bring them along inside your soul,*
> *unless your soul sets them up in front of you.*
> *Hope your road is a long one ..."*

A little Cavafy to fit the situation! But the road was not a long one. Only three days and nights to go.
> *"The Laistrygonians and the Cyclops I will not see*
> *but Scylla and Charybdis now beckon me*
> *and Estrella's frightened heart will tremble to be free!*
> *And if these beasts do not shake the heart*
> *Of this Senorita, from the start,*
> *may poor Cephalonia never dot my chart!"*

"Idiot!" He chided himself for his improvised verses half-heartedly bringing his open palm up to his face in a typical Greek gesture meant to show self-disgust.

But at least he had come up with a scenario: They would pass through the straits at midnight, the witching hour. It is the time when people feel most vulnerable. He would call her to the bridge and recount the myth of Scylla and Charybdis. In the dark, moonless night, the mountains in the straits would appear menacing, like wild beasts. He would recite the *Odyssey* to her in a sonorous voice, like a tragedian, and it would frighten her. She would turn to him and huddle against him for protection; then he would take her to his cabin to comfort her, to make love to her.

Everything had been thought out except for three details: how would he manage to get her up to the bridge since she was obviously avoiding him now? How would he get her to his cabin since he was on duty till 4? And where was he going to find a copy of the *Odyssey* to memorise the passage? Because even though he remembered parts of the text, he wouldn't be able to put enough melodrama into the recitation without the details.

The first difficulty could be overcome. Wherever she might be, he would go and find her and tell her straight out. 'Come up to the bridge if you want to experience the thrill of passing through the Straits!' No, better write her a note. If she saw him the blood might rush to her head again. A letter, a note would build confidence. She would feel that he was thinking of her, that he had taken the effort to write a few lines and she might read and re-read it and even be moved! That takes care of that! His watch? Nothing could be done about that. He couldn't ask someone else to take my watch but as soon as we pass the straits he would take her to my cabin and tell her to wait there while he was gone. She'll be tired and probably lying down on my bed and will have plenty of time to feel closer to me! He rubbed his hands together. He had found the answers so easily, one after the other.

"*The Odyssey*? Damn it, I'm stuck! Who would have a copy of the *Odyssey* on board?" But he didn't want to concede defeat after getting so far. "I've got it! I'll call my friend Evgenios in Athens on the ship's radio. He was the best student in the class and especially good in ancient Greek. He's certain to have a copy of *The Odyssey* at home. I'll have him dictate that section to me." He was excited about the idea. He felt he was living his own intellectual Odyssey.

He turned to the helmsman: "Take over for a while. In any case, it's the open sea, there aren't any boats around and if the Captain shows up, tell him I just went out for a minute and stamp your foot on the deck. The radio room is right below, and I'll hear the knock and get the message."

The radio operator will make fun of me, he thought; but what the hell! I'll tell him that ... when we're passing through the Straits I want to compare it with the description in Homer and if he swallows it, fine, if not ... who cares!

He knew his friend's telephone number by heart. "Sit down and I'll try to make radio contact," the radio operator told him, "but there may be a delay in getting through."

"Make it urgent. I have to have it before this afternoon."

He had to learn the text by heart and he didn't have much time. It never passed through his mind for a moment that he was doing something crazy.

As he waited in the radio room and the operator called Athens-Radio he suddenly heard another conversation between a Greek boat and the homeland.

"Hello, Yiannis, how are you? Over."

"Fine, Argyro, and you? What about the children? Over?"

"He had a pimple on his cheek – Vassilakis that is, but now it's over. Over."

"Take care Argyro, they're only children. Over."

"Yes, Yiannis, do you love me? Over."

"I can't hear you, I can't hear you. Over."

"I said, Yiannis, do you love me, Over."

"I can't hear you, I can't hear you. Over."

Then addressing the radio operator at Athens-Radio:

"Oh dear, could you act as a relay for us?"

Without any hesitation, the operator replied in a deep voice:

"He loves you, madam, he loves you!"

Alexis and the radio operator burst out laughing.

"Come in Athens-Radio, Athens-Radio. The *Semiramis* here, the *Semiramis* here, Sierra, Victor, Athens, Kobra ..." the operator called out.

"Come in *Semiramis*, do you read me?" he heard the voice at Athens-Radio.

"You're coming in loud and clear. I want Athens 318-224. I repeat, three one eight two two four."

"Hold on *Semiramis*. You're second in line and I'll call you back. If you can't hear me, we'll try frequency 2900. Over."

"I can hear you well. I'm on hold."

"Fine, hold on."

"Well, you're lucky," the Radio Officer told Alexis, "only one connection before us."

"I hope he's at home."

Then to prepare the radio operator for what was coming.

"It will seem a little strange to you but I'm calling my friend to get him to read me a passage from *The Odyssey*."

"Nothing you might do would surprise me, Alexis," the answer came back like a cold shower.

He and Andreas had known each other from way back, when, as a child, he went to travel with his grandfather and grandmother to his island.

"You were a little devil from the time you were a toddler!"

"Hold it, I'll tell you all about it while we're waiting, so you don't think I'm an utter fool! An English Naval Officer who I met in Alexandria told me once that after the war he was going to travel in a sailboat on the trail of Odysseus with *The Odyssey* in his hand. He wanted to find out how near the truth the descriptions of Homer were and to write a book comparing sailing in that day with his own experiences. For instance, no-one ever doubted that it was in the Straits of Messina that Scylla and Charybdis were waiting in ambush, but were they? So I want to remember the lines of *The Odyssey* when we're passing through the Straits." He felt very proud about the story he had made up.

"Come in, *Semiramis*. Your number in Athens is ringing."

"Thank you, Athens-Radio."

He could hear the ringing and immediately afterwards:

"Hello?"

It was a female voice he didn't recognise.

"You're being called by the ship *Semiramis*; please wait for your caller to finish before you answer."

He turned to Alexis. "Here, take the receiver."

"May I speak to Evgenios please?"

"From a boat? Dear me! I'll get him right away. Can you call from a boat?"

The voice on the other end of the line sounded frightened. Evgenios wasn't slow in coming. "Hello, this is Evgenios, who is this?"

"It's Alexis on his way to Barcelona."

"Swimming?"

"On the *Semiramis*! It's a long story; I'll tell you when we get back."

"OK. It's so sudden. I thought you were still in the Army."

"I want something from you."

"Tell me what."

"Get a modern translation of *The Odyssey* and read out the passage about Scylla and Charybdis."

"Are you crazy?"

"I knew you would say that but I hoped you would know me better. For me to ask you on the ship's radio means I have a reason. In the evening we're passing through the Straits of Messina."

"Ah! All right then ... be careful you're not one of the six companions who gets taken. I'm going to get it, just a minute."

"Fine, I'll wait."

Evgenios came back on the phone quickly. "Where shall I start?"

"Right from Circe's warning about Scylla and Charybdis."

"Are you ready?"

"I'm all ears."

The operator's eyes were bulging with interest, perhaps even admiration, as his receiver declaimed Homer for the first time and Alexis wrote it down, like dictation. Nothing like that had ever happened before and it certainly lightened the boredom of the endless hours in the radio room.

Suddenly there were two thumps on the ceiling.

"Damn, it's the Captain," Alexis said while Evgenios was reading.

"Enough, enough," he kept repeating in agitation, having forgotten to push the button on his speaker; Evgenios couldn't hear him and went on reading. "I've got all I wanted, thank you very much," then turning to the operator: "The flood gates have opened and I can't stop it," he shouted into the speaker again: "You've passed the straits ... stop. Evgeeeenios! Stop!"

"Push the button pal," the operator said in a calm voice.

"Ah! Of course, sorry ..." And again; "Evgenios, Evgenios, that's fine, thanks. Over."

"You mean you don't want me to go on?" Evgenios asked in surprise.

"No, for what I want it for it's plenty. So long!"

"What time will you be passing through the straits so I can think of you?"

"Midnight!" And, like a cautious sailor, he added, "God willing!"

"Be careful of Scylla and Charybdis!"

"Don't joke about this to my mates in Athens. Thanks, so long and over."

"That, I cannot promise. It's too good a story!", were Evgenios' last words. And the voice of the operator at Athens-Radio was heard:

*"*Andra moi – ennepe mousa – polytropon*," Come in *Semiramis*. Have you finished?"

"Finished Athens-Radio. Thank you."

"I've got to hurry to the bridge. The Captain will be furious with me!"

"Aren't you going to finish the story about the Englishman for me?"

"You'll be off duty soon, won't you? Come on up to the bridge."

"I'm through now. I'll lock up and we'll go together."

"Well, Captain Alexis. Do you just go off and leave the bridge?" the Captain asked.

"With the bosun at the wheel there's nothing to worry about, Captain; he knows a lot more than I do. And I kept an eye out as I came up from the radio room to see if any boats were about."

What a lie! Captain Gerasimos didn't like to offend anyone and he was always ready to look at both sides. "And what were you doing down there, if I may ask?"

The radio operator took the initiative as the Captain seemed to be bursting with curiosity. "Tell the Captain about the Englishman, Captain Alexis."

"As I was telling Andreas, there was an English Naval Officer I met in a bar in Alexandria during the last year of the war. He had roamed the Mediterranean for three years on a destroyer. We became friends. We went to the cinema together and chased girls and he was always talking to me about Homer who he had been studying since he was a boy. His dream was to retrace the routes of Odysseus and to find out if indeed Homer had travelled in these parts himself or just imagined the whole thing or maybe just enhanced the tales that he was told. We corresponded from time to time. Recently, he was in Greece. He'll be continuing his voyages for many years to come. But he has already made a few observations on many of the tales and, by coincidence, he

---

*"Oh Muse, tell me about the man of many talents ..."

mentioned the conclusions he had reached on Scylla and Charybdis. Let's look at the chart and I'll show you."

At that moment the doctor joined them on the bridge.

"I want to hear this too," Alexis said, "I'll explain later. Captain, you know better than I do the rock called Scylla on the north side of the promontory of Calabria at the entrance to the Straits, when you're sailing north to south. Right here, opposite the cape"; and he pointed to the chart with his finger, "the rock has a vaguely female form and is full of gullies and deep caves. When the wind is blowing and the waves are crashing against it, they make an infernal noise, as Circe warned Odysseus.

"Scylla lived in a dark cave. Half of her head was outside the cave. She had twelve legs, six long necks and hunted dolphins and swordfish. This is poetry. But, as you know, Captain Gerasimos, this region is full of dolphins and swordfish and when the mistral is blowing, dead octopus and other exotic sea life are washed up on the beaches which in the imagination of Homer could very well have taken the form of Scylla. On the other side of the Straits, Charybdis sucks in dark waters. There are whirlpools throughout the entire strait, on both sides. But the largest one is near the north cape of Sicily, right here on the map and the currents run two to three miles to the north. 'Hold close to Scylla and move at full speed ahead because it's better to lose six companions to Scylla than to lose everyone to Charybdis', Circe counselled. Of course, with its 1800 horsepower engines, the two and three mile wide currents and whirlpools wouldn't affect our ship the *Semiramis*, but imagine Odysseus' small ship with tired sailors at the oars! Even today, it seems, when smaller sailing boats pass through the straits they keep close to Scylla on the Calabrian side to avoid the whirlpool, Charybdis."

Captain Gerasimos, with his nautical experience, had a broad mind open to all theories and he nodded his head in agreement and said with a look full of wisdom: "These are facts of the sea, and nobody can deny that they didn't happen like that."

"Now listen to Homer's narration." Alexis said, inflated by the Captain's approval of his theory and he gathered up his papers as Captain Yiannis entered the chart room to relieve him.

"What's going on? Any problem?"

"We're having a small performance. Alexis is going to recite Homer for us!" the doctor said brightly in a mocking tone.

Captain Yiannis cast a glance at the open chart for the Straits and got the meaning: "I understand," and began to declaim himself:

"Etsi thrinontas, to steno pernousane yi'apano …"*

"Do you know Homer by heart, Captain Yiannis? And I went to the trouble of calling Athens to have a friend read out to me the passage I needed."

"Ye Gods! Just think if Homer had known that 3000 years later his description of the Straits of Scylla and Charybdis would travel over radio waves in a tenth of a second!" Captain Yiannis always had to make a witty comment.

"Since it is Captain Yiannis' watch I'll leave it to him to recite to you …" Alexis said. "But start at the beginning. Circe's description is more dramatic than the description of the passage through the Straits. See you!"

He was in a hurry to leave, to write a letter to Estrella, to translate the long text of *The Odyssey* into English and to memorise it. He went to his cabin and took up paper and pen: 'Dear Estrella' – too formal – 'My dear Estrella' – too insipid. 'Estrella' – her name! Just that – without embellishments. The sweetest sound to a woman is her own name. I'll write her a simple note. I'll let her imagination work without anything to go on. Let her think whatever she likes. 'Estrella! At just before midnight we will be passing through the Straits of Messina, exactly as Odysseus did 3,000 years ago! Two terrible monsters, Scylla and Charybdis, guard the Straits. If we make any mistake as we pass between the two creatures, we're lost!' Here she would begin to feel a little afraid, he thought and continued: 'I don't think you would want to miss an experience like that.' Since she had set off in quest of adventure he would offer her adventure. 'I'll be waiting for you on the bridge. At the sound of the

---

* "Thus weeping, they started sailing into the straits".

ship's bell, three doubles and one single tone, it will be 11.30.' It was an invitation it would be hard for her to turn down.

Now just a polite closing and a signature. 'With Love?' Not on your life! 'Tenderly?' Closer to the way he felt, but he still didn't like it. 'In expectation?'

No, I don't want to sound too persistent. Now I'm beginning to play around with words, losing my concentration! Why do letters have to have a closing line anyway? It's very simple. I started with 'Estrella' and I'll close with 'Alexis'. And let's hope that my name will move her as much as her own! He put the letter in an envelope and wrote 'Estrella' on it in large flowing letters with a long tail on the final 'a' sealed it and rang the bell for the officer's orderly, a young fellow, just sixteen years old, on his first trip. "Hello, Babis! Do me a favour and slide this under the cabin door of the Spanish nurse – you know who I mean or give it to her by hand if you see her. That's a boy!" And he gave him a friendly slap on the neck.

"For Captain Alexis I would jump into the sea," the orderly said craftily.

"If I ever ask you to do that then *you* throw *me* in the sea!"

The rest of the evening he spent translating and memorising *The Odyssey*. By the time night came he almost believed that he would soon be coming face to face with those terrible monsters and he was filled with dread.

When he went up to the bridge a little before the bell struck three and then one, he felt like Odysseus, ready for the great trial and oddly enough wasn't worried about whether Estrella came or not. If you are the King of Ithaca, you are sure of yourself, you are wise and you are patient. Or at least ... you think you are! Despite the cold, the Spaniards had come out on deck to watch the passage between the tip of the boot of Italy and Sicily.

The usual group had gathered on the bridge. They had left the lights of Messina to the left and were proceeding at full speed toward the Straits. The bleak coast of Calabria loomed up to the right. Only the scattered lights of the few houses on the coast brought you forward in time, far from Odysseus' nightmare, but not for long, because now the sea narrowed and the closer they got the higher the mountains got, looking menacing in the dark.

Silence had fallen on the bridge and not even the breathing of Odysseus' companions could be heard. Everyone, except Alexis, who was fixing the mountains with his gaze, turned their heads at the squeak of the sliding door as Estrella opened it, and came to stand next to him without saying a word, motionless in the silence.

And when the colossal rocks rose up like giants before them in the pitch black night he grabbed her hand and pulled her outside onto the side wires of the bridge. Funnelled through the Straits, the 'mistral' was howling madly and the sea hissed forming white snake-like shapes as the foam swirled in the air.

The deep voice of Alexis echoed as if it were coming down through the ages:

One is sharp mountain
piercing the sky with storm cloud round the peak
dissolving never, not in the brightest summer
to show heaven's azure there, nor in the fall.
No mortal man could scale it, nor so much
as land there, not with twenty hands and feet,
so sheer the cliffs are – as of polished stone.
Midway that height, a cavern full of mist
opens toward Erebus and evening. Skirting
that is the lugger, great Odysseus,
your master bowman, shooting from the deck,
would come short of the cavemouth with his shaft;
but that is the den of Scylla where she yaps
abominably, a new-born whelp's cry,
though she is huge and monstrous. God or man,
no one could look at her in joy. Her legs –
and there are twelve – are like great tentacles,
unjointed, and upon her serpent necks
are born six heads like nightmares of ferocity,
with triple serried rows of fangs and deep
gullets of black death".

He paused to see what impression he had made, but he had been influenced as well, and shuddered. The mountain of Scylla was dead ahead without any opening appearing in the sea. He felt Estrella trembling.

"It's like we're caught in a trap. I don't see any exit. We'll run into the rocks!" She said in anguish.

Alexis didn't reply but continued:

*Half her length she sways
her heads in air, outside her horrid cleft,
hunting the sea round that promontory
for dolphins, dogfish or what bigger game
thundering Amphitrite feeds in thousands.
And no ship's company can claim
to have passed her without loss or grief; she takes
from every ship one man for every gullet.*

"And now Estrella, turn left. Where the water appears to be frothing. Near the inhospitable mainland."

*"A great wild fig, a shaggy mass of leaves,
grows on it, and Charybdis lurks below
to swallow down the dark sea tide. Three times
from dawn to dusk she spews it up, a whirling
maelstrom; if you come upon her then
the god who makes earth tremble could not save you.
No, hug the cliff of Scylla, take your ship
through on a racing stroke. Better to mourn
six men than lose them all, and the ship too."*

Estrella huddled up next to him, to feel the protection of his body. "I'm afraid. The rock is getting closer, do something!"

'Everything is going according to plan,' he almost said and grew even bolder. Now it was his triumph and he would shout it to the two monsters, Scylla and Charybdis, so they could hear him.

But suddenly, his eyes froze. It was as if the rock had changed form and become a woman's figure. Olga! And from the roaring wind incomprehensible cries reached his ears. Her voice! But her shape and her voice were transformed.

More severe, more unapproachable! He touched Estrella's hand, maybe the vision would go away, but the roar, as Circe had described it, grew louder and louder. He quickly went on with the recitation to stop thinking.

> "And all the time,
> in travail, sobbing, gaining on the current,
> we rowed into the strait – Scylla to port
> and on our starboard beam Charybdis, dire
> gorge of the salt sea tide. By heaven! When she
> vomited, all the sea was like a cauldron
> seething over intense fire, when the mixture
> suddenly heaves and raises.
> The shot spume
> soared to the landslide heights, and fell like rain.
>
> But when she swallowed the sea water down
> we saw the funnel of the maelstrom, heard
> the rocks bellowing all around, and dark
> sand raged on the bottom far below
> My men all blanched against the gloom, our eyes
> were fixed upon that yawning mouth in fear
> of being devoured.
> Then Scylla made her strike,
> whisking six of my best men from the ship.
> I happened to glance aft at ship and oarsmen
> and caught sight of their arms and legs, dangling
> high overhead. Voices came down to me
> in anguish, calling my name ... for the last time.

Estrella was now shivering. "Stop it, stop it, enough, I want to get off the bridge."

"Then go."

"I'm afraid to walk down alone."

The distance between them and the mountain was no more than half a mile and in the night it seemed as if you could touch it by stretching out your hand.

"Port easy," the calm voice of Captain Gerasimos was heard, as the head of the cape toward the Tyrraneum Sea appeared and they slid with all the power the 1800 horse-power of the *Semiramis* could muster through the tentacles of Scylla and the whirlpools of Charybdis.

Bong-bong, bong, bong, bong-bong, bong-bong! The bell on the prow rang out midnight. The nightmare had passed. The water, the wind and their nerves calmed and Alexis' voice resumed its normal tone.

"The bell of Aghios Soulpikios is striking midnight. A coincidence? Do you remember Jules Vernes' *20,000 Leagues Under the Sea* from your childhood?" he asked Estrella.

"I remember Captain Nemo and a huge octopus in the deep waters. Like Scylla. Please take me down."

"I'll escort you down and come back. I'm on duty."

He took her around the waist and helped her down the stairs. Estrella looked petrified, without will. Alexis' cabin was just beneath the stairs leading from the bridge. He opened the door and took her inside without asking her. His bed was made up this time and everything in place. He took off his cap and hung it on one of the hooks on the door.

"Lie down here. Take a nap. I'll return at four," his voice was almost tender. "Everything is fine now, don't be afraid."

He caressed her cheek as though she was a child. "Everything is fine now," Estrella repeated.

He didn't kiss her.

"Sleep like Odysseus on the shores of the Island of the Phaiakes, when his torment had at last ended. I'm going to the bridge. We still have to pass by the islands of the Sirens tonight!"

"I'm jealous. Tie yourself tightly to the mast."

Even now he didn't kiss her but ran up to the bridge, because he was late in relieving Captain Yiannis. The feeling of triumph had faded and he was filled with a sense of peace. Of the companions on the bridge, only the doctor was left, waiting for Alexis to come and give him the evening report and, of course, Captain Yiannis, who greeted him: "What a weight you've taken off me! I thought we'd lost a comrade to the tentacles of a Spanish girl!"

The doctor added: "Come on, Captain Yiannis, you have to admit she is no Scylla."

"No-one doubts Captain Alexis' taste. But a dreamer like him would see her as Scarlet O'Hara, even if she *was* Scylla!"

"Why Scarlet O'Hara, Captain Yiannis?" the doctor asked.

"Eh! Scarlet Haralambopoulou if you like. I'm leaving. Goodnight and stay on your toes, Captain Alexis, the course is set for Bonifacio – stay on your toes off the Aeolian islands so you won't get blown away! Don't forget that everything around here is Odysseyland. Thank God we have passed the land of the Cyclops! But stay on course or you may end up in the arms of the Sirens, the Lotus Eaters or land in the embrace of Circe! That is, if you're lucky and she doesn't turn you into a pig. Your course is 318," and he left.

"What a man that Captain Yiannis is," the sailor at the wheel said. "I like to be on duty with him. A few days ago he told me stories about ships' dogs."

"Do you remember any?" the doctor asked.

"I do. His freighter was based in Lisbon during the war. He was Second Officer onboard. They had a mongrel puppy who took the tram every midday and evening to meet the ship's crew who ate in Rodrigo's tavern – five stops from the harbour. He would get in through the back door of the tram, crouch under the last seat and at each stop wiggle a little further ahead and move from seat to seat, figuring on being under the front seat at the fifth stop, when he'd jump off. When the ship was set to sail, he knew it somehow and never budged off the boat."

He felt that Alexis was ignoring him as if to say: 'Keep your eyes on the compass and forget the gab!'

The truth was that Alexis had his mind elsewhere, on his own tale and he wanted to talk to the doctor again. "Do you remember what Captain Yiannis said?" he asked him. "That even if she was a Scylla I would see her as Scarlet O'Hara. He meant Estrella of course. Well, you know that as we are passing the straits, it seemed to me that Scylla had taken on the shape of Olga. I even heard her voice! But her face was different, severe and savage, and her voice a cry of rage!"

"Quite natural," the doctor answered without curiosity.

"You find everything natural!"

"Natural, that is, considering your fevered imagination and your sickened sensibility!"

"And what's your explanation this time, Mr Know-it-All?"

"CGP"

"What did you say? CGP? Have you started to talk gobbledegook too?"

"CGP I said. C.G.P. Conscience – guilt – punishment!

"Even though you shut her out of your mind and replace her with Estrella, your unconscious mercilessly spreads out its tentacles and punishes you."

"And why can't it just mean that she still exists in my mind? CGP! Listen to that!"

"Well, decide then. You're giving us a rough time. You're staging a whole theatrical performance to get in the Spanish girl's pants and then you talk to us about Olga, who takes on the voice and form of an inaccessible monster from *The Odyssey*!"

"But didn't you say yourself that I had a ... how did you put it? That I suffered from ... fusion, wasn't it? I really like that."

"Since you like it, go on with your complexes and let the women alternate in your imagination like the ads for 'Pil-Poul' hats or the 'Father Akakios' on his donkey going off to buy MISKO spaghetti, which you must have seen as a kid, gazing out of the window on the underground running between Piraeus and Athens, without ever touching them!"

Alexis launched a counterattack. "What about yours – did she stand you up tonight? Why wasn't Michelle on the bridge?"

"She was keeping the Spanish men company, but don't worry. She's waiting for me in the salon. To each his own ... nurse!"

"Why not? Do we have to get old before we're entitled to nursing care?"

"I am now going for my injection! You better try to glue your shattered mind together because you've lost your senses! I keep asking myself how they trust you to run a ship especially at night. Imagine! Seeing a rock and mistaking it for a woman! Goodnight, have a pleasant watch!"

"All I care about is that I don't see a woman and take *her* for a rock. Then I *will* really feel uneasy, doctor! Goodnight!"

The doctor left and Alexis was glad he hadn't had to admit that Estrella was waiting in his cabin. That was his secret for tonight: "The doctor thinks that women are only in my dreams. So I'll keep reality from him!" he thought stubbornly.

Bong bong, bong bong, bong bong, bong bong!

Four in the morning. It was the longest watch he had ever spent. The hours seemed endless and when the second in command came to relieve him, he was more than relieved. All he could do was to give him the course and run. As soon as he was out in the fresh air however he slowed down as, from this point on, he didn't have any set plan and was somewhat at a loss. He was unpretentious by nature and his feeling of triumph had had plenty of time to fade away during his hours on duty. From here on he had to play it by ear. He walked down the steps from the bridge, opened the door to his cabin carefully, trying not to make any noise. The first thing he saw was Estrella's white stockings fluttering from his desk. The white flag of surrender! What could be more … flattering and disarming!

Estrella, curled up under the covers, with her back turned toward the door, seemed to be sleeping. He saw her clothes hanging from the wardrobe handle and her bra over his papers on his desk. Only her underpants were missing. She had to keep up some pretext. The pants – the last line of defence!

The only light came from the deck, through the opaque porthole on the door

He didn't have that many choices. He undressed and thought that it would be thoughtful if he too kept his shorts on. They would enter the battle with the same weapons. Each one feigning peace! Just like the generals when they discuss disarmament. Oh well, what the hell!

He slipped in beside her and embraced her, putting his arms around her from behind and fitted together like two spoons in a drawer. Half awake Estrella kissed his hands and placed them on her breasts. They stayed like that for quite some time, without speaking, without moving, each feeling the warmth of the other, giving their senses and their souls a rest. Peace.

When they both stripped, almost simultaneously, and turned around, they grabbed each other like two old well-attuned loves, freed of all prejudice, till the moment when Estrella was ready to receive him, offering herself to him. At that moment Alexis thought he heard the same roaring wind as in the straits of Scylla and Charybdis and recoiled, bombarded by a new image, once more a prisoner to mixed emotions. Was it the voice of Olga he'd heard just in time to stop him? Am I afraid that she might latch on to me? But do I really desire Estrella? Do I? He asked himself and kissed her more out of a sense of obligation, and caressed her all over her fresh, young body without passion while she, liberated, wriggled with pleasure. But soon Estrella realised she was giving without getting. "Why, why?" she asked. "You know I want you."

"It's for your own good," was his excuse. "Pleasure is the song of freedom. It is the hatching of your desires, the time when you think with nothing but your sex. The word love has not been spoken. I respect you. I don't want you to repent. The fruit of love has consequences. The roots of one's upbringing run deep. I don't want your tears!"

"Mi vida, mi vida!" she cried out at the last spasm, lost deep in the past.

"Thank you," she told him simply and fell asleep in his arms. When they woke in the morning they knew they had only one night left but they were at peace. Each was conscious of what he wanted or didn't want from the other.

Finally, there was the peace of understanding, as it should be.

They got up together and looked each other in the eyes. People in love do not communicate as well as Alexis and Estrella did at that moment.

> "*Oh noche, que guiaste,*
> *Oh noche amable mas que el alborada:*
> *Oh noche, que juntaste*
> *Amado con amada,*
> *Amada en al Amado transformada!*"

(Oh night that was my guide!
Oh darkness dearer than the morning's pride,
Oh night that joined the lover
To the beloved bride
Transfiguring then each into the other.)"

Estrella recited the lines of St. Jean de la Croix in a flat voice drawn from the vaults of a Gothic church. How beautiful she was! Why didn't he feel any jealousy, uneasiness, all the emotional factors of love? But he knew that he was going to lose her. Maybe because he didn't love her? Even if she was beloved. You don't love a goddess. How strange!

He was ready to kneel before her. He watched her as she dressed and it was like a holy ritual. A reverse strip-tease, intensely erotic, as she slipped her white stockings over her divine legs. And then he again felt a contraction in his solar plexus as "Olga" invaded the cabin once more in her silk stockings. But the cabin was narrow and confined, so Estrella left and Olga stayed to destroy his peace.

He was enraged. The roles had been reversed. What right had Olga to walk in and out of his mind whenever she felt like it? I know, if the doctor were here he would say: '*You* and no-one else gave her this right!' No, I mustn't rebuke poor Olga. Poor Olga already?

Estrella left and didn't say whether they would meet again in the evening. Maybe she thought it would be self-evident. But where? What time? By midnight she hadn't appeared and at midnight he was on duty. He had waited for her in his cabin till the last moment, with the certainty that she would show up. He found her on the bridge waiting for him.

"It was so beautiful last night," she told him. "I was afraid of one more night with you. Tomorrow we arrive. I'll be occupied with the Spanish prisoners and then we will meet thousands of people. I first spoke to you here on the bridge. Here is where I will say adieu to you."

Now *she* was running the game again. "Had she won after all? Had he lost? Was she still playing? What difference did it make." Whatever the case, Alexis would follow her lead. He made no attempt to try and dissuade her. "Give me a few more hours, three, two, one, just few minutes," he would have said in another situation. He would have dug his nails into time as if he could hold it back. But not now. Not to Estrella, not to the most beautiful woman he had ever come across, to the goddess that is beyond love.

Alexis stared at the prow. He didn't speak. Estrella squeezed his hand and Alexis knew she was preparing to leave. He turned his head toward her, touched his hat with the three fingers of his right hand, imitating a salute, half military, half goodbye and as if giving a naval command said to her: "Stay on course. You're sailing well."

Estrella opened the door of the bridge, her cape and her hair whipping in the mistral. "I'm leaving on the windy side, the way I came in. Forgive me if I'm not following the rules of the sea."

The helmsman was distracted, trying to follow what was going on. Alexis saw that the waves, instead of coming from the prow as they should have, were breaking on the starboard side of the *Semiramis*. He glanced at the compass. The *Semiramis* was 20 degrees off course, to the left.

"The performance is over, helmsman. Try to correct your course too!"

The next morning he was awoken by the noise of low-flying aeroplanes. He leapt up and saw a formation of fighters circling above the ship, and the Spaniards out on deck waving at them and shouting with emotion. Alexis caught up in his own problems had nearly forgotten their existence in the last couple of days. The coast of Spain was not yet in sight; their estimated time of arrival in Barcelona, was around two in the afternoon and they were still about fifty miles from shore. There was still about four more hours to go.

He dressed and went up to the bridge long before his watch. Where would Estrella be? In the salon? In her cabin? On one of the decks? Would she be alone? With whom would she be speaking? Did she at least feel sad?

Smoke appeared far ahead and soon Spanish destroyers came into view while the airplanes continued their aerobatics above the *Semiramis*.

Like gigantic dolphins, the destroyers cleaved the frothing waves with their prows as they approached at more than twenty-five miles an hour. They passed on the portside of the *Semiramis* and when they were a half-mile off the stern, turned back in a closed circle, and quickly caught up with the *Semiramis* to escort her all the way to Port, like a guard of honour, one on each side. The sailors on the two destroyers, lined up on the deck and gave military salutes, while the *Semiramis* returned the salute by raising and lowering the ship's flag on the stern three times, according to the rules of the sea, and the warships replied. The sea was calm but the sky overcast.

Invited by the Captain, Monsieur Dupont, Captain Palladio, and the leader of the Spanish mission, who had embarked at Constantinople, had gathered on the bridge for the last time. Alexis looked around. The doctor was missing, Michelle was missing, Estrella was missing.

By noon, the coast first appeared while at the same time, dozens of black dots swarmed on the sea.

"What's that supposed to be, a Spanish Armada?", the Captain muttered as Alexis took up the binoculars.

"Yachts, row-boats, motor-boats, fishing-boats, all coming toward us!" he exclaimed.

"Are they coming to give us a reception?" the Captain asked the leader of the mission Captain Palladio in an Hercule Poirot tone of voice, Alexis translating.

"Certainly. All of Spain is waiting for its children," the Head of the mission answered and Captain Palladio couldn't hold back his tears.

"All of Spain! Who would ever think this wasn't pure exaggeration?" the Captain murmured in Greek.

At the estimated time, they slowed down at Pilot Skotia, and as soon as the Pilot boarded the ship, they entered the harbour of Barcelona, escorted by airplanes, two destroyers and over one hundred small craft, which were truly dancing on the sea with their passengers waving multi-coloured handkerchiefs and flags while on the piers, jetties, on the rocks and the docks, tens of thousands of people had gathered ready to break out in a frenzy. The other ships in the harbour were hooting madly as the *Semiramis* advanced in a proud and stately manner, the same way the Battleship Averof must have returned to Port after the Battle before the Dardanelles, or the Victory to Portsmouth after Trafalgar.

"Blow the whistle, Captain Alexis," the Captain commanded.

Alexis pulled the cord proudly and felt like a conductor of an orchestra who had signalled the trombone to sound the final notes of a symphony, the crowning point of the voyage.

The crowd on the docks grew larger and larger. Now they could make out the streets behind the harbour where another mass of people, pushing and straining, while trying to get nearer to the ship resulting in some of those standing near the waterfront falling into the murky waters of the harbour, fully clothed. Alexis picked up the binoculars again and followed the tragi-comic scene. At the Estacion Maritima, where the *Semiramis* would dock, you couldn't have wedged a pin in. The *Semiramis* eased gently to; the captain ordered two cables to be thrown ashore, one for the bow, one for the stern in the hope that someone in that mass of people would slip them over the stanchions in the harbour.

But before they had secured the ship and before they had even lowered the gangway, people started jumping aboard from the lower weather deck of the stern and streaming across the ship to embrace and kiss the prisoners. The officials who were waiting to enter the ship had been lost in the human flood and only with great difficulty, managed to reach and walk upon the gangway to attend the welcoming ceremony amid the shouts and the cries of the joyful crowd.

The ship began to list dangerously to port as more people were pouring in. So many heads, all knit closely together, made Alexis slip off again as before his eyes instead of the crowds he saw pictures from childhood books of the battle fought by Alexander the Great at Issos, then the Battle of Nafpaktos by Vincentine, in the drawing by Bush and Pegnet.

He was brought back to his senses when he made out in the crowd a flag with a swastika on it. It brought the blood rushing to his head and at that moment he decided not to make a report to the newspaper in Athens. "I'm not the one to judge political systems, but I don't want to report about what the men now being welcomed with Nazi flags, told me about Olga's Russia." He felt almost ashamed.

The loudspeakers on the Estacion Maritima began to plead with the crowd to stop boarding the boat and instructing those who had boarded the ship to get off, but in the general pandemonium no-one paid any attention to the instructions.

Unperturbable Captain Gerasimos, who knew better than anyone else how much of a list his boat could take, didn't seem too worried, but he did mutter: "Damn it, they're going to overturn my boat!"

Alexis took it upon himself to save the situation. He called on the bosun and two sailors to go and seal off the opening on the weather-deck with tarps. To do that, they had to fight the crowd and push it back.

Then they ran and pulled up the gangway. At least no more could get on.

The boat returned to a more or less even keel as people began to distribute themselves among the inner spaces and the decks and Alexis calculated there must have been well over a thousand onboard.

But now the officials had to get off, followed by the ex-prisoners, and when there was no purpose any longer the other visitors would also leave. They lowered once more the gangway and disembarkation began in a more orderly fashion.

Alexis had bade farewell to Captain Palladio as well as Dupont and Michelle. He had no reason to stay at the gangway. The bosun, the mate and a sailor had taken it upon themselves to preserve order. He went back up to the bridge to gaze at the officials and the captives who, as they disembarked, were seized and whipped away by the crowd. In reality, he was on the lookout for another reason.

"Estrella?" he asked the doctor who had also come up to the bridge.

"She got off with the first group," the doctor answered.

"Why didn't I see her going down the gangway? She must have walked down while I was on my way to the bridge and then she was lost in the crowd."

"Maybe."

"Maybe for the better. That way I will be left with the image of her as she left the bridge with her hair streaming in the wind. Proud, confident, at peace with herself."

"You mean, Captain Alexis, that you've been doing nothing but saying 'bye-bye', all the way from Odessa to Barcelona? Come on, I'll take you to a whorehouse, and maybe your luck will change!"

Alexis started to recite:

Red sun, whose flame polishes
and colours the high heavens dark red,
have you ever seen on this earth such a beauty
as that peaceful, happy glow of hers?
Oh sweet, tender and beloved zephyr,
you caress us with your soft wings
like the light which spreads its golden veil
have you ever touched a shock of hair like hers?

"Fernando Herrera, for you ... illiterates! Don't worry and don't get any complexes either. My memory is not all that good. Look it up in the ship's library."

"Since you seem to be satisfied with touching her shock of hair, I have nothing more to say, except that you belong on the stage, not the bridge!" the doctor concluded.

Alexis had decided not to tell the Doctor about the night he had spent with Estrella. A night without any future but which left behind the sweetest of memories. You don't share such an experience, you keep it all to yourself. "Did I say memory? Is it a memory, already?" Estrella had been lost for ever in the sea of people, around the harbour.

As he said to the doctor: "I'm going to change, to put on my civvies and then we'll go into town," he still had a faint hope, however, that he might encounter her in the streets of Barcelona.

It had been eleven days since Alexis had been off the boat, four days from Piraeus to Odessa and another seven to Barcelona. Except ... of course, during the night in Odessa on the wild ride through the Russian steppes to conquer the tower! And now he was stepping onto the land of Don Quixote. But he had nothing to conquer this time ... unless ...

"Doctor, what did you say about the whorehouse?"

"I said I would take you to a house of ... easy virtue to close the circle."

"What circle?"

"Since Odessa you've been living in a dream. The first act was called Olga, the second Estrella. One more act to play in a Barcelona brothel, your dream will have been resolved and then you can draw the curtains. What is more, you will have the choice of your partner."

The doctor had pinpointed the lurking suspicion that was in his mind.

"Let's look around Barcelona and then we'll see," Alexis replied.

"Spain!" As on the way to Russia, images of Spain, one after the other came to his mind. They were scenes of contradiction, conflict, mystery. Spain with the severe face of Fernando Nino de Guerrera, the Inquisitor under Philip II. Religious fanaticism which unleashed forces of cruelty and torture. The burning at the stake. Spain of the Second Coming, when the naked figures of the martyrs who died for the word of God, will be resurrected to be judged according to the Apocalypse.

Crime and forgiveness, portrayed by the steady hand of El Greco.

Spain, as in the Burial of the Count of Orgath. For the Hidalgos, death was nothing more than the beginning of life.

The Spain of the Conquistadores, as seen through the eyes of Lorca, but also Spain in the ease of luxury and of wealth as in Goya's 'La Maja' surrendering in the embrace of the relaxing 'dormeuse'.

The two worlds of Goya; the Duchess of Alba, in black lace, gold jewellery and red silk, as opposed to the unanswered questions of the hallucinating nightmares, where everyone wants to appear to be what one isn't, where one deceives the other, without even really knowing the other, as he himself said.

Spain through the Cortegas, through the monsters and demons of the painter of madness.

But Alexis saw Spain above all in the thin and fleeting form of Don Quixote, riding on a white horse, accompanied by his shadow Sancho Pancha in the painting by Daumier. With his long lance ready to tilt at the drop of a hat, he was the expression of a deeply rooted proud loneliness.

"The duel with Eros, the duel with the bull, the duel with oneself. That is Spain," he said to the doctor as in conclusion to his imagination's promenade. Alexis seemed to walk smartly through the streets of Barcelona, lost in his visions of Spanish painting as if he knew where he was going. The doctor, who had learned not to interrupt him when his eyes were staring at other worlds, followed him silently, just like another Sancho Pancha.

At some point he couldn't take it any more.

"Where are you headed if I may ask?"

"To Gaudi's Church of course!"

"Why is that?"

"Because it contains the whole haunted, dreamy and magical atmosphere of Spain, uniting truth with a fairy tale element, just like the 'Vision of Toledo' by El Greco."

"How do you know you're going the right way when you don't ask anyone?"

"I don't know but I'm being drawn by instinct, to the centre of the city by instinct and further on I'll ask."

"I'd like to see Christopher Columbus' 'Santa Maria' and the Gothic Quarter," the doctor ventured. It was six and they were casting off at midnight. "If you want to see everything and still go to the whorehouse then we had better start asking or even better get a taxi to take us around the sights and then leave us with the girls. He'll know."

"I don't have any objection. I only hope we can communicate with the taxi driver. Neither my Spanish nor yours is at University level."

"Now just a minute, with a little French and Italian from you and a little Spanish from me, I think we'll manage."

As soon as they reached the first plaza, the doctor went to the first taxi. "Por favor, queremos, but first, andare: 'Santa Maria'. Vapor Columbus' Christofor!" the doctor ventured.

"'Vapor' doctor? You mean it was a steamship? I thought the Santa Maria was a sailing ship!" Alexis told the doctor ironically.

"So how would you say it, come on, show me!"

"La caravella de Cristoforo Columbo!" and he struck a pose.

"Si Senor, 'La Santa Maria', e despues?" the cab driver asked.

"E despues ... how do you like that doctor?"

"Forward, impetuous one, don't stop now."

"E despues ..." Alexis was stuck. "How do you say the Gothic Quarter in Spanish?"

"Now I've got you wise guy. That's the easiest," the doctor took up the cudgels. "Quarter Gothico Barcelona; despues iglesias gaudi. Understand?"

"E despues?" the cab driver asked again.

"La chiquitas mucho lindas por compagnia!"

"Si, Senor, todo bien!"

The taxi driver had got the message.

"There, I arranged your visit to the city and I found you women – what more could you ask?"

"Let's have a look at the women first and then we'll talk about it again. If they're anything like the ones in Troumba in Piraeus ... forget it!"

Since their tongues had loosened and conversation was free and easy they went on to personal questions. "Where are you from? Da donde esta usted?" the doctor asked the cab driver.

"Catalan, y usted?"

"Nostros tribulacion *Semiramis* arrivados prigionieres, Compania Azul!" the doctor answered in Italofrancospanish.

The sudden braking nearly threw them into the front seat. The driver turned around and shook their hands and his excitement was such that he talked on and on without them understanding a word and only remembered to set off again when a row of cars behind him started leaning on their horns.

The first thing the taxi driver did as he restarted the motor was to shut the meter off.

"Nada pagar. Paga la Espana."

"What's he saying? That Spain is paying?" Alexis asked.

"It seems so!"

They tried to argue. "No, no, es impossible ..."

The taxi driver wouldn't listen to them.

"What can we do Alexis? After all, we did bring them their boys from Russia. Sit back in the seat and let them take care of us. Make believe, that we're conquistadores!"

The driver took them back to the harbour.

The tiny *Santa Maria* was anchored close to the *Semiramis*, but they hadn't seen her as they were getting off the ship.

"Did Columbus cross the Atlantic in that tub? That's no more than a large caique," Alexis said in amazement.

"What did you expect?" the doctor grabbed at the opportunity; "They were the real sailors. Not like your kind who need a radiometre, and a radar to navigate, as well as an engine with a propeller to push you forward."

"You're absolutely right! One more duel – man against nature. At the peak of adventure!"

They just managed to get to the church in the Gothic Quarter while the organ was playing the final notes of a fugue and choir of young boys and girls were singing Spanish while the two Caballeros were trying to make out the words and translate them as best they could.

'May the light be blessed
and blessed the Cross
and blessed the Lord
and the Holy Trinity.
Blessed this morning
and may the blessing last till night.'

It was the prayer of the young sailors on the 'Santa Maria', the driver who had accompanied them into the church explained. This was immediately followed by another little song, one the sailors sang as they lit the navigation lamp before dark:

The lookout is at his post
the sand rolls on the beach
we are having a good journey
but we are in the hands of God.

And when they sighted the new world, the voices of the choir filled the Gothic domes of the church as they sang in unison, "God, we bless you."

"Faith, in the service of Ferdinand and Isabella," Alexis said to whoever wished to listen.

This time, the taxi stopped before Gaudi's church. Alexis climbed the steps into the fairy-tale cathedral with a sense of awe. He looked up at the unfinished roof and gazed at the sky, then turned to the doctor. "I've never felt so close to God in a church. As if your soul rose out of you, and taking off for heaven, slides up those fantastic tortuous spiral columns, on its greatest adventure, towards the truth that remains unexplored."

"First time I've been in a see-through church," the doctor said prosaically.

Alexis ignored him. "Look at the unbridled fantasy of Gaudi, as expressed through organic shapes, forming a cathedral that is a masterpiece of the Soul, in triumph!"

"You mean you're in your element, although you have become a little pedantic ..."

"If you close your eyes, the dream-like forms of El Greco, the nightmares of Goya, the paranoia of Dali, even the broken-up forms of Picasso will pass before you all in one composition which had its start many years ago and lives on today in the architecture – what am I talking about? In the *sculpture* of Gaudi destined to reach the universe, the infinite!"

"I must admit that even with my eyes open I get the shivers in here."

"Can't you see I'm right?"

"You're right all right! Even my dick has shrivelled ... and if I'm not able to perform at the whorehouse it will be your fault."

"Doctor, don't you ever feel any reverence?"

"In the Gothic church I was an angel – you have to admit. While in here I feel like I'm in a madhouse. That Gaudi must have been nuts!"

"And you're nuts yourself. Go on outside – I'll be along soon. I want to be by myself for a few minutes.

"You're delirious again. I'm leaving."

"Thank you for pointing it out to me. Delirium is like bubbling water, a dissonant music which wraps itself around the 'daedalian' forms of Gaudi being caressed by them."

The doctor left shaking his head.

Alexis stood in the middle of the church. He again lifted his eyes to the sky and for a few minutes stopped thinking. He felt he had become one with the universe.

"Aren't we going to shop for my souvenir to bring back home?"

"Like what, doctor?"

"May be a small bullfighter's sword, one of these colourful scarves, a pretty Spanish doll?"

"Were you so much influenced by the Sacrada Familia that you now want a doll as a replacement for Michelle instead of some Senorita at a whorehouse?"

"Why of all the nerve!"

"All those times you came to me for consolation and interpretation of your tormented soul. Now since you're on firm ground, I see you're putting on airs!"

"The psychoanalysis has ended, doctor. You cured me for good!"

"On the contrary, you've lost your marbles now. You forget that to be cured by a doctor isn't enough, you need a nurse too, and you let yours slip away. And since we're talking about shops, there's a little place over there. Tell the driver we're going to look around."

The driver eagerly escorted them into the shop and announced to the boy and the girl behind the counter that the two 'senors' were members of the *Semiramis* crew. Another excited round of handshakes and attentions followed while the girl said in excitement:

"We too were at the harbour, you know. All the radio stations and the newspapers in Spain are talking about your ship."

They chose some small skewers for spearing 'aceitunas' – olives – and a statuette of a bull.

"Gifts to you from Spain!" The boy said as he was wrapping up the souvenirs. No matter how much they protested it was impossible to pay.

"If we screw for free too I'm ready to shout 'Viva Franco'!" the doctor said.

Carrying their booty from their expedition they got back into the taxi for the crowning moment of their Spanish sortie.

The cab stopped in a narrow side street in a neighbourhood that couldn't have been too far from the centre. The facade of the building gave no clue as to what was going on behind the walls. They gave the taxi driver a large tip which he took only after a great fuss. They started to bid him farewell, but he was determined no matter what to introduce them himself to the priestesses of love!

They waited for the door to be opened by a classic Madame with hair dyed red, plump rosy cheeks and fleshy lips; but instead they found themselves facing an ascetic figure, full of wisdom, like the woman by Velasquez, frying eggs! She was around forty years old and was wearing an ash grey scarf, a blouse of the same colour and a long skirt. When she looked you in the eyes you felt she was reading the depths of your soul.

If she hadn't politely invited them in, they would have thought they'd knocked on the wrong door. Behind the door, a double red velvet curtain concealed a large hall with wide couches all around covered with dark green velvet fabric thrown casually over the soft feather cushions, completing the steamy atmosphere of Velasquez.

When a while later Alexis saw the Venus of Velasquez coming down the stairs, a stark naked woman with a virginal appearance and her hair in a braid, he couldn't help feeling bewildered and he believed that nothing in life is by chance. Other girls came down the stairs, some half-dressed, some dressed in filmy clothes, but all well apportioned and well groomed. Blue-eyed blondes, swarthy Catalans, Spanish ladies from Andalusia, brown-skinned Castilians, a bouquet of beauty for Alexis' and the doctor's Spanish collection, all orchestrated by the Madame.

The cab driver had remained standing next to the curtain by the entrance, and when he had seen them settled in on the comfortable couches he announced in the voice of a majordomo: "The gentlemen come from Greece; they are officers on the *Semiramis*, and they have liberated our prisoners."

All eight girls ran up to them and covered them with kisses.

The driver made his exit through the curtain and the performance began. Like two pashas from the Orient, they lolled indolently on the velvet couches, enjoying the attentions of the girls of the house, while the 'lady with the fried eggs' filled their glasses with sangria every so often. Alexis had no trouble in making his choice. The Venus of Velasquez was right next to him; she was looking him in the eyes the same way she would look in a mirror. When she realised that she was his choice, she took him by the hand and showed him into a room on the floor above. This room too had an air of the 17th century, with all the comfort that comes from the passing of time.

Up till that moment they hadn't spoken. He didn't even know her name. After the Venus of Velasquez had closed the door she began to undress him slowly and ceremoniously, first the jacket, then the tie and the shirt ('it seems she knows how stupid a man looks in a shirt without his pants on,' Alexis thought). Then his shoes, his socks and finally his pants and underwear. For her the problem of undressing didn't exist – she didn't have anything on to take off. She kissed him tenderly on the mouth, on his chest and on his groin. Then she lay down next to him and waited. Alexis also lay down and they looked at each other without touching.

"What's your name?"

"Alexis, and you?"

"Concita. Do you have a father and mother?"

"Yes."

"Brothers and sisters?"

"Two."

"Are you married?"

Strange, neither Olga nor Estrella had asked him these simple, first questions that one asks if they have the slightest interest in the other. He hadn't felt such tenderness in a long time and then he caressed her supple body, passing his hand over her hollowed out waist, which was like a soft wave, two, three, four times slowly. Concita took the initiative while he closed his eyes and let her do whatever she wanted to. Now she kissed him from his head to his toes and every so often asked him what pleased him. He didn't answer and she took her own sweet time with feminine patience.

And when they were ready to unite, there was no Olga or Estrella but only Concita, the woman, outside of time, outside of matter, in a harmonious interval of escape, as you imagine life beyond life, the definitive surrender, when you only give and ask for nothing, because you have everything. When she whispered 'Mi vida' he didn't know if she meant his life or her life.

"Are you happy?" she asked as they stretched out next to each other.

"I'm free," he answered. "Estoy libero!"

As they left the whorehouse, the Madame, after filling their pockets with sweets, pulled the two velvet curtains behind them.

"You were right, doctor. The curtain has closed!"

"Lovemaking in three acts!" the doctor added.

"I accept your money so that you won't feel you owe me anything" Concita told me. Only a prostitute can liberate the soul of a man. A brothel is the highest school," Alexis added epigrammatically.

"Now that one appetite has been satiated, I think we should go and have a bite. It made me hungry."

"Which one did you go with?"

"That blonde with the big tits. She was half French, from Gascony. It was a change from Michelle who had practically no bosom at all."

"You are in Spain and you weren't curious to try Spanish fruit?"

"You know I've always had a preference for French women ... and then ... if you know the ins and out of the ... language!"

"Along with your appetite, your dubious humour has come back too, I see!"

"Gallic wit, my good man, Gallic wit!"

"Where should we go to eat?"

"I think we should end the evening in style with Spanish food and flemenco!"

"Where do you go for flemenco?"

"Paseo de la Republica cinquenta y dos!"

"How do you know?" Alexis asked, surprised.

"I got my information from the Madame! She told me how to get there. It's not far."

ANDALUSIA, stated a large illuminated sign at Paseo de la Republica 52.

Two guitarists were singing at the time they entered the narrow salon. They sat wedged at a table not far from the stage.

"Who's going to order?" the doctor asked.

"Let's get some real Spanish food."

"What would you say to 'gaspacho'? Gaspacho for you, Sopa a la Alentejena for me."

"What's that?"

"Fortunately, it describes it for tourists like yourself. Soup with herbs and garlic and poached eggs."

"To your good health and happiness, but you messed it up like the tourist you are! That is Portuguese food and you didn't read it right. Afterward I'll have Almejas a la Marinera or better yet Zarzuela de Meriscos. The name alone fills your mouth. A ragout of lobster and shrimp, mussels and ham and other goodies, – oh, and there's also a little garlic."

"Good! My soup has garlic too, but stay away from me just the same. I'll have pork for a second course. Porce con pimientos vermellos. What do you think?"

"What do I think? Read it and find out – more garlic?"

"Thank God we went to the girls before eating!"

They turned to the waiter and ordered.

"Brazo de gitano para mi. Bunuelos de platanos para el Senor, for dessert," the doctor concluded. And to Alexis: "We'll share the desserts and try both of them. One is with rum and the other with fried bananas." "God protect us! But since we started with Madam's fried eggs we may as well end with fried bananas."

"What fried eggs?"

"Velasquez's of course."

The doctor didn't understand, but at that point he didn't even try to.

They ate at their leisure, listening to the lacy notes of the Spanish guitar, with that inner peace that men have when they share each other's company after coming out of a whorehouse. When the sex drive is satiated, when, with no-one else present, they don't have to play games and the conversation flows freely with no restrictions.

They had eaten enough garlic and drunk enough sangria that they felt a little tipsy, just enough that the images took on a magical dimension – as the three flamenco dancers came out in their long dresses with the fringes and with the tall combs crowning their jet black braids. Three serious figures, given over to the dance in body and soul, hands and feet drawing figures in space, tapping out the rhythm with their heels and the castanets, their arms raised in the air, as the guitarists spurred them on with cries: Ida, Ida … Asa Asa … Olé!

Three dancers. One dressed in red, one in green, one in blue, swirled before the eyes of Alexis who wanted to play his game for the last time. He put the head of Olga on the one in red, Estrella's on the one in green and Concita's on the one in blue.

And as they whirled around and around the three colours blended into one, the colour of the spectrum of the sun, and their three names fused into one as well. The name of woman – of the woman without a face.

THE END